CHATHAM HOUSE PAPERS

Russians Beyond Russia

The Politics of National Identity

Neil Melvin

THE ROYAL INSTITUTE
OF INTERNATIONAL
AFFAIRS

Pinter *A Cassell Imprint*
Wellington House, 125 Strand, London WC2R 0BB, United Kingdom

First published in 1995

British Library Cataloguing in Publication Data
A CIP catalogue record for this book is available from the British Library

ISBN 1-85567-233-2 (Paperback)
     1-85567-232-4 (Hardback)

Typeset by Koinonia Limited
Printed and bound in Great Britain by
Biddles Limited, Guildford and King's Lynn

CHATHAM HOUSE PAPERS

A Russia and CIS Programme Publication
Programme Director: Roy Allison

The Royal Institute of International Affairs, at Chatham House in London, has provided an impartial forum for discussion and debate on current international issues for 75 years. Its resident research fellows, specialized information resources, and range of publications, conferences, and meetings span the fields of international politics, economics, and security. The Institute is independent of government.

Chatham House Papers are short monographs on current policy problems which have been commissioned by the RIIA. In preparing the papers, authors are advised by a study group of experts convened by the RIIA, and publication of a paper indicates that the Institute regards it as an authoritative contribution to the public debate. The Institute does not, however, hold opinions of its own; the views expressed in this publication are the responsibility of the author.

Contents

Acknowledgments

This volume has grown out of a project conducted under the auspices of the Russia and CIS Programme of the Royal Institute of International Affairs (Chatham House). The project was generously funded by the Leverhulme Trust and field research was greatly aided by financial assistance from the Nuffield Foundation. The project has benefited in numerous ways from the wise guidance of Neil Malcolm and Roy Allison. I would also like to thank the staff of Chatham House for providing unstinting support throughout my time at the RIIA. Thanks are also due to the participants (too numerous to mention here) of the series of study groups conducted at Chatham House in connection with the project. Unfortunately, no volume could ever hope to incorporate the rich range of ideas produced in these sessions. Margot Light, Andrew Wilson, Charles King and Rein Müllerson read draft versions of the chapters on Russia, Ukraine, Moldova and the Baltic states, respectively. Any errors in these sections of the book are because I failed to heed their advice. A special debt of thanks is owed to Evgeni Kovalev and Yuri Kulchik for their research assistance and for their insights into post-Soviet politics. During the course of the project, I drew heavily on the hospitality and knowledge of many local researchers in the former Soviet republics. Without their patient explanations of the nuances of local politics, this project would not have been possible. Over the past two years I have interviewed more than 150 officials, diplomats, politicians, cultural leaders, businessmen, military personnel and journalists in connection with this study. I am forever grateful that they managed to find the time to answer my endless questions. Finally, a special thank you to Shyama Iyer who offered unfailing encouragement throughout the project.

July 1995   N.M.

A note on names

Since the late 1980s, a large number of places in the former Soviet republics have had their names altered from the Russian or Russified form to the name used, or invented, by the titular population. This process has been particularly controversial in areas populated by Russian communities and the struggle to rename districts, towns, and even streets has emerged as a particularly controversial issue in many localities.

In this book a combination of anglicized Russian and titular place names are employed. In Ukraine, for example, the Ukrainianized forms of local names are utilized – hence *Kharkov* becomes *Kharkiv* – where these have won acceptance among the local population. In most areas, however, Russified forms remain current. In Kazakhstan, with the exception of *Akhmola* (formerly *Tselinograd*), which is widely employed by different ethnic groups, the Russified place names are used. Most towns in the north and east of Kazakhstan contain Russian majorities who are fiercely opposed to changing the names of towns which have never had a Kazakh equivalent. The area formerly known in the West as *Moldavia* is given as *Moldova* because this is the form now generally accepted in that country.

Regional map

Chapter 1

Introduction

The twentieth century has been dominated by nationalism. Nationalism is, of course, not a new phenomenon; its foundations lie in the seventeenth and eighteenth centuries. However, only in the past hundred years has it become a dominant force in world affairs. In this period, the nation has become a basic unit for the organization of human society, and serves as one of the main building blocks for the modern international system. If this situation was obscured by the post-Second World War confrontation between the socialist and capitalist systems, the intellectual defeat of Marxism-Leninism and the collapse of regimes that espoused communism have left the world in no doubt that the national idea remains primary among political principles.

Recent scholarship has provided rich pickings for those interested in understanding nationalism. A range of multidisciplinary studies has made nationalism one of the most theoretically lively areas of contemporary inquiry. Together, these studies have mounted a powerful critique of the primordial view of nations – that they have existed through the mists of time, either oppressed or waiting to be 'awakened' – so popular among nationalists. Instead, research has suggested a more instrumental understanding whereby the origins of nations and nationalism lie in modern forms of economic activity, bureaucracy, secularism and inter-state relations. Moreover, the dynamic forms of contemporary social, economic and political institutions mean that the character of nations is not fixed for eternity. Rather, nations are the subjects of a continual process of re-creation or reinvention.[1]

It is a principal assumption of this volume that the forces driving nationalist politics in the former Soviet Union are not fundamentally dissimilar to those in other regions of the world: that in the ex-USSR we

1

are not witnessing the 'rebirth' of nations but their ongoing construction. Nations and national identities are being forged and remade amid the apparent chaos of the post-Soviet collapse, a process originating not in some historical destiny or 'natural' community but in the prosaic modernization that has been sweeping across the former USSR since the late nineteenth century and in the development of the contemporary bureaucratic state. While the broader processes of urbanization, education and enhanced communications promoted by the Soviet authorities destroyed traditional forms of social organization and identification, the particular administrative practices and public policies pursued in the USSR linked peoples and territories and developed ethnic identities as national ones.[2]

Thus, in the late 1980s and early 1990s, nationalist movements emerged as the primary form of mass political mobilization, and it was they that in large part brought about the final disintegration of the USSR. With the communist order shattered, national self-determination became the basic justification for a new political order. The national-territorial arrangement of the USSR provided the political architecture for the post-Soviet political system – union republics became sovereign states. That is, with the collapse of the socialist project, national belonging was institutionalized as one of the main conceptual frameworks through which each community conceived of itself as a legitimate social and political form. Individual and collective identities became, more than ever before, national in form.

The sudden demise of the communist system brought together an unprecedented set of challenges: to establish markets, to develop new forms of political and social life and to build relations with other states. Since independence, nationalism has been used to define and strengthen the new states in order to tackle these challenges. Within this context, it is primarily elites that have sought to influence the evolution of the new states and that have therefore played the key role in the development of nationalist forms of politics. Nationalism has provided the post-Soviet elites with their political discourse, framework for action, and justification for developing the apparatus of the state. Most significantly, nationalism has provided these elites with a way to consolidate themselves at the pinnacle of the new system. This process has had both a domestic and an interstate dimension.

The empirical focus of this study is on the Russified settler communities living outside the Russian Federation. As these communities straddle many of the main fault lines of post-Soviet society – ethnic, class, urban/

rural – developments within and around them are of crucial significance to the political, economic and social orders that emerge in the former USSR. Through detailed analysis of the role of the Russian-speaking communities in the development of national identity in six former Soviet republics[3] – the Russian Federation (Chapter 2), Estonia and Latvia (Chapter 3), Moldova (Chapter 4), Ukraine (Chapter 5) and Kazakhstan (Chapter 6) – this study seeks to examine three broad issues. First, how has the establishment of a series of new states in the former USSR affected the development of new political identities among the Russified settlers? Second, what role have these communities played in the emergence of national identities among the broader populations of the newly independent states? Finally, what light does the issue of the Russian communities shed on the complex relationship between ethnicity, nation and state in the ex-USSR?

Chapter 2

Russian identity in Empire, Union, nation-state and diaspora

Introduction

Independence for the Russian Federation at the beginning of 1992 marked a triumph for Russia's opposition forces. While nationalist movements on the periphery of the inner Soviet Empire – the republics of the USSR – had driven the process of change from the late 1980s, Russian national sentiments provided the final *coup de grâce* to the Soviet system. During the anti-reform putsch of August 1991, the symbols of an emerging Russia – the Russian flag, the Russian parliament and above all the Russian President, Boris Yeltsin – served as the rallying points for opposition to the coup.

However, while the transformation of Russia and the other Soviet republics into independent entities solved the immediate problem of finding a form of political organization to replace the USSR – the Union became fifteen separate sovereign states – it also raised basic questions about the social, economic and political systems that were to operate within the new order, and about the definition of the post-Soviet nations. Were they to be ethnically or territorially based? The most acute problem was to determine the nature of the relationship between ethnic Russians, the Russian nation and the Russian state after the fall of communism.

Within the Russian Federation, the Russian national question is of fundamental importance because Russia is far from being ethnically homogeneous. Indeed, in certain areas – e.g. Tuva and Chechenia – Russians constitute a minority.[1] At the same time, implicit in the assertion of the Russian Federation's territorial integrity is the notion that Russian settlement throughout the Federation, even if only sparse in places, constitutes a basic justification for the political unity of the

4

country. Indeed, protection of the Russian community was cited as an important initial rationale for the harsh action by the Russian authorities against the secessionist movement in Chechenia.

However, linked to the question of the status of Russians in the Russian Federation is a second element: the question of the Russians outside Russia. During the Russian Imperial and Soviet periods, extensive settlement by Russian-speakers[2] – ethnic Russians, Ukrainians and Belorussians as well as a variety of non-Slavic, but heavily Russified, ethnic groups – had developed in areas traditionally populated by non-Russian peoples. The disintegration of the USSR created a situation in which these 'Russian' settlers (estimated at 25–35m) suddenly found themselves living in newly independent states controlled by governments seeking a firm break with a past in which Russia, the Russian language and culture, and ethnic Russians had occupied a leading position. From 1992, the fate of the Russian settler communities and the role that Russia should play in ensuring their well-being emerged as a central issue in the domestic and interstate politics of the Russian Federation – indeed, as one of the main elements in the development of a post-Soviet Russian national identity.

The relationship between the Russian state and the settler communities became a matter of basic contention because Tsarist and Soviet nationalities policies had created little sense of a well-defined ethnic or civic Russian nation, and certainly not one that coincided with the current territory of the Russian Federation.[3] Therefore, at independence the link between an ethnic Russian settler (*russkii*) and Russia (*Rossiia*) remained highly ambiguous. Equally uncertain was the relationship between Russia and the Russified non-ethnic Russians of the settler communities. Who qualified to be a Russian citizen (*Rossiianin*)? Was it only those resident in the Russian Federation at independence, or did ethnic Russians and Russian-speaking settlers outside Russia also have an automatic right to citizenship?

Following the collapse of the USSR, reconciling *russkii* and the Russified settler with *Rossiia* quickly became a central element in Russian politics. Domestic and interstate politics provided a crucible within which understandings of kinship were recast and given political significance.[4] With only a weak sense of national identity, the boundaries constituted by history, culture, language and kin emerged as powerful alternative definitions of the Russian nation to the one provided by existing political borders. Distinctions between the social and the political became steadily more blurred and ethnicity increasingly became political identity. The terms *russkii* and *Rossiianin* were fused and their meaning expanded to embrace a broad range of different peoples – ethnic Russians, Russian-speakers and other groups with some link, real or imagined, to Russia.

In short, the notion of a Russian diaspora was forged from a hotch-potch of different peoples, and concepts of ethnicity and political belonging were moulded around this understanding. The notion of the diaspora was subsequently integrated into the definition of the Russian nation. In this way, the debate about the diaspora became a central part of a conceptual and linguistic process of defining modern Russia and its place in the post-Soviet world.[5]

The transformation of the settler communities into a part of the Russian nation provided an important justification for Russian state involvement beyond the borders of the Russian Federation. Protection of the diaspora became one of Russia's 'vital national interests' and therefore a cornerstone supporting its claim to have the leading role in the former Soviet Union. This justification for Russian external action was also interwoven with ideas about Russia's status in the international community: its 'objective' national interests outside the Russian Federation made it a 'great power' in world affairs.[6]

As well as providing a justification for its external policies, the creation of a Russian diaspora also offered Russia a new identity, a *raison d' être* as a kin-state, a 'historic homeland' for the Russian communities abroad.[7] A leading Russian political observer has noted the close links between external and domestic politics in contemporary Russia:

> With us, foreign policy does not emanate from the precepts and priorities of evolved statehood. On the contrary, foreign policy practice ... is helping Russia become Russia. Dealings with the surrounding world are helping shape Russian statehood and helping Russia recognize its interests.[8]

The creation of the notion of a Russian diaspora was at the heart of domestic efforts to forge a new Russian identity. In the immediate post-independence period, the intellectual debate about it became a central part of the bitter struggle among Russian political elites to gain control of the Russian state. The eventual redefinition of the settler communities as a Russian diaspora (*Rossiiskaia diaspora*) marked a victory for the political ideas of one particular elite. Subsequently, the understanding of the Russian nation-state and its place in world affairs promoted by this group became a core element in the self-identity of the Russian political establishment, and a justification for its foreign policies.

The Russian Empire

Until at least the late nineteenth century, Russia was defined not as the land of the Russians but as the territory of the Russian Empire-state. The political legitimacy of the Russian state rested not on popular sovereignty expressed through the Russian nation but on Tsarist rule. Early ideas of Russianness and Russian identity hinged on allegiance to the God-appointed Tsar, autocracy and the Russian Orthodox Church. While the expansion of the Russian Empire may have diluted the territorial sense of Russia, it did not pose a direct threat to the underpinnings of this political system.[9]

In the nineteenth century, the emergence of significant internal political challenges to the Tsarist order and the debate between Slavophiles and Westernizers placed the question of Russian identity at the centre of late imperial politics. Towards the end of the century, nationalist agitation by intellectuals and the introduction of a deliberate policy of Russification by the government began to foster a sense of Russian national identity among the mass of the population. As a result, despite the lack of a consensus among Russian elites about the actual extent of 'Mother Russia', Russian nationalism began to emerge as a significant political identity.[10] However, although there were important ethno-nationalist dimensions to this process, there is evidence that the emergence of a Russian national identity at a mass level was based upon a multicultural and cosmopolitan view of Russianness which was gradually supplanting the traditional one of loyalty to Tsar and Orthodoxy.[11]

Thus, although the last years of the Tsarist Empire were marked by a rising national consciousness, the basis of this new identity remained ambiguous. Even immediately prior to the Bolshevik revolution, Russian patriots were likely to identify the entire state, not just the lands populated by Russians, as their *otechestvo* (fatherland); important sections of the Russian intelligentsia were just as taken with the state as with the ethno-nationalist idea.[12] Moreover, despite the strong drive for ethnic consolidation brought about directly by policies of Russification and indirectly by rapid modernization, notions of Russian ethnicity remained weakly developed – a basic impediment to the development of ethno-nationalism – with Russians being divided into a variety of ethnographic subgroups.[13]

7

The Soviet period

Following the Bolshevik revolution, the relationship of Russians to the new political order remained as ambiguous as it had been to the Tsarist Empire. The Soviet regime relied on the political acquiescence of the Russians who were encouraged to regard the successes of the USSR as advancing the interests of Russian people. The bond between Russian and Soviet reached its apogee during the Second World War – 'the Great Patriotic War' – when the Soviet leadership actively promoted Russian nationalism.[14]

The close relationship between the notions of Russian and Soviet ensured that Russians enjoyed a powerful but not completely dominant position in the USSR; they had advantage rather than guaranteed privilege. Indeed, Russian nationalists faced repression along with other nationalists. The position of advantage was reinforced by the centrality accorded to a sanitized Russian culture in the Soviet system, and the role assigned to the Russian language, which was not only the lingua franca of the USSR, but also the language of success. Moreover, Russo-Soviet culture served as the primary means by which other ethnic groups were assimilated into a general Soviet way of life; it was therefore central to the regime's ultimate goal of creating the Soviet people (*Sovetskii narod*).

The powerful advantages enjoyed by Russians and those conversant with Russo-Soviet culture, coupled with the replacement of the policy of indigenization – the promotion of ethnically indigenous cadres within each republic – with one of Russification in the 1930s, ensured that Russian identity exerted a strong pull on the rest of the population of the USSR. According to Soviet census results, the period 1926–39 was a time of massive reidentification with the Russian *ethnos*. As many as 10m non-Russians may have registered themselves as Russian in this period; this compares with a figure of 4.7m from 1939 to 1959.[15]

Expansion of the Russian linguistic and cultural space under Soviet rule was reinforced by the migration of Russians, other Slavs and Russian-speakers to urban industrial regions outside the Russian Federation and the linguistic Russification of non-Russians who settled in these enclaves. Although policies of Russification were toned down after Stalin's death, Russian and Slavic-based migration to many non-Russian republics continued until the 1980s.[16] The Soviet regime relied on the immigrant communities and large-scale migration by Russian-speaking, predominantly ethnic Russian, settlers to dilute the powers of the titular groups and to consolidate Soviet rule. These communities and migrants to the Soviet periphery were encouraged to see themselves as political and economic benefactors, as *Kulturträger* for the ambiguous meld of Soviet and Russian culture. In return for their loyalty, they were rewarded by political and economic power disproportionate to their numbers in the local population.

However, the settler communities were not composed simply of ethnic Russians, nor was the primary identity of the Russians in these enclaves an ethnic one.[17] Rather, as the most mobile group in the USSR, Russians formed the nucleus of highly Sovietized, predominantly urban-based, largely industrial, settler communities composed of a number of ethnic groups (see Statistical Appendix). The non-ethnic, socio-cultural identity of the settler communities was further reinforced by their position in the Soviet political and economic system. Although geographically scattered, they were strategically at the heart of the Soviet political economy. Their enclaves developed around heavy industry, particularly the military-industrial complex. As a result, they were tied to the all-Union rather that to an individual republican economy. The importance of the enterprises located in the settler enclaves ensured that the powerful Moscow-based economic ministries and the Central Committee of the Communist Party of the Soviet Union (CPSU), rather than republic-level institutions, generally served as the focus for the communities.

Despite the close links between ethnic Russians and the Soviet Empire, in the 1970s a loss of 'imperial will' became apparent within significant parts of the Russian population.[18] As national sentiment among other peoples of the USSR rose, polls conducted by the Institute of Ethnography in Moscow identified a rising ethnic consciousness among the Russians, especially those on the periphery.[19] That is, Russians began to see themselves as a group with an identity other than Soviet. However, overall ethnic identity among Russians remained comparatively weak and there is little indication that rising ethnic consciousness developed into a national identity.[20] Moreover, unlike the other ethno-nationalist movements, the Russians lacked a clear territorial identity – a homeland – other than the USSR as a whole.[21] It was only with the Gorbachev reforms of the 1980s, and the rise of nationalist politics, that Russian identity really began to undergo significant change.[22]

Russian national identity during perestroika

The *perestroika* period challenged the identity of Russians in two key areas: the rise of national movements on the periphery of the Soviet Union led many of the settlers to question for the first time their role in, and relationship to, the USSR and their host republic. And the emergence of a political movement in the Russian Federation that campaigned for an independent Russia accelerated the decoupling of Russian and Soviet identities.

On the Soviet periphery, rising nationalist mobilization based on a volatile admixture of anti-Soviet/pro-independence and anti-Russian sentiment, presented the settler communities with the choice between supporting independence, being passive, or actively opposing the Popular Fronts (local independence movements). Although the settler communities showed important support both for and against independence, most of their members were passive. While the Russian communities in the Soviet periphery were being pulled in a variety of directions simultaneously, Russians in the Russian Federation faced a far simpler choice.

The confrontation that developed between the Soviet centre and the Russian Federation from 1989 fostered the rise of what has been termed the Russian national idea. The Democratic Movement (the variety of groups that united to oppose communist domination and which was led by Boris Yeltsin) sought to use the institutions of the Russian Federation to assert the independence of Russia and to challenge Soviet rule. This conflict was personified in the struggle between Boris Yeltsin and Mikhail Gorbachev. Behind the personal struggle lay a battle to create and gain power for Russian institutions which, after the August 1991 coup, culminated in the creation of an independent Russia.[23]

The construction of a notion of diaspora and the domestic roots of Russian foreign policy

Following independence, the relationship between the Russians abroad and the Russian Federation became a dominant issue in Russian internal politics and in the development of Russian national identity. Owing partly to events in the former Soviet republics[24] and the historically weakly defined sense of Russia and Russianness, the importance attached to this issue was primarily a reflection of the poorly developed nature of Russian domestic political institutions, whose structure was inappropriate to the new demands placed upon them, and of competing ideas about Russia and its interests.[25] The debate about the diaspora between Russia's political elites initially served to accelerate political disintegration and then provided a catalyst for the formation of new political alliances.[26] Between late 1991 and December 1994, the issue of the settler communities passed through three main stages in the domestic politics of the

Russian Federation: the defeat of the Democratic vision of settler relations; the consolidation of a Centrist consensus on the diaspora;[27] and the institutionalization of diaspora policy within the Russian state.

The defeat of the Democratic vision of settler relations (autumn 1991– autumn 1992)
The sudden collapse of the USSR presented the Democrats with a dilemma. Prior to summer 1991, little in the way of a clear policy agenda, other than the overthrow of the USSR, had been developed. As a result, the policies that emerged in late 1991 and early 1992 often had a strongly idealistic quality, particularly Russian foreign policy which drew its main principles from the Gorbachev/Shevardnadze 'New Thinking' of the 1980s.[28]

Foreign policy in this early period of independence was primarily based on a vision of Russia's national interest defined in economic terms, as in Gorbachev's last years. Economic prosperity was viewed as the motive force of external policy, a goal that could most successfully be achieved by rapid integration into the international economy, coupled with Western financial and technical assistance. At a political level, these economic goals could best be achieved by membership of international institutions such as the IMF and the World Bank; this presupposed good relations with Western states. This view of Russia's main foreign policy aims and position in the world was supported by the leading members of the Democratic bloc, including Boris Yeltsin, and the leading 'Atlanticist', the Foreign Minister Andrei Kozyrev.

With attention focused on improving links with the West, relations with the newly independent states of the former Soviet Union seemed to have low priority for the Russian government. Independent and sovereign over their populations, these states were viewed as having primary responsibility for the well-being of the predominantly Russian settler communities. A specific Russian policy towards the settler populations therefore seemed unnecessary.

While there were obvious historical and kinship bonds to these populations, there is no sense at this time that the settlers were perceived as an integral part of the Russian nation or that Russia had a *special* interest in them. Russian national identity was presented in primarily civic terms: all those resident in the Russian Federation at independence were granted Russian citizenship irrespective of ethnic belonging. The Russian settlers should become citizens of their host state and therefore any problems could be dealt with within the republic or through international forums such as the United Nations or the Conference on Security and Cooperation in Europe (CSCE).[29] It was not Russia's place, nor indeed in its interest, to interfere in the internal affairs of its neighbours. Such policies belonged to the imperial and Soviet past.[30]

However, the Democratic vision of foreign relations quickly came under attack. Opposition was divided between two main political currents: Soviet/Russian chauvinists (the Red/Brown alliance), a movement composed of communists and so-called Russian patriotic forces; and the Statists (*gosudarstvenniki*) or National-democrats, former members of the Democratic camp who had embraced a more assertive Russian nationalism.[31] While boundaries between these movements were fluid – indeed they operated as loosely arranged networks of actors and ideas rather than coherent, united forces – they shared a strong sense that Russian foreign policy was ill-judged, believing in particular that the Russian state and the Russian settler communities outside it were inexorably bound together, and that it was a basic responsibility of the Russian state to defend these populations.[32]

The dominance in the Supreme Soviet of deputies who were critical of the Democratic position made parliament a centre for opposition to government policy on the settler communities and for establishing links (especially through organizations of a Nationalist/Communist orientation such as the National Salvation Front) with radical elements among the settlers themselves.[33] Continual criticism was levelled at the government, particularly Andrei Kozyrev, by the deputies from early 1992, and a series of provocative resolutions was passed about the settler communities in the Baltic states and Moldova, and on the status of Crimea and the Black Sea Fleet. Vladimir Lukin, Chairman of the Committee for Foreign Affairs and a leading advocate of the Statist position, initially led the parliamentary assault on government policy, supported by a range of intellectual critics outside parliament including Sergei Karaganov, Andranik Migranian and Yeltsin's political adviser Sergei Stankevich, who also supported the Statist vision of Russia's place in the world.[34] Together, this group used the issue of the settlers to mount a sustained attack on government policies. As Migranian noted in August 1992:

> Within the framework of the CIS, Russia both legally and practically is called upon to play a special role across the whole geopolitical space of the former USSR. This role is conditioned by several extremely important factors. After the break up of the USSR close to 30m Russians and Russian-speakers found themselves

resident on the territory of foreign states. Arbitrarily established borders, recognized by nobody, have given rise to inter-national and inter-ethnic conflicts. The development of several autonomous national areas and Russian-speaking compact settlements within the newly created states and their request to Russia for protection raise questions about the legitimacy of these states. Many of these territories (Ossetia, Karabakh, Crimea and Transdniester) were part of the Russian Empire for a long time before they became part of the newly independent states. It seems to me that Russia ought to announce to the world community that the whole geopolitical space of the USSR is the sphere of its vitally important interests.[35]

The position of the government's critics was greatly enhanced by the support of Vice-President Aleksandr Rutskoi, who soon emerged as a leading figure in the Red/Brown alliance of political forces. Rutskoi's championing of the 'plight' of the Russian-speakers and his trip to Transdniester and Crimea at the height of tension in the two regions (early summer 1992) was crucial to the development of Russian policy towards the communities and indeed, by publicly establishing a link between the two regions and Russia, to the creation of a firm notion of a Russian diaspora.

Although the Ministry of Foreign Affairs (MFA) and Kozyrev made some concessions to the opposition, throughout the first half of 1992 government support for the settlers remained half-hearted, with foreign policy still focused on the West.[36] However, during the summer the introduction of a law on citizenship in Estonia, coupled with fighting in Moldova and growing tension in Ukraine, especially over the status of the Crimea, forced the government to address the criticism from its domestic opponents.[37]

For the first time too, the Democratic view of inter-state relations was being called into question by a variety of alternative visions of Russia's place in the world.[38] The issue of the settlers was also being used to challenge the MFA's monopoly over foreign policy-making within the executive. In the late summer, the publication of the draft new Russian military doctrine indicated that the Ministry of Defence was planning to use protection of Russians abroad as a basic justification for future external military action.[39]

By the autumn, events within the former Soviet republics and sustained domestic criticism of existing foreign policy finally forced those supporting the Democratic view of settler relations into retreat. Some of the leading Democrats who had advocated a moderate line on the diaspora were forced from office.[40] In addition, the MFA became increasingly tough in its criticism of other states and their policies towards the settler communities. The Baltic states were warned against 'ethnic cleansing', and at the end of October Russia suspended military withdrawal from the region, citing the failure of the Baltic states to protect the rights of the Russian minorities as the main cause of the action.[41]

Consolidation of a Centrist consensus on the diaspora (winter 1992– autumn 1993)

By winter 1992, the original Democratic version of settler relations had been severely modified and defence of the settler communities had become a basic tenet of Russia's external and domestic politics. The government had accepted that the settler communities constituted a Russian (*Rossiiskii*) diaspora and concomitantly that the Russian state bore a basic responsibility for them.[42]

Domestic debate about the settlers now began to shift to more practical questions about how Russia's relationship to the Russian-speaking communities was to be formalized. At the same time, with growing support for the position of the Statists on the settler issue, and with the Atlanticist thrust of Russian foreign policy heavily constrained, the domestic political struggle over diaspora policy increasingly involved a battle against the more radical Soviet/Russian patriotic forces.

A comprehensive state policy towards the Russian communities could not be developed effectively without high-level supervision. From early 1992, Sergei Stankevich had identified with the issue of the settlers. In a series of articles published in 1992–3, he stressed that Russia's relationship to the diaspora was central to the future of the Russian state and society. At the end of 1992, he became the government's main spokesman on the settler issue.[43]

The main goal of Russia's external policy, Stankevich argued, should be stability around existing borders, and one of the best ways this could be secured was through ensuring the rights of the Russian settlers and by building close ties between Russia and its diaspora. The settlers, a diaspora made up of populations 'ethnically connected to Russia', were clearly part of Russia's responsibility although the territories where they lived were considered part of independent states. The settlers could only be protected, therefore, through international agreements. Russia had a basic responsibility to conclude such agreements with the other newly independent states, to promote the cause of the diaspora in international forums and to ensure that international agreements were observed in the former Soviet republics. However, Stankevich argued that the settlers should not be seen simply as a potential problem for Russia. With the right policies, they could be discouraged from moving to Russia; as a self-identified Russian diaspora they could even function as powerful levers of Russian influence, helping Russia fulfil its role as the leading power in the former USSR.[44]

These two main principles were formulated in a report on the Russian diaspora entitled 'On urgent measures for the implementation of socio-cultural cooperation of citizens of the Russian Federation with Russian (*Rossiiskie*) compatriots abroad'. It was issued by Stankevich in January 1993 at Yeltsin's request. It also recommended that all relevant government departments draft measures aimed at building links with the Russian communities. The Federal Migration Service was established with the rather paradoxical role of providing resources for those who wished to migrate to the Russian Federation, but not encouraging them to do so.[45]

The main thrust of Russia's policy towards the diaspora was to be conducted by the MFA. Its consular sections were to be expanded within the CIS and Baltic states with the specific purpose of developing links to the Russian-speaking communities. The 'plight' of the diaspora was also to be of central importance in negotiations between Russia and the other former Soviet republics.[46] The MFA was to be supported by the State Committee for Nationalities, then headed by Sergei Shakhrai, which created a special section to deal with the diaspora.[47] On the domestic front, the MFA also sought to pacify its opponents by establishing a series of regularized contacts and consultative forums for members of parliament, leading public figures, the policy-oriented academic community and Russian public organizations working with settler communities.

A major aspect of the new initiative to develop a coordinated policy towards the diaspora involved creating a terminology to encapsulate and indeed legitimize the link between the settler communities and the Russian state. As noted earlier, these settler communities are far from purely *russkii* (ethnically Russian). The most obvious appellation for them, *russkaia diaspora*, was therefore not appropriate. Finding an alternative linguistic term to encapsulate the political link between Russia and the settlers presented a major difficulty.

Reflecting the diverse nature of the communities, a range of terms has been used to describe them.[48] The most neutral is *russkoiazychnye* (Russian-speaking). However, while this comes closest to capturing the essence of these populations, it holds no clear political dimension, and also includes communities which are not considered to be part of the diaspora, such as Russified Kazakhs in Kazakhstan. From the beginning of 1993, the MFA and other government departments therefore began to employ the terms *sootechestvenniki* (compatriots), *Rossiiane* (technically Russian citizens, although it has a strong connotation of those who are in some way historically tied to the Russian state and may well be resident outside the Russian Federation but within the area of the former Russian Empire or the USSR), *etnicheskie Rossiiane* (ethnically citizens of Russia),[49] and *vykhodtsy* (literally those who have left, with its implication that Russia is their 'natural' homeland).[50] The adoption of these terms served to tie Russia to the settler communities via a mixture of ethnic, political, cultural and historical bonds. Implicit in them is the understanding of Russia as a *rodina*, a homeland, for the *Rossiiskaia diaspora*.

The strategy outlined in the report did not rely on state activity alone. Stankevich argued that it was also important to establish links between Russian public organizations and the diaspora. In late 1992, Stankevich was instrumental in the establishment of a semi-official organization known as the Russian (*Rossiiskii*) Club, intended to fulfil three functions. First, it was to act as a focal point for the range of existing public organizations with links to the diaspora. Second, it would serve as a lobby group for diaspora interests. Finally, the Club was to act as a link to the diaspora communities themselves, fostering political, cultural and particularly economic ties with Russia.[51]

The creation of the Russian Club represented the first attempt to set up an organization to implement the practical policies derived from the Statist notion of Russia's relationship to the Russian settlers. However, the Russian Club was not the only public organization seeking to build links to the diaspora. By 1993 there were nearly a dozen involved with cultural ties, human rights and the migration and resettlement of 'returnees'. The best-organized and best-funded was the Congress of Russian (*Russkii*) Communities (CRC), headed by Dmitri Rogozin. In contrast to the Russian Club, the CRC was politically close to the radical Russian nationalist position. From spring 1993, Rogozin began to receive support from the leadership of the Russian Supreme Soviet.[52]

Reflecting the nationalist sympathies of the leadership of the CRC, the vision of Russia's relationship to the Russian populations which underpinned the CRC's approach to the settler was very different to that outlined by the Statists. Unlike Stankevich, Rogozin lays particular stress on developing the ethnic Russian nation as the core of a revival of Russia as a whole.

We are convinced that Russia is not contained within the borders that have been assigned to it today. Russia is a special, unique civilization, uniting the most diverse people and ethnic groups. The Congress of Russian Communities considers Russians (*Rossiiane*) to be all those who recognize that they belong to this civilization, value its great history, care about the development of its culture and believe in the future of Russia. In the struggle for survival several tasks stand before the Russian (*Russkii*) people. Without a revival of the Russian national ideal and the Russian Idea it will not be possible to return to the age-old bases of Russian spiritualism and Russian (*Rossiiskii*) Statehood ... We are striving to build up the contemporary relations and spiritual organization of the nation which were damaged during the times of trouble in the twentieth century.[53]

The Russian Idea – the revival of the ethnic Russian nation – is therefore central to the well-being of all the *Rossiiskii* peoples. Rogozin argues that only on the basis of uniting ethnic Russians within and outside Russia can this task be achieved. The Russians beyond Russia must therefore be integrated directly into Russia and given full political and economic rights as part of the Russian nation. For Rogozin, it is ethnic-based national identity that defines the Russian populations. Indeed, these are hardly diaspora communities because the territory of the former Soviet Union is viewed as the natural extent of the Russian state.[54]

During 1993, the significance of Rogozin's organization grew as these ideas often found strong support among sections of the diaspora elite. The CRC quickly emerged as an important challenge to government policy, a development greatly assisted because of the failure of the Stankevich initiative.

Stankevich's proposals were circulated within the government in spring 1993 but were soon bogged down in a bureaucracy that had little interest in devoting scarce resources to the diaspora. Stankevich himself lacked the political weight to drive through the necessary measures; moreover, he was a theoretician more than an administrator. By late summer 1993, it was clear that a new initiative would be required to rejuvenate official diaspora policy, but this was delayed by the autumn struggle between the government and the Supreme Soviet.

During summer 1993, there were signs of renewed confrontation between the government and parliament. In the sphere of diaspora relations this was signalled by the decision of the Supreme Soviet to give the city of Sevastopol in Crimea – a city with a great emotive significance to many Russians because of its link to the Russian Imperial navy – the status of a Russian (*Rossiiskii*) city. The destruction of the Supreme Soviet in October and the subsequent elections did not, however, signal a return to the Democratic vision of settler relations. Rather, together these two events contrived to reinforce the Centrist consensus about diaspora policy, derived mainly from the ideas developed by the Statists, that had emerged at the end of 1992. The Soviet/Russian chauvinist bloc was the principal loser of the political events at the end of 1993.

During the elections, it became *de rigueur* for all shades of political opinion to demand protection for the Russian diaspora.[55] But at the same time, apart from Vladimir Zhirinovski, almost all leading politicians accepted that the existing territory of the Russian Federation constituted the modern Russia, following the Statist conception of Russia and its place in the world. Economic and diplomatic pressure, not territorial annexation, were to be the means to influence neighbouring governments in regard to their Russian minorities.

Institutionalization of diaspora policy (winter 1993–winter 1994)
Despite the intellectual victory of the Statists, without adequate funds or bureaucratic support to develop policy, actual links to the diaspora had remained undeveloped throughout 1993. Following the December 1993 elections, however, the nature and significance of the Russian diaspora issue began to undergo important changes. With broad agreement among the Russian political elite that there was such a thing as a diaspora and that Russia bore direct responsibility for its wellbeing, the issue largely ceased to be a divisive element within the Russian body politic. Instead, as measures were taken to develop an official policy towards the settlers, the issue began to serve as a means for integrating diverse political elements. In addition, representatives of the settler communities were drawn into policy-making structures within Russia and, for the first time, the institutions of the Russian state began to engage seriously with the diaspora, seeking to coordinate and develop it.

The new emphasis on Russia's relationship with the diaspora was signalled by President Yeltsin in his 1994 New Year Address:

> Dear compatriots! You are inseparable from us and we are insepara-
> ble from you. We were and will be together. On the basis of law
> and solidarity, we defend and will defend your and our common
> interests. In the New Year, 1994, we will do this with greater
> energy and greater resoluteness.[56]

The centrality of the diaspora issue for Russia's domestic politics was reiterated in Yeltsin's address to parliament in February 1994. The President argued that the problems faced by Russians within and outside the Russian Federation provided a basic justification for strengthening the Russian state. He stressed, however, that Russia would pursue its interests through initiatives aimed at international organizations.[57] In fact, a new state policy towards the diaspora communities was already nearing completion.

During summer/autumn 1993, relations between the President and Sergei Stankevich had soured and in September responsibility for a new diaspora policy passed to the Commission for Citizenship (attached to the Presidency) together with the MFA and leading academic policy experts.[58] Its general emphasis was on building political, economic and cultural links to the diaspora, establishing provisions for dual citizenship and developing a series of international/bilateral agreements on the rights of the Russian-speaking minorities.[59]

From late 1993 into the first quarter of 1994, this Commission, together with the MFA, worked on developing the state programme and organized an extensive series of conferences to promote this goal. These meetings brought together for the first time the large range of individuals and organizations involved with diaspora issues, including representatives of the MFA, other ministries, parliament, the Federal Migration Service, Russian public organizations and leaders of the settler communities.[60]

The development of the state programme to support the diaspora was only one of the functions of the Commission for Citizenship, whose president, Abdullah Mikitaev, was also called upon to produce provisions permitting settlers to take Russian as a second citizenship.[61] In April, it was announced that increased efforts would be made to assist those who wished to take Russian citizenship. New Russian consulates would be opened in predominantly settler areas of the newly independent states.[62]

The MFA also began to take a more active role in the promotion of diaspora issues in the CIS. At the end of 1993, the MFA underwent a serious reorganization, refocusing away from global issues and onto the 'New Abroad'. Henceforth, it was to concentrate on promoting bilateral treaties with neighbouring states which incorporated provisions for dual citizenship.

The dual citizenship agreement concluded with Turkmenistan in December 1993 was to serve as a model. Initially, the Russian drive for dual citizenship treaties was pursued in Central Asia.[63] However, these proposals faced strong resistance from governments in the region suspicious

19

of Russia's motives, and talks quickly stalled.[64] Nevertheless, Russia continued to press for dual citizenship arrangements and also opened negotiations with Ukraine and Moldova on the issue.

By June, the report produced by Mikitaev's commission had been completed and circulated to ministries and departments for comment. In early summer 1994, a Government Commission for the Affairs of Compatriots in the New Abroad was established to pursue the policies outlined in the report and coordinate all policy developments in the area.

The final form of state policy towards the diaspora contained important changes from the earlier drafts. In particular, the preamble was toned down: the original claim that as the historic homeland (*rodina*) of the Russians (*Rossiiane*), Russia 'bears responsibility for their well-being'[65] was replaced with the more cautious assertion that 'the Russian Federation is prepared to help governments of the new independent states to satisfy the needs of the Russians (*Rossiiane*) living there and in guaranteeing their legal rights'.[66]

In the state programme a role for Russian diplomatic activity was outlined that focused on the establishment of bilateral agreements with ex-Soviet republics on minority rights and on using CIS and international human rights organizations to ensure their observance.[67] Dual citizenship arrangements and measures to promote Russian as a state language were also to be pursued. Great significance was attached to the further development of organizations concerned with settler issues in Russia and the diaspora.[68]

The document also contained important social and cultural commitments, including the aim to protect the poorest sections of the diaspora, the creation in Russia of regional societies for links with the Russian diaspora, assistance for returning military personnel, support for Russian and Slavic centres within the diaspora communities, help for Russian media and general support for the restoration of Russian culture via aid to libraries and funds for the preservation of Russian monuments.[69]

Particular emphasis was given to economic measures, which were to serve two main goals: to promote contacts between Russia and the diaspora and thereby help to consolidate the communities themselves; and, if diplomatic and international mechanisms fail to ensure the rights of the Russians, economic sanctions, perhaps involving energy resources and raw materials, could be used.[70]

Following the destruction of the Supreme Soviet in autumn 1993, the Russian parliament was far more limited in its ability to influence the development of policy. The new Russian constitution, which came into force in December 1993, severely restricted the activity of the legislature in foreign affairs, and so from the end of 1993 policy towards the settler communities was almost exclusively concentrated within the government; the parliament, however, continued to fulfil some important functions.[71] Responsibility for foreign affairs was divided between two committees: Vladimir Lukin was chairman of the Committee for the 'Far Abroad', while the centre for diaspora relations in parliament came to rest within the Committee for CIS Affairs and Compatriots Abroad, headed by the hawkish Konstantin Zatulin.[72]

Zatulin's committee enjoyed close ties to the government and particularly the MFA. Indeed, it formed an important element within the new Russian foreign policy establishment. During 1994, it became a leading vehicle for championing diaspora issues within both Russia and other CIS states.[73] In summer 1994, the committee began a prolonged series of hearings on diaspora affairs.[74] It also established close links with the Russian communities themselves and so became an integral element within the broader aim of organizing and coordinating the settler populations as a Russian diaspora.

The new government programme and the series of consultations undertaken during the drafting process helped to bridge the political schism that had opened between different organizations working with the diaspora during 1992–3. Nevertheless, criticism of government policy did not disappear completely.[75]

Decreasing confrontation within the domestic politics of the Russian Federation over the diaspora was reinforced by important changes in the external sphere. In 1994, the centrifugal political forces that had promoted the disintegration of the USSR began to be reversed. Between 1992 and 1993 the settler issue played a fundamental role in stemming the process of disengagement between the former Soviet republics. Fear of Russian action to 'protect' the diaspora or of opposition from the settler communities themselves, slowed implementation of some of the more radical policies designed to break the links with Moscow. The was especially true following the war in Moldova in 1992. From 1993, the development of the concept of a Russian diaspora served, to some extent, to bind the newly independent states to Russia once again.[76]

The wide support for the broad definition of the Russian nation and the responsibilities of the Russian state signalled by the introduction of a comprehensive, state-led policy towards the diaspora in autumn 1994 did not, however, mean the diaspora became the dominant theme of Russia's external policy. Rather, as the importance of the Russian communities for the internal politics of most other newly independent states declined,

21

as Russian foreign policy became increasingly complex and policy towards the settlers was institutionalized within the Russian state, the significance of the issue was transformed.[77]

That the Russian communities are part of the Russian nation and that the Russian state has a basic responsibility for their well-being has become an uncontested principle of Russian policy on which Russia's other political, military-strategic and economic interests hinge. With this principle in place, attention has turned to other more pressing concerns. The issue of the diaspora has thus become a vital thread that holds together the broader fabric of Russian domestic and foreign policy, but is no longer the primary issue in Russian external relations with the Baltic and CIS states. Increasingly, diaspora issues provide the backdrop for more urgent debates about reintegration and the future of economic relations between the ex-Soviet republics.[78]

Conclusion

Following independence, the settler communities outside the Russian Federation became a central issue in Russian domestic and interstate politics and a defining element in the struggle to determine Russia's national identity. During this struggle, the initial Russian understanding of the relationship between ethnicity and the new states, of interstate relations, of the nature of sovereignty, and of Russia's post-Soviet role was transformed.

As a result of the internal Russian political battle, the two alternative definitions of the Russian nation – the ethnic *Russkii* and the civic *Rossiiskii* – were fused together in a highly ambiguous relationship. The Russian-speaking settler communities of the CIS and Baltic states have become a Russian (*Rossiiskii*) diaspora by virtue of the fact that they are largely composed of ethnic Russians (*russkii*). However, for policymakers in Moscow, the Russian diaspora includes Russified groups across the former USSR – Koreans in Kazakhstan, Ukrainians in Tallinn and Jews in Ukraine. Russian ethnicity and national identity have therefore been defined in terms of an admixture of sociological, political, cultural-linguistic and genealogical definitions. Settler communities are part of the diaspora because they are composed of *etnicheskie Rossiiane*, compatriots, Russian-speakers, those who have left their 'historic homeland' and individuals who 'identify' with *Rossiia*.

Despite the ambiguities, the Russian diaspora has become a central concept in defining Russian national identity.[79] In particular, since 1992 the settler issue has helped to consolidate a new political elite around a self-image of Russia as the historic 'homeland' for the Russian-speaking communities outside Russia (the diaspora) with Russia directly responsible for their well-being.

These definitions have been institutionalized within the Russian state; that is, notions about Russia and its relationship to the settlers provided the conceptual foundations for state policy and for the further development of the institutions of the state itself. Russian state power is now being exercised to mobilize public organizations and shape society around this definition of the Russian nation. Indeed, the Russian state is to be used to help foster a *Rossiiskii* identity within the settler communities, to create a sense of being part of a Russian diaspora.

The Russian diaspora has therefore functioned as a powerful myth – in the Platonic sense of an allegory – on the basis of which a variety of other myths have been constructed, notably that of Russia as a great power. Cherniavsky argues that the emergence of an independent, centralized Russian state at the beginning of the seventeenth century created an important problem:

> The ideological problem was to associate the population with the
> government in a unity called Russia; the psychological problem was
> to make this 'Russia' convincing, and, perhaps more important, to
> convince oneself, as a member of the governing class, that the unity
> did exist and that one was also a part of it.[80]

In response to these new conditions, Russian thinkers began to develop new concepts of the ruler and the state; and the myths of 'Holy Russia', the 'Russian God', 'the Russian soul', and 'the Russian Tsar' were born.

The collapse of the USSR presented the Russian political elite with a similar problem: how to foster a set of collective and individual identities that tied the population of the Russian Federation to the political unit of the Russian state. This crisis of identity was most acute among the elite itself. Within this context, the myth of the diaspora became a crucial element in cementing together a new ruling elite.

The construction of the idea of the Russian diaspora did not simply involve recognizing that the settler communities had some particular tie to Russia, it also involved viewing Russia as a 'homeland' and a 'kin state', and in this sense the diaspora also defined Russia. The diaspora both provided a central legitimacy for the existence of the Russian state as a protector, a powerful state with broad responsibility – indeed a 'holy

23

duty' – to defend the Russians[81] and most importantly a common sense of identity and purpose for the new political elite.

This argument is not to suggest that there was no discrimination or anti-settler sentiment in the former Soviet republics. Rather, it is to recognize that the extension of Russian political responsibility to these communities involved a crucial process of definition within Russia. There was no 'objective' Russian diaspora simply waiting to be recognized by Russian politicians. After all, despite the presence of large numbers of Ukrainians and Belarussians in the settler communities, Ukraine and Belarus remained silent about alleged 'ethnic' cleansing in the Baltic states and Central Asia.

The construction of the idea of a Russian diaspora was not, however, simply a product of Russian domestic politics. Rather, Russian internal politics was one part of a political dynamic that also included the newly independent states and the settler populations. The role of the settler issue within five of these states will be discussed in the remaining chapters.

Chapter 3

Russian settlers and the struggle for citizenship in Estonia and Latvia

Introduction

The fate of the Russian settler populations in the former Soviet Union first emerged as a central issue of post-Soviet politics in the newly independent states of Estonia and Latvia.[1] Controversy about the settlers initially developed there as a reflection of three main factors: the size of the settler communities relative to the titular populations; the nature of the independence struggle and post-independence politics in the Baltic republics – reactionary ethno-nationalist directed against perceived Russian colonialism; and, finally, the fate of the Baltic settler communities became a major issue in the domestic politics of Russia itself.[2]

The main factor responsible for the politicization of the settler issue in Estonia and Latvia was the form of popular mobilization that emerged there in the late 1980s. Without the developed political institutions of civil society, it was the bonds of culture, language and family that provided the foundations of political organization against Soviet rule. The cultural-linguistic basis for mobilization was further reinforced by perceptions of Russian expansion in the region and gradual assimilation of Baltic and Finno-Ugric peoples by Russian society. In this context, Baltic national identities became even more closely wedded to language and culture than in other Soviet republics. Protecting Estonian and Latvian language and culture therefore became the central justification for political activity in the Baltic states during *perestroika*.

As a result of these factors, manipulation of the settler issue became central to a variety of nationalist movements – Russian-Soviet and Estonian/ Latvian – seeking to shape Baltic and Russian national identities.

In the post-independence period, the powerful ethno-political impulse

Distribution of Russian settlers in Estonia and Latvia

that had emerged in Estonia and Latvia during the latter years of Gorbachev's tenure became their central political dynamic. The legislative agenda promoted by radical nationalists in the two parliaments and governments – the background for inter-ethnic tension in the region is formed by the initial decision of Estonia and Latvia to adopt very narrow definitions of citizenship – provided radicals in Russia with significant ammunition to be used against Democratic politicians, particularly the Foreign Minister, Andrei Kozyrev. As a result, the political struggle over citizenship in Estonia and Latvia became one of the most powerful forces shaping perceptions of the Russian diaspora and the relationship between the Russian Federation and the other former Soviet republics. The battle to shape the national identities in the Baltic states therefore developed at three different levels simultaneously: between the indigenous and settler populations; among the Russians themselves; and between Russia and the Baltic states.

Although the Baltic states have faced similar challenges with regard to their respective settler communities, each republic has followed different approaches. In Estonia, despite a greater initial divide between the autochthonous population and the Russian-speakers, the preconditions for the emergence of relatively harmonious inter-ethnic relations have been established. The Russian population has emerged as the most developed settler population in the former USSR and the Estonian politicians and officials have shown themselves willing to support the cultural and political development of the non-Estonian community. In Latvia, on the other hand, the prolonged debate about a law on naturalization froze inter-ethnic tension and prevented the internal development of the settler community. At the same time, the Latvian authorities did nothing positive to structure or organize the non-Latvians. As a result, the Russian population of Latvia remains disorganized, lumpen and uncertain about its loyalty to the new state.

The local Russian populations themselves are also struggling to define their own identity. Under Soviet ideology, the migrants largely lost their cultural roots. At present most Russian-speakers have great difficulty identifying themselves with any one particular culture. Multiple and often competing identities are therefore found among the settlers. The minorities tend to view themselves as being simultaneously representatives of overlapping Baltic (Estonian or Latvian), Soviet, Russian and world cultures. In terms of self-identification, the settler communities are not as yet ethnic-based minorities. Being a Russian-speaker continues to form the main substance of their identity. Challenged by both the Baltic and Russian authorities to define their national identity, the Russian-speaking settlers are seeking to determine what role ethnicity (Russian, Ukrainian, Jewish etc.) will play in it and whether it will be linked primarily to a Baltic or Russian (*Rossiskii*) identity.

Russians and the Russification of Latvia and Estonia

Prior to 1940

The majority of the Russian-speaking population in the Baltic states are immigrants who have come to the area since the Second World War. However, the history of Russian settlement in the Baltic region stretches back for over 900 years. Prior to the crusades, Russian princes controlled significant territories in the area. When the region fell under the control of the Teutonic Knights, Russian influence declined although a few small settlements populated by Russian merchants and traders remained. From the sixteenth century, these communities were enlarged by political refugees and dissidents fleeing Ivan the Terrible and his descendants. Among these migrants were many Old Believers escaping religious persecution. Estonia and Livonia were finally brought under Russian control by Peter the Great. The region remained closely bound to the Russian Empire from this time until the First World War.

The experience of Russian empire in each of the Baltic provinces differed in important ways. The Lithuanians and the Latgalians participated in the uprisings of their Polish-speaking rulers against Russian rule, while the Estonians and Latvians lived in relative peace owing to the loyalty of their German masters to the Russian Empire, whose dominance of the area had been guaranteed by Peter the Great in 1721. Although the size of the Russian population in the Baltic region gradually increased as traders, officials and soldiers moved there, the absolute numbers of Russians remained relatively small until the 1890s. The balance of social relations was then beginning to change as new demographic and economic forces appeared. Rapid growth in the rural population accompanied by industrialization in the urban areas drew Estonian and Latvian peasants to the cities and towns. This large-scale migration challenged the hegemony of the German-speakers in these areas for the first time in 600 years. Within a few decades, sizeable Estonian and Latvian communities had grown up in most urban areas. At the same time, increasing Russian migration to the Baltic cities as a result of economic development outflanked the previously dominant Germans.[3]

Historically, the relationship between Latvians-Estonians and Russians has been ambiguous. Before the 1917 revolution many Baltic nationalists sided with the Russians to counter the economic and political dominance of the Germans. However, this alliance was rather fragile. There was little support for Baltic nationalism within the leadership of the Russian Empire and under Alexander II and Nicholas II, imperial policy sought to exert greater control of the Baltic republics by instituting policies designed to produce thorough Russification.[4]

During the 1905 revolution, the Latvians and Estonians rose against the Germans but their insurrection was quickly suppressed. However, the chaos that accompanied the Russian revolution of 1917 finally allowed the Latvians and Estonians to replace governing German institutions with their own. During the struggle for power following the revolution, the Bolsheviks attempted to consolidate their hold in the Baltic region with the support of the local Russian working class. By April 1918 the whole region had been overrun by Germany. Over the next two years control of the area fluctuated between Bolsheviks, Germans and the local forces. By the early 1920s the Estonians and Latvians had successfully seized political control in their respective territories and had begun to build the foundations for independent and sovereign states. The independent status of the new states was formalized in the Treaty of Tartu in February 1920 (Estonia) and the Treaty of Riga in August 1920 (Latvia).

While a sizeable German minority remained in the region, the Russian population had been substantially reduced during the war. In the following years, however, significant numbers of Russians began to arrive in the Baltic states, repeating the migration patterns of hundreds of years before. Russian refugees – White Russian officers, priests, aristocrats, Russian-speaking Jews and much of the intelligentsia from St Petersburg – came fleeing persecution in the USSR. Between the two world wars, Riga became host to the largest Russian émigré community after Paris and a centre for Russian arts and letters.[5]

Annexation and the end of independence

After Soviet annexation of the Baltic states in 1940, Stalinist terror was immediately unleashed. Not only Latvians and Estonians but Russians and Russian culture were particular targets for Soviet repression. The Russian communities in Latvia and Estonia were ruthlessly broken up by a combination of terror and the influx of Sovietized Russian-speakers. By 1945, the prewar Russian communities of the Baltic region had been all but completely destroyed by war and Soviet policies.

The extermination of potential opposition to Soviet rule was accompanied by a policy aimed at inducing significant demographic change in the Baltic states. Indigenous officials were purged and replaced. Russian-speaking Soviet personnel from Moscow were assigned to help establish political control and to develop a core of reliable administrators in the area. However, the new Soviet order in the Baltic region did not simply rely on Russian cadres to consolidate its position. As a result of the First World War and the Bolshevik revolution, about 200,000 Latvians ended up in the USSR. Tens of thousands of them were used by the Soviets to establish their rule in the Baltic states in 1940.[6] The subjugation of the Baltic countries was not simply a new form of Russian imperialism.

With peace, the Soviet authorities returned to the demographic policies that they had begun in 1940. The settlement of Russian-speakers began immediately, with Red Army officers and soldiers being demobilized in the region. Postwar economic reconstruction brought further migration, especially to the cities, and whole neighbourhoods grew up to accommodate new settlers. In the 1960s and 1970s, the economic development of the republics envisaged by the Soviet state planning ministry, Gosplan, brought further migrants to the region. Large all-Union, Moscow-directed industrial enterprises, often connected to defence, were sited in the Baltic republics with little regard for the availability of labour. Indeed, labour in the form of Russian-speaking workers was considered to be the most easily transportable of all resources.

Alongside the workers and technical intelligentsia who moved to the republics, military personnel were stationed in the area and often retired there. Because released prisoners were not allowed to return to many of the big cities of the Russian Federation, many ended up in the Baltic republics. Some sources suggest that 23% of immigrants between 1980 and 1988 were released convicts.[7] In the 1970s, the comparatively higher standard of living of the Baltic republics drew a further wave of migrants from other areas of the USSR.

As well as providing the workforce necessary for steady industrialization and developing a population largely loyal to Moscow, the rising numbers of Russians and Russian-speakers changed the cultural milieu of the Baltic republics. The Russian-speakers acted as *Kulturträger* for the strange admixture of Soviet and Russian culture that formed the core of Soviet identity. At the heart of this culture was the Russian language. The Soviet authorities promoted one-way bilingualism (Estonians and Latvians were expected to know Russian as well as their native language but migrants needed only Russian) based largely on Russian, Belarussian and Ukrainian settlers.[8] Gradually indigenous culture and language were displaced from their previous dominance. By 1989 in Latvia 227,783 non-Russians considered Russian their first language but only 34,429 non-Latvians spoke Latvian as their first language.

Although the majority of settlers identified themselves as ethnic Russians in the Soviet census, the settler communities also contained significant numbers of Ukrainians, Belarussians and Jews. However, ethnicity was not the primary element of the migrants' identity. As with settler populations in the other Soviet republics, the principal element of the Baltic settler identity was Soviet. The core of the migrant population was drawn from those sections of the Soviet population most closely tied to the successes of the regime – industrial workers and members of the military and security apparatus. They were largely rootless in an ethnocultural sense. Their migration to the Baltic region was thus not Russian colonization in a new guise but Sovietization by a Russian-speaking, de-ethnicized immigrant population.[9]

The most extreme case of Sovietization took place in Latvia. As early as the 1950s, a number of leading officials of the Latvian Communist Party expressed concern to Moscow about the number of migrants coming to the republic. The officials were promptly removed from their positions by Khrushchev. The scale of migration to the republic can be seen in Table 3.1. In fact, shortly before annexation the percentage of Latvians was even higher, reaching 83% in 1940. In Estonia, during the Soviet period there was also large-scale in-migration. In 1945, the figure for ethnic Estonians living in the republic reached 97.5%. In all, only 23,000 non-Estonians lived in Estonia at that time (see Table 3.2).

The large number of migrants to the Baltic states was reinforced by the strategic positions that the Russian and Russian-speaking settlers occupied there. They came to dominate the machine-building, energy, transport, construction and manufacturing sectors. Estonians and Latvians occupied important political positions, but to ensure that they complied with Moscow's instructions they were almost always shadowed by a Russian-speaker. In addition, there was an ethnic division of political labour such that non-Balts were over-represented in the republican Communist Party and in crucial areas of the local state administration.

Economic and political domination was reinforced by the geographic concentration of the settlers. In both Estonia and Latvia, rapid urbanization and the large scale of migration led to a two-way structural shift in the distribution of the population. Non-indigenous Russian-speakers were consolidated in the two capitals. The indigenous share of the total populations of Tallinn and Riga fell dramatically, in Riga's case to less than half. At the same time, industrially developed towns and districts became dominated by non-Balts. Thus, under Soviet rule, Latvian and Estonian control was gradually confined to the rural areas.

By 1989, Latvians were minorities in the seven largest cities of their country and in Riga they constituted only 36.5% of the population. In Estonia, migration followed a similar pattern with 80% of the non-Estonian population concentrated in the cities of the north (Tallinn), the northeast and Paldisk, while only 8.5% lived in the countryside. However, unlike the integrated form of settlement that emerged in Latvia – districts and even blocks of flats often contain mixed populations of settlers and Latvians – in Estonia the migrants concentrated in Russian-speaking enclaves.

By the 1980s, the age structure and rates of natural increase among the

Table 3.1 Population of Latvia by ethnic origin: 1935–89 (thousands)

Ethnic Origin	1935	%	1959	%	1970	%	1979	%	1989	%
Latvian	1,467.0	77.0	1,297.9	62.0	1,341.8	56.8	1,344.1	53.7	1,387.8	52.0
Russian	168.3	8.8	5564.	26.6	704.6	29.8	821.5	32.8	905.5	34.0
Belarussian	26.7	1.4	61.6	2.9	94.7	4.0	111.5	4.5	119.7	4.5
Polish	48.6	2.6	59.8	2.9	63.0	2.7	62.7	2.5	60.4	2.3
Ukrainian	1.8	0.01	29.4	1.4	53.5	2.3	66.7	2.7	92.1	3.4
Lithuanian	22.8	1.2	32.4	1.5	40.6	1.7	37.8	1.5	34.6	1.3
Jewish	93.4	4.9	36.6	1.7	36.7	1.6	28.3	1.1	22.9	0.9
German	62.1	3.3	1.6	0.1	5.4	0.2	3.3	0.1	3.8	0.1
Estonian	6.9	0.4	4.6	0.2	4.3	0.2	3.7	0.1	3.3	0.1
Gypsy	3.8	0.2	4.3	0.2	—	—	6.1	0.2	7.0	0.3
Tatar	0.04	0.0	1.8	0.1	—	—	3.8	0.2	4.8	0.2
Other	3.9	0.2	7.1	0.4	19.3	0.8	13.3	0.6	24.7	0.9
Total	1,905.4		2,093.5		2,364.1		2,502.8		2,666.6	—

Source: Juris Dreifelds, 'Immigration and ethnicity in Latvia', *Journal of Soviet Nationalities*, vol. 1, no. 4 (Winter 1990–91), p. 48.

Table 3.2 Population of Estonia by ethnic origin: 1934–89 (thousands)

Ethnic Origin	1934	%	1959	%	1970	%	1979	%	1989	%
Estonian	992	88.1	893	74.6	925	68.2	948	64.7	963	61.3
Russian	92	8.1	240	20.1	335	24.7	409	27.9	475	30.3
Ukrainian	—	—	16	1.3	28	2.1	36	2.5	48	3.1
Belarussian	—	—	11	0.9	19	1.4	23	1.6	28	1.8
Finnish	2	0.2	17	1.4	19	1.4	18	1.2	17	1.1
Jewish	4	0.4	5	0.4	5	0.4	5	0.3	5	0.3
German	16	1.5	2	0.1	8	0.7	4	0.3	3	0.2
Swedish	8	0.7	—	—	—	—	0.2	0.0	0.3	0.0
Latvian	5	0.5	3	0.2	—	—	4	0.2	3	0.2
Other	5	0.4	10	1.1	18	1.1	17	1.3	23	1.7
Total	1,126		1,197		1,356		1,464		1,565	

Source: Estonia and Soviet Census Data. Pre-1940 and post-1940 figures are not directly comparable due to border revisions undertaken by the Soviet authorities. In 1945, territory that had been occupied by Estonia in 1920 was returned to the Russian Federation.

Russified settlers meant that even if migration stopped completely, Latvians and Estonians would still continue to dwindle relative to the non-indigenous population. Demographically, linguistically and culturally, they faced a precarious future. Despite the growing threat to the indigenous population, relations with the migrants were not always tense. Latvia in particular enjoyed relatively high rates of intermarriage: in 1988 33.1% of marriages involving Latvians were of mixed nationality, which was close to the rates in the predominantly Slavic republics of Belarus (34.6%) and Ukraine (35.6%) and is significantly higher than Estonia's 16.1%.

Russian-speakers during the independence struggle
The struggle for independence that developed in Estonia and Latvia in the late 1980s exposed the complex identity of their Russian-speaking populations. In response to the appearance of powerful independence movements (the Popular Fronts), these populations were, for the first time, forced to question who they were and what functions they performed in Baltic society. Two main political tendencies appeared within the Russian-speaking populations: the Soviet-Russian and Baltic-Russian trends, the former more noticeable and better organized, being able to rely on the existing structures of the Communist Party, the security apparatus and the military for support. The Baltic-Russian trend tended to be swallowed by the Popular Fronts and had little organization of its own, although polls taken during this period suggest that among the immigrant population there was more support for the Baltic-Russian tendency than the Soviet one.[10]

Soviet organizations and Soviet enclaves As reformist elements gained control in the Baltic communist parties, local hardline communists and groups in Moscow joined forces to create shadowy Soviet loyalist organizations – Interfronts (*Interdvizhenie*) in both republics: the United Council of Workers' Collectives (OSTK) in Estonia and the All-Latvian Salvation Committee, which were to appeal to the Russian-speaking populations.[11] In both republics, these organizations sought support from the workers and administrators of all-Union industrial plants and from the military and security apparatus – precisely those people who would be most vulnerable if the Soviet Union disintegrated. The Interfronts opposed independence for the Baltic republics and championed the economic rights of workers in place of the Popular Fronts' emphasis on human rights. Although a great deal of attention was directed towards these organizations, political mobilization among Russian-speakers was modest. However, in a number of heavily Sovietized enclaves, where old-style communist leaderships retained control, these movements were particularly powerful. In Latvia, Daugavpils emerged as a centre for the Interfront. In 1989, the city soviet called for regional autonomy for the area and in 1990 it adopted a resolution proclaiming the Latvian Declaration of Independence of 4 May 1990 inoperative. In Estonia, the cities of the northeast, particularly Narva, became the centres for Interfront activity. Here too, claims for local autonomy were made by the local leadership.

In both republics, Soviet front organizations also had significant parliamentary representation. In Latvia, the Equal Rights faction was formed from hardline Latvian Communist Party and Interfront deputies in the Supreme Soviet on 4 May 1990. In Estonia, the Interregional Council of People's Deputies was created in May 1990, based on the Committee of the Defence of Soviet Power and Civil Rights in Estonia. Its main goal was to oppose the political and economic sovereignty of Estonia.

The Popular Fronts and the Russian settlers In both Latvia and Estonia the Popular Fronts deliberately sought support among the non-indigenous population and in particular tried to co-opt representatives of the Russian-speaking intelligentsia; special Russian cultural organizations were set up and the Fronts published Russian-language papers.[12] While the presence of representatives from the Russian communities in the independence movements was important, they always played a secondary role to the Estonian and Latvian activists. However, from 1989 to 1991, the Russian-speaking populations demonstrated increasing support for Baltic independence.

Russian settlers in Latvia A good example of the growing support for independence among the Russians and Russian-speakers was the parliamentary election of March 1990. The ethnic distribution of the deputies indicates that far more Russian-speakers voted for the ethnic Latvian candidates of the Popular Front than for the ethnic Russian candidates put up by Equal Rights. In the new parliament 74% of deputies were ethnic Latvians; the Russian-speakers had clearly voted for independence and trusted ethnic Latvians to represent their interests better than other Russian-speakers.

Two-thirds of Latvia's Russian residents indicated support for the Latvian Supreme Soviet and Council of Ministers in a poll taken two days before the Soviet crack-down in Riga in January 1991.[13] The same poll indicated declining support among the Russians for the Interfront and the All-Latvian Salvation Committee. In January 1991, many non-Latvians were reported to be on the barricades in Riga when the Soviet internal security forces launched their attacks. On 3 March 1991, a non-binding consultative plebiscite on Latvian independence and democracy was called by the Latvian Supreme Council to pre-empt the referendum called by the USSR Supreme Soviet. Despite the efforts of the local Communist Party and Interfront to organize a boycott, turnout was 87.6%; 73.7% voted for independence and not a single district or city, including Daugavpils, voted 'no'.[14] Although data on voting by ethnic group is not available, the size of the pro-independence vote and its distribution suggests that considerable numbers of Russians voted for it.

Russified settlers in Estonia Polls conducted during the independence struggle indicated growing support for independence among non-Estonians. Between April 1989 and June 1990, those supporting independence rose fivefold (from 5% to 27%).[15] A poll conducted by the polling group EMOR in December 1990 showed that independence was supported by 28% of non-Estonians born in the republic and by 14% of those who had settled there.[16] In the 1990 elections for the Supreme Soviet, votes for pro-Soviet organizations totalled only 28.2% (CPE-CPSU – 13.3%; OSTK – 9%; Interfront – 5.9%). In the referendum in spring 1991, 37–40% of non-Estonians supported independence. An EMOR poll published in September 1991 indicated that 55% of Russian-speakers supported an independent Estonia during the August putsch.

Work conducted by the sociologists Hallik and Kirch indicates that by 1991 important changes in perceptions of the Estonian republic had taken place among different ethnic groups. In 1986, 72% of Estonians identified with the Estonian nation as an integral whole, 18% identified with all the population of the Estonian Republic and only 10% with the all the people of the USSR. Russians in Estonia identified with the whole USSR – 78% – while only 14% of Russians felt close to Russia and only 8% identified with the Estonian Republic.[17] By 1991, Russian-speakers in Latvia and Estonia were the least pro-Soviet of the settlers in the USSR. Only 52% of Russians in Latvia considered themselves to be citizens of the USSR while in Estonia the figure was 59%. In Georgia the comparative figure was 68%, in Kazakhstan 77% and in Uzbekistan 88%.[18]

Russians and Russian-speakers and the post-independence period

The defeat of the August 1991 coup in Moscow marked the triumph of the pro-independence forces in the Baltic republics. However, the Russian-speaking populations of the Baltics were ill-prepared for the dissolution of the USSR. The struggle for independence had done much to affirm the ethnic and national identities of the Estonians and Latvians; the settler community, by contrast, faced a major identity crisis. The Russian settlers in the Baltic republics lacked significant indigenous social and political institutions to promote new identities and were confronted by powerful ethno-nationalist movements. As a result, by the beginning of 1992 both Soviet-Russian and Baltic-Russian movements were facing severe difficulties.

Most of the Soviet organizations in the Baltic region were banned after the August coup, while the end of the USSR meant that significant support for them from Moscow ceased. In addition, the pro-Soviet organizations faced an ideological crisis because their underlying communist value system was totally discredited. While some former Soviet politicians began to reorient themselves towards Russia and Russian nationalist organizations, many blamed Russia for the collapse of the USSR and left politics altogether.

Like the pro-Soviet organizations, the Baltic-Russian movement was facing an identity crisis. The transformation of the Baltic independence movements into largely ethno-nationalist movements placed increasing pressure on the settlers. The Russian-speaking activists within the Popular Fronts were quickly marginalized and support for Russian cultural organizations ceased. At the same time, the emergence of the Russian Federation as an independent state meant that there was another political entity that could claim the political allegiance of the settlers. There were important differences between the responses of the settler communities in Latvia and Estonia to these challenges.

In the absence of independent civil structures and democratic institutions, nations and ethnic groups appeared as the only collective actors capable of representing anti-totalitarian and anti-imperial interests.[19] However, following independence the dynamic induced by these movements quickly led to the creation of a new enemy. With the Soviet threat destroyed, the fragile institutions and weak democratic culture of the Baltic states led to wide political fragmentation within the independence movements. The only element that united the former allies was fear of the enemy within: the fifth column of Russian-Soviet influence, the

Russian-speaking population. In this climate, the issue of citizenship quickly emerged as the focal point for the political struggle to define the new nations in both Baltic republics.[20]

Latvia

After the coup, the political composition of the Latvian parliament changed dramatically. Until August 1991, political power in Latvia was distributed between three groups of deputies in the Supreme Soviet: the Popular Front of Latvia (PFL), which comprised just under two-thirds of the deputies; the Equal Rights group (*Ravnopravie*) and Communists, which made up about a third of the deputies, many of them ethnic Russians and the majority pro-Soviet; and a small independent group who generally voted with the PFL. On 24 August 1991, the Supreme Council decided to ban organizations that aimed to overthrow the government and legislature of Latvia, including the Communist Party. The Equal Rights group lost more than half its strength because these deputies had supported the Communist leader Alfred Rubriks who was accused of trying to seize power in the republic during the August coup. In October 1991, the Supreme Council dissolved the Soviet loyalist city councils of Daugavpils and Rezekne, along with the Leningrad district of Riga.

The arrest of Rubiks and the loss of fourteen mandates for Equal Rights gave the Latvian nationalist forces a large majority in parliament. They were therefore able to set about transforming Latvian society and defining the new Latvian state with little effective opposition. On 15 October a law on citizenship, based on a Latvian law of 1919, was adopted. Under its terms, most non-Latvians were not entitled to Latvian citizenship. The implementation of the 5 May 1989 language law, which required that Latvian become the official state language, also posed a serious threat to Russian-speakers.

With the collapse of the Soviet Union, the Popular Front quickly disintegrated into a range of factions and independent deputies with no place for the Baltic-Russian forces.[21] With both the Soviet and Democratic settler institutions severely weakened, non-Latvians were largely excluded from the political process. Latvian nationalism became the main substance of post-independence politics.

Neither the Latvian government nor parliament developed a strategy to deal with the Russians and Russian-speakers. This allowed the emergence of groups whose stated aim was ridding Latvia of all migrants who had come during the Soviet era. The philosophy of the three Ds – deoccupation, debolshevization and decolonization – became the language of politics and extremist organizations like the Citizens' Congress – which had originally tried to act as an alternative to the Supreme Council and government of Latvia – became particularly active with the support of a cluster of radical groups. Many leading Latvian politicians spoke openly about the need to encourage non-Latvians (especially Russians and Russian-speakers) to leave.[22]

The Latvian state initially did almost nothing in either political or financial terms to assist with the creation of the institutions of civil society among the non-Latvians. Indeed, organizations designed to act as a bridge between Latvians and non-Latvians, such as the Nationalities Department of the Council of Ministers, were ignored or downgraded.[23] Unlike Estonia, where the government of Edgar Savisaar laid the foundations for a system to manage inter-ethnic relations, Latvia lacked a leader with the foresight to tackle ethnic problems directly. The only potential leader, Janis Jurkans, was never sufficiently powerful and was ousted from his position as foreign minister in November 1992 for his support for non-Latvians. Moderate Russian-speakers and Latvians sympathetic to the problems of non-Latvians were largely driven out of mainstream politics. With indigenous settler organizations crucially weakened, the Russian-speaking community emerged from the immediate independence period highly fragmented and essentially powerless.

The non-Latvian population During 1991–4 the Russian and Russian-speaking population remained leaderless, unstructured and divided.[24] Of the approximately 63 organizations that claimed to represent the Russian-speakers none represented more than 500 people; together they represented at most 10% of the non-Latvian population. Approximately 4,000 non-Latvians out of a total of nearly one million were involved in activities in the non-Latvian subculture.

While attempts have been made to establish moderate Russian political organizations, the lack of citizenship for their potential leaders has prevented them achieving any sort of success. This has left settler politics dominated by ex-Soviet, fomerly anti-independence organizations, foremost of which is Equal Rights. Originally very close to the Latvian Communist Party, its leaders Alfred Rubiks, Sergei Dimanis and Tat'iana Zdanok are descended from pre-1941 citizens of Latvia and gained citizenship automatically.[25]

Before independence, Equal Rights campaigned for the retention of the Union, economic rights in Latvia and citizenship issues. Following the 1991 putsch, nine deputies left the faction to join the Centre for

Democratic Initiative (CDI, formed to organize Russian-speakers around support for human rights and a liberal citizenship law, and headed by Gavrilov, formerly of the Latvian Communist Party), while others were banned for their support for the coup. Since independence, Equal Rights has tried to distance itself from communism and has concentrated on the citizenship question. In the 1993 elections, it gained seven deputies in parliament. It also picked up seats in the local elections of 1994. Of all the parliamentary parties, Equal Rights was the only one to support the 'zero option' for citizenship.[26]

In the post-independence period, the other leading ex-Soviet organization to claim support among the settlers was the reformed Interfront. As it had become clear to the Soviet authorities that Interfront was failing in its aim to mobilize non-Latvians against independence, so efforts were made to set up a new organization to achieve this goal. Established in March 1991, the Russian Community of Latvia (*Russkaia obshchina Latvii* – ROL) was to be under the control of the Soviet loyalist organizations and was initially led by leading members of the Interfront. Membership of ROL was drawn primarily from the technical intelligentsia and was initially put at 1,000. The organization established a Russian-language paper, *Russkii Put* and the Russian Technological University, the first independent higher education institution in Latvia to teach in both Russian and Latvian.

However, internal conflict between the Soviet loyalist leadership and the rank and file who supported Latvian independence soon arose. At ROL's second conference in December 1991, a number of moderate members walked out in protest against authoritarian leadership. It also emerged that ROL leaders had been involved in financial irregularities. By September 1992, discontent led to the leadership being removed and Vladimir Vladov, leader of the moderate pro-Latvian wing of ROL, became the new president. However, the power struggle had left ROL very weak. It quickly disintegrated, leaving only a small Russian cultural organization.[27]

Reflecting the high numbers of military personnel in Latvia, a range of reactionary organizations developed during the independence struggle based largely on the Soviet armed forces.[28] On 5 October 1993, following the putsch in Moscow, the Latvian government announced it was banning three 'illegal and pro-communist' organizations: the Latvian Communist Union, the Veterans' Rights Defence Union, and the Russian Citizens' Association of Latvia. Their leaders – Igor Lopatin, Oleg Kapranov and Viktor Alksnis – were reportedly with other Union of Latvian Communist members, veterans, and rights groups at the Congress of People's Deputies of the USSR near Moscow on 20 September 1993,[29] allegedly plotting a coup with former members of the Soviet internal security service in Latvia.[30]

Although settler society has been politically dominated by ex-Soviet institutions, some attempts were made to form more moderate cultural and political groups. The cultural organizations that emerged from the Baltic-Russian movement during *perestroika*, however, fared little better than the pro-Soviet political organizations after independence. During the independence struggle, the Latvian Popular Front sought to counter Interfront influence through the promotion of Russian cultural organizations. In March 1989, the Russian Cultural Association of Latvia (LORK) headed by Iurii Abizov was formed and immediately declared solidarity with the Popular Front. The Latvian local council in Riga provided it with a house and money. LORK representatives went to Moscow with the Latvian intelligentsia to meet Gorbachev and lobby for independence. As the Popular Front became more nationalistic, support for LORK was withdrawn and it collapsed after independence.

The Balto-Slavic Association for Cultural Development and Cooperation was formed in 1988 by elements of the Slavic cultural intelligentsia. After initially seeking an intermediate position it became closer to the Interfront than the Popular Front. After the August 1991 putsch, its leadership accepted Latvian independence although it subsequently also embraced a fairly strong form of Russian nationalism; but, lacking financial support, it could do little.

Although new Russian cultural organizations were founded after independence, they were short of funds and could reach only a tiny percentage of the Russian-speaking population. Established in 1991, ART-ROL (which incorporated *Russkii Put* and the Russian Technological University after the collapse of ROL) aimed to unite the young professional non-Latvian artistic and cultural intelligentsia of Latvia. It strongly supported Latvian independence and opposed the former Interfront. Since financial assistance from the Russian Ministry of Culture ceased in 1991, ART-ROL has been unable to function effectively.

A number of attempts have also been made to develop moderate parties with support from the settlers. During the 1993 elections, the CDI united with Andrei Vorontsov, a journalist from the Russian-language paper *SM-Segodniia*, to form the Russian Democratic List. Formerly an expert on national relations and democratization within the LCP and with close ties to the thriving settler business class, Vorontsov has argued that the only solution to the current problems is a system of two national states and two parliaments in Latvia, with a Latvian President and Russian Vice-President. These separate national states would be based on language, not *ethnos*. However, as most of the leadership of the party lacked Latvian citizenship, the list failed.

The non-Latvians have also been unable to find powerful allies among the Latvian political elite. In public opinion polls, Janis Jurkans is consistently rated as one of most popular non-Latvian politicians. His party, Harmony for Latvia, has received assistance from leading settler businesses.[31] The nationalist thrust of post-independence Latvia has, however, kept Jurkans on the margins of mainstream politics.

The most dynamic sphere for the settler community has been its new economic role adopted in the early 1990s. Forced out of the state sector by the requirement of fluency in Latvian, many non-Latvians have moved into the private sector and have used former Soviet institutions, particularly the *Komsomol*, as the basis for new economic activity. By late 1993, most of the country's 60 banks were controlled by non-Latvians. The Russian-speaking community has close business links with Russia, and Riga has emerged as a major 'offshore' centre for capital from the Russian Federation, although much of this money appears tied to criminal activity. Unfortunately, the more traditional economic links such as joint manufacturing ventures have often been rejected by the Latvian authorities, who fear losing control of the national economy.[32] The close economic interests between Latvian and Russian-language businessmen may provide a basis for some inter-ethnic reconciliation.[33]

Although Riga contains by far the largest concentration of settlers in Latvia, the towns of Daugavpils and Jurmala have also become important centres for settler political activity. During the independence struggle, Daugavpils emerged as a focus for Soviet resistance to the Popular Front. After the Second World War, the town was designated a centre for the Soviet defence industry and employed large numbers of Slavic migrants.[34] The local party-state *nomenklatura* became immensely powerful and promoted thorough Sovietization of the town. This political network was used to build up a powerful base of support for the Interfront in the late 1980s. In August 1991, the Daugavpils soviet tried to rally support for the coup from towns similar to itself in the ex-USSR like Narva in Estonia and Tiraspol in Moldova.

With independence, the Latvian authorities disbanded the local soviet and imposed a new mayor on the town, Valdis Lauskis. His main task was to break the grip of ROL (Interfront) through a policy of support for different national-cultural organizations in the area. Alongside Jewish, Polish and Ukrainian societies, he has fostered the development of the Baltic-Slavic Society based on the Old Believer community. The deliberate development of ethnic-based identities has helped undermine the Soviet Russian-speaking one formerly dominant in the area.

The Jurmala Russian Community (JRC) arose in the last years of *perestroika*. It includes those in mixed marriages, Russians who have worked in Latvia all their lives and young Russian entrepreneurs. Headed by Victor Iurkov, the JRC wants cultural-national autonomy and has developed in four directions – education, culture, medical and social welfare programmes. The JRC has built close ties to the Congress of Russian Communities of Dmitri Rogozin in Russia, but is largely isolated from Latvia's other settler communities. Like the central settler organizations, those in the regions are disorganized, poorly funded and exhibit little coordination between themselves.

The 1993 elections The Latvian elections of June 1993 highlighted the problems facing the non-Latvian community.[35] Under the electoral law only citizens of Latvia were allowed to vote; of these 28% were ethnic Russians. This meant that 34% of the country's residents could not vote. The elections signalled a general drift to the right, with 75% of the vote going to centre-right or far-right parties. Anatoli Gorbunovs, leader of Latvian Way, emerged as victor (32% of the vote) and formed a coalition with another centre-right party, the Farmers Union (10.6%).[36] Both parties aimed at a 'gradual naturalization' of the non-Latvian population.

In parliament, two factions represent the interests of the non-Latvian population: Jurkans' Harmony for Latvia and Equal Rights. Equal Rights gained 5.77% of the popular vote. Its support was not wholly non-Latvian – it gained one mandate in a primarily Latvian area, Vidzeme, while only receiving 40% of the vote in Daugavpils. Harmony for Latvia gained 11.98% of the vote and 13 seats. Vorontsov's Russian List and Gavrilov's CDI ran on a programme of citizenship for all those resident in Latvia on 4 May 1990, use of the Russian language in regions of compact settlement, and rapid privatization. However, unable to find strong candidates fluent in Latvian, they failed to get through the 4% barrier, gaining only 13,006 votes or 1.163%.

The law on naturalization and local elections in 1994 Latvian nationalist control of the parliament made it possible to introduce a law on naturalization. On 25 November 1993, the parliament (*Saeima*), after a heated debate, chose from among five draft laws the one formulated by Latvian

Way as the basis for further discussion. Immediately, the issue of quotas on the rate of naturalization emerged as the central issue of the legislation. After prolonged debate, parliament eventually passed a version of the law that would have severely limited the numbers of non-Latvians who could naturalize every year. Under strong international pressure, President Ulmanis sent the bill back to parliament.[37] A revised law without the quota element was passed at the end of July. Under this law 400,000 of the 700,000 registered non-Latvian residents of Latvia will be able to apply for naturalization and the process should be completed by 2003.[38]

Although Latvia has developed a legal basis for citizenship and naturalization, the continued disempowerment of the settlers makes them unable to influence the political process in any meaningful way. Thus, the local elections of 29 May 1994 led to another victory for Latvian nationalist parties, while the majority of the Russian-speaking population were unable to vote. Of Riga's population of 800,000, only 340,000 were eligible to vote.[39] Although fears about the quota system led to the formation of a new settler organization – the League of non-Citizens – all such organizations remain weak. Until a sizeable nucleus of Russians holds citizenship, the settler community will remain on the margins of Latvian politics.

Estonia

Although inter-ethnic relations in Estonia initially developed the same pattern as in Latvia, since independence there have been important differences between the two republics. While Latvia continued to pursue the construction of an ethnocratic state and society, key sections of Estonian society and many leading politicians gradually came to accept that the settler minorities would have an important role in the new society. This is partly because Estonia began the process of state-building earlier and therefore had the foundations of the new social and political order before Latvia; but other factors have also been important, notably international pressure, a greater willingness to compromise among Estonian politicians and a more active non-Estonian community. Estonia therefore entered the post-nationalist stage of development – when nationalist slogans begin to lose their resonance, domestic issues become more complex and socio-economic questions begin to dominate – well before Latvia.

The period of mono-ethnic state-building in Estonia lasted from August 1991 until mid-1993. During this time, Estonia became a member of the UN, the CSCE and other international bodies, and the fundamental principles of the state were laid down in a series of basic laws. Originally the Estonian Popular Front had proposed a zero variant for citizenship based on residence on 30 March 1990. This was opposed by the nationalist Congress of Estonia. Following independence, Estonian nationalists used their position of strength to reinstate the citizenship law of 1938, thereby granting automatic citizenship to all those who were citizens on 16 June 1941 and their descendants, regardless of ethnicity. The vast majority who received citizenship by this method were, of course, Estonian.

On the basis of this law, elections were conducted in September 1992 that resulted in only one non-Estonian, an ethnic Swede, being voted into the new parliament. Since the majority of the non-Estonian population were not citizens, they were unable to stand as candidates or vote. The new mono-ethnic parliament subsequently passed a series of laws – of which the Law on Foreigners of 21 June 1993 was the most important – which further institutionalized the ethnic division of society. The new language law, taking into account the recommendations of international observers, came into effect on 10 February 1993.[40]

In the climate of strong ethno-nationalism that followed independence, a number of extremist organizations emerged, including the Decolonization Foundation, set up in early 1993 to promote the 'peaceful' repatriation of Russian and Russian-speaking immigrants so that the percentage of Estonians could rise from 63.5% to 80%. The Foundation particularly targets former KGB, intelligence and Soviet army officers for deportation.

Under this early pressure, the Russian settlers of Estonia developed as a far more integrated community than those in Latvia. Well-organized non-Estonian political, cultural and economic bodies have emerged and work together to promote their common interests. And the institutions of civil society are well developed among the non-Estonians. However, they still face fundamental questions about whether their identity is primarily Baltic, Slavic, Russian or Russian-speaking.

Although the emergence of an organized Russian community owed much to leaders within the community itself, a central role was played by the first leader of independent Estonia, Edgar Savisaar. Before his government fell in January 1992, Savisaar promoted several items on the Russian agenda: a relatively liberal citizenship regime for individuals currently living in Estonia, self-governance for the northeast and a less strident position on the withdrawal of Russian troops. More importantly, he laid the foundations for an indigenous non-Estonian political movement.

The Russian-speaking community was traditionally organized around enterprises, the Communist Party and the Soviet military. During the independence struggle, Russian-speaking intellectuals were increasingly marginalized by the growth of Estonian nationalism and Soviet imperialism focused on the Russian-speaking working class. With independence, the settler intellectuals were almost completely excluded from the Estonian political system. In an attempt to draw the Russian-speaking intelligentsia back into politics, Savisaar encouraged the establishment of the Russian Democratic Movement, to represent the interests of the non-Estonians. At the same time, increasing pressure on the Russian-speakers, for example citizenship legisation, forced the settlers to organize themselves. During the independence struggle, the Russian-speaking leaders had participated without a constituency behind them, campaigning only for a range of abstract ideals. The policies of Savisaar and the citizenship law forced them to look for a social base and led to the emergence of the Representative Assembly.

Originally, the Representative Assembly was to function as an alternative parliament, although it has subsequently become more like a pressure group. The Assembly served as an umbrella organization for the various political, economic and cultural groups within the Russian-speaking community, including the Russian Democratic Movement, the Narva Trade Union Centre, the Russian Entrepreneurs' Association, the Union of Slavic Education and Charitable Societies in Estonia (which manages a Russian theatre in Tallinn, and has its own literary-cultural journal, as well as art and music schools), and the Russian Cultural Society of Estonia (though affiliated with the Representative Assembly, this organization developed from the Russian society set up by the Popular Front and remains close to the Estonian state).

Central to this well-organized Russian community has been investment by Russian-speaking businessmen. The Representative Assembly was housed in the former Officers' Mess in Tallinn, which it rented at a very favourable rate from the Russian Auction Society, an umbrella organization for Russian businesses in Estonia that has representatives from the Assembly on its board of directors. The building also served as a centre for all Russian-speaking cultural and political activity.

Unlike in Latvia, the Estonian government and parliament have undertaken initiatives to foster the development of separate national and ethnic identities. While there is little doubt that these form part of a divide-and-rule strategy – to split the Russian-speaking population into Russians, Ukrainians, Jews, etc. – such assistance has improved Estonian/non-Estonian relations. A central part is played by the Estonian

Union of National Minorities, a quango that grew out of national cultural societies formed by the Popular Front. Established in September 1988 to counter Soviet-Russian organizations, it is headed by the only non-Estonian in parliament, Ants-Enno Lohmus.

Lohmus is especially keen to fund research into the historical roots of each community in Estonia. The aim of the Union is 'to create national cultures as a way of destroying the communist mentality'. Although much of the work has been directed against the Representative Assembly, which Lohmus regards as pro-Soviet, the leaders of the Assembly support his Union. Lohmus was the main force behind the law on cultural autonomy enacted on 11 November 1993 to allow minority groups to form councils with elected representatives at the municipal and national levels and to provide partial government funding for cultural activities.

In response to international pressure, the government has undertaken a number of initiatives to help integrate the non-Estonian population. From July 1993, President Lennart Meri began a series of round-table discussions on the problems of ethnic minorities with the leaders of their main groups. He also used a clause in the Estonian Constitution that allows the President to grant citizenship for 'special services' to co-opt the Russian-speaking elite. The editors of Russian-language papers, leaders of moderate political groups, and businessmen have thus been granted automatic citizenship. Prior to the local elections in October 1993, the 15 candidates on the Representative Assembly list were granted citizenship so that they could stand for election.

Although the Estonian Russian-speaking community is far better organized and more united than any other in the former Soviet republics, it also contains divisions. An important split has emerged between what are basically Russian nationalist groups, although they also still have a strong Soviet orientation, and the non-ethnically based and westward-looking Representative Assembly leadership. On 17 April 1993, the Russian Council (*Russkii Sobor)* was set up as a rival to the Representative Assembly. Led by Aleksei Zybin, a former Estonian Supreme Soviet deputy, its goal was to unite ethnic Russians to fight 'for Russian cultural and national identity'. It demanded unconditional citizenship for all residents and for Russian to become the second official state language. In summer 1993, the Russian National Union was established, headed by Sergei Kuznetsov. This has become the political wing of the Russian Council. Both organizations are strongly anti-Semitic and have sought links with radical nationalists in Russia, especially the former Supreme Soviet.

The most serious confrontation in Estonia emerged in the northeast, particularly the town of Narva. Presented as an ethnic conflict, it was essentially a political and economic one in which ethnicity was exploited by both sides. The problems in Narva and the northeast did not stem from Russian separatism or a popular will to reunify with Russia but from democratization and marketization, a process initiated and supported mainly by Estonians but which had its most direct impact on the local non-Estonian population. The struggle that developed between Tallinn and the cities of the northeast in 1992–3 was thus due to a complex mix of anti-market sentiment, pro-Soviet sympathy, a centre–region struggle and a degree of ethnic-based anxiety.

Before the Second World War, Narva had a sizeable Russian population. However, as the Red Army advanced, the population fled and the town was almost totally destroyed in subsequent fighting. After the war, the original Russian residents were not allowed to return and instead, Sovietized Russian-speaking migrants flooded the area. Before 1940, Estonians made up 79.1% of the district's population. By 1989, this figure had fallen to 18.5%. The share of Russians in Narva rose from 29.7% before 1940 to 85% in 1989. Narva and the other towns in the northeast became fortresses of Soviet control within Estonia with little connection to the local economy and being tied instead to the all-Union economic system, especially the military-industrial complex, like the towns of Daugavpils and Tiraspol.

The independence movement in Estonia constituted a direct challenge to the leadership in the northeast for a number of reasons. First, their power base was built on control of local industry; these were Soviet company towns in which the political and economic elites dovetailed and their control of the locality was total. The policies of marketization and privatization promoted by the Estonians were therefore anathema to the local elite. Second, the democratic changes advocated by the Popular Front posed a direct challenge to their political control over the local population. Thus, although the local leadership claimed citizenship as the central issue in their struggle with Tallinn, their main aim was to retain economic and political control over the area.

Opinion polling conducted in Narva suggests that despite the claims of the local leadership, there was considerable support for an independent Estonia.[41] On 2 February 1990, the day the Supreme Soviet of Estonia declared independence, a group of deputies, mostly representing Tallinn, Kohtla-Jarve, Sillamae and Narva, created the Committee for the Defence of Soviet Power and Civil Rights in Estonia. In May, they created the Interregional Soviet as a parallel structure to the Estonian Supreme

Soviet. However, a survey taken in Narva at the time suggests that only 26% of the population opposed the decision of the Estonian Supreme Soviet and only 37% of the population recognized the Interregional Soviet as the 'real expression of the will and interests of the non-Estonian population', while 35% actually opposed the proposition.[42]

With support from the local Soviet elite, a number of organizations were set up in Narva, notably the Russian Citizens' Rights Movement, headed by Yuri Mishin. Mishin campaigned among the local population, encouraging them to take Russian citizenship. In February 1993, the Russian Foreign Ministry sent a consular group to Narva to arrange Russian citizenship for those who wished to take it. At one stage 1,500 people a month were requesting citizenship. By January 1995, there were estimated to be 20,000 Russian citizens in Narva.[43]

On 16 and 17 July 1993, the Sovietized leadership of the northeast held a referendum on national-territorial autonomy for the region. Amid reports of major irregularities, the turnout was low (54% in Narva and 60% in Sillamae). The local government of Kohtla-Jarve (an area with a 70% non-Estonian population) refused to hold the referendum. In Narva, 97% of those who voted supported autonomy, in Sillamae 98.6%. The Estonian State Court ruled the referendum illegal on 11 August 1993. By mid-1993, new, more moderate political forces were emerging in the area. The Narva Independent Trade Union Centre began to gain influence as unemployment became more of an issue. Mayor Yuri Mishin and other Soviet loyalists were gradually marginalized from politics.

In early 1993, the Russian and Estonian governments had agreed to cooperate to prevent extremists travelling to the northeast from Russia; however, Mishin and the others had successfully established contact with Red/Brown organizations grouped around and within the Russian parliament. The failure of the October 1993 putsch in Moscow was therefore a severe blow to the northeastern leadership. The Estonian local elections of October 1993 marked the final defeat of the the old party-state *nomenklatura* in the northeast region. Unable to stand for election because they lacked citizenship, they moved into commercial activities.

The local elections of October 1993 also marked a new stage in interethnic relations in Estonia as a whole. For the first time since independence, significant numbers of non-Estonians were able to vote and even stand as candidates. Two non-Estonian parties stood in the elections: Our Choice (*Nash Vybor*) and *Revel*. Our Choice was the political wing of the Representative Assembly and its candidates were mostly from the Assembly's leadership. Its election programme contained no direct reference to narrowly Russian-speaking issues and concentrated instead on economic and social questions. *Revel* represented the Russian patriotic bloc, in particular the Russian Council, with strong echoes of the old Soviet identity. Thus, in the *Revel* bloc alongside Russian nationalists such as Sergei Kuznetsov, there were the ethnic Estonians, and more importantly former communists, Lembit Annus and Vladimir Kukk.

The municipal elections marked a major success for the Russian and Russian-speaking blocs. In Tallinn, Our Choice received 17 mandates and *Revel* 10.[44] Estonian parties thus became a minority in the capital. Lembit Annus, former editor of the journal *Estonian Communist* and still a hardliner, won 4,120 votes, the second highest figure in Tallinn, after Arnold Ruutel, the former Estonian Communist Party leader. Mart Laar's ruling *Isamaa* party gained only five of the 64 seats. In Narva, the old communist leadership was swept away and replaced by a less confrontational council.[45] Despite the problem of citizenship, three-quarters of seats went to ethnic Russians. The success of the non-Estonian parties was primarily due to a much greater turnout among the non-Russians. In Narva and Sillamae, the turnout was 67%, while in the predominantly Estonian south the figure was only 34% (Tartu).

Parliamentary elections in 1995 The integration of non-Estonians into Estonian society was further accelerated by parliamentary elections in early 1995. As with the local elections of 1993, the Russian-speaking politicians broke into two main blocs: a moderate, pro-Estonian group (Our Home is Estonia) and a radical Russian nationalist one (The Russian Party of Estonia).[46] Although the parties were split over many issues, shortly before the election they succeeded in uniting around a mild leftist agenda demanding slower privatization, more social guarantees, and closer ties to Russia.[47]

The coalition won six seats (5.9% of the vote) in the 101-seat parliament, the first Russian-speakers to enter the independent parliament. However, it was clear that many settlers had voted for Estonian centre and left parties on economic grounds. The elections of 1993 and 1995 showed the population was becoming more concerned about economic questions than narrowly ethnic issues. The nationalist impetus in the Estonian parties and population is diminishing.[48] As a result ethnic polarization is beginning to break down.

Human rights, troop withdrawal and the role of Russia

During the period of common struggle against the Soviet centre, relations between Russia and the Baltic states were generally good. Yeltsin fiercely opposed the January 1991 Soviet crackdown in Latvia and Lithuania and, following the August 1991 coup attempt, he quickly recognized Baltic independence. Goodwill between the Balts and Russia was formalized in treaties between Latvia/Estonia and Russia in 1991. The Latvian–Russian Treaty recognizing Latvian independence was drafted in summer 1990 and signed on 13 January 1991. A similar treaty had been signed with Estonia on 12 January. However, while relations were generally friendly, even at this stage there were important areas of tension, especially over the issue of citizenship.

In negotiations with Latvia, Russia had originally wanted a system of dual citizenship but the Latvians were firmly opposed to it. The treaty was due to be signed in September 1990 but representatives from Equal Rights, the Latvian Communist Party, the Soviet military, the Interfront, and the Council of War and Labour Veterans travelled to Moscow to lobby the Supreme Soviet against it. As a result, ratification was delayed. Eventually, when the Latvians gave some ground on a territorial dispute resulting from the Soviet–Latvian Peace Treaty of 1920 and the status of Russian troops in Latvia, and in the context of the Soviet crackdown in Latvia, Yeltsin signed the treaty, but the Russian Supreme Soviet never ratified it. It also faced opposition from the Committee of Latvia, the governing body of the Latvian Citizens' movement, which felt it gave citizenship to Soviet 'occupants'.

Negotiations with Estonia were not so protracted and, as well as being signed by Yeltsin, the treaty was ratified by the Russian parliament in December 1991. In Article 3, both sides agreed to a 'zero variant' on citizenship whereby all persons living on the territory of the RSFSR or the Republic of Estonia at the time of signing 'have the right to maintain or achieve citizenship in the RSFSR or the Republic of Estonia according to their expression of free will'.[49] The subsequent adoption of laws that limited citizenship, thereby rejecting the earlier agreements with Russia, severely strained Baltic–Russian relations and moved the question of citizenship for the Russian settlers to the top of Moscow's foreign policy agenda in the region.

As ethno-nationalism grew stronger in the Baltic states following independence, Russian nationalists and Statists used the issue of citizenship to attack their government. At the height of the Soviet-nationalist campaign against the Democrats, President Yeltsin issued a decree (29 October 1992) which linked the withdrawal of troops from the Baltic states with human rights guarantees for Russians.[50] On 10 June 1993, addressing leaders of the armed forces, he again linked human rights and troop withdrawal, saying that Russia could not withdraw without citizenship for the Russians in the Baltic.[51] He argued that Russia had to guarantee the rights of servicemen and expressed 'profound concern over numerous infringements of the rights of the Russian-speaking population in the Baltic countries'.

Baltic leaders made much of comments in the roundtable discussions between Russian diplomats and foreign policy advisers in autumn 1992, published in *Diplomaticheskii Vestnik*, arguing that they constituted a blueprint for a new Russian imperialist policy (see above, Chapter 2, note 36). These fears were compounded by Yeltsin's appeal in early 1993 for a mandate from the United Nations to intervene in 'trouble spots' in the former USSR. Speaking to a Russian military audience in Kaliningrad in March 1993, the Russian Foreign Minister, Andrei Kozyrev, spoke of the need to maintain troops in the Baltic.[52]

In late June 1993, tension between Russia and Estonia reached fever pitch over the introduction of the Law on Foreigners, legislation which codified the position of the (mainly Russian) non-citizens and required them to apply for residence permits or face deportation. President Yeltsin and the Russian foreign ministry threatened economic, political and 'other' sanctions. Yeltsin appealed to the UN for measures against Estonia and noted: 'Russia will take steps to defend its national interests in Estonia.' On 24 June, he said: 'It must be understood that Russia cannot remain a disinterested observer if the Russian-speaking population should show a natural desire to defend itself against crude discrimination.' On 28 June, Kozyrev accused the Estonians of 'apartheid' and 'ethnic cleansing'. Speaking to a Congress of Young Russians Abroad in August, Russian Deputy Prime Minister Vladimir Shumeiko noted that Estonia had no choice but to set up an autonomous region in the northeast populated by Russian-speakers.[53]

By autumn 1993, there seemed to be some progress in Russian–Baltic relations. On 17 November Russia pledged to pull its troops out of the Baltics by the end of August 1994. The Baltic governments seemed to react favourably to the proposal, or at least accept it with resignation. By the end of 1993, approximately 22,000 Russian troops were left in the Baltics. In November, Estonia made a major concession to Russia by amending the Law on Foreigners to grant the right of residency to retired

Soviet officers.[54] However, after the Russian elections in December 1993 the tone of relations changed again.

During the election the Russian diaspora, particularly in the Baltic, became an important issue not just for Zhirinovski but for a number of other conservative and nationalist forces and even members of the Democratic blocs. Deputy Prime Minister Aleksandr Shokhin vowed that his Party of Unity and Accord would defend the rights of Russians in the ex-Soviet republics through concerted 'external political' and 'economic' measures.[55] Following the success of nationalist and communist forces, the tone of Russian foreign policy became increasingly harsh. Speaking to a meeting of Russian ambassadors in Moscow in January 1994, Andrei Kozyrev claimed that Russia should not withdraw from regions which had been in its sphere of influence for centuries.[56]

However, despite bellicose statements from leading Russian politicians, little has actually been done to 'protect' the Russians in Latvia and Estonia. The Russian government has maintained control of more radical Russian groups that sought to exploit the issue and at the same time has secured important rights for ex-Soviet servicemen and women living in the region. The final withdrawal of its military units from Latvia and Estonia on 31 August 1994 signalled that the Russian government remained commited to independent Baltic states.

Conclusions

While it is still far too early to say that the Russian-speaking populations of Latvia and Estonia have developed a new non-Soviet national identity, its basis is clearly in place, at least in Estonia. Ironically, while the Latvians and Estonians complained that their countries were being Russified under the Soviet system, it now appears that there was also a high degree of reverse Balticization of the immigrant community. The Baltic Russian-speaking settlers emerged from the independence struggle as the most market-oriented and democratic of the settler communities in the former Soviet Union. The majority in these communities have consistently expressed support for the independence of the Baltic states and lack a strong affinity with Russia. Moreover, the comparatively high standard of living in the Baltic region – at least compared with the Russian Federation – is a powerful stimulus for loyalty to the new states.

A comparison of the two cases shows that if the institutions of civil society and a new Baltic identity is to emerge quickly among the immigrant communities, it will largely depend on the actions of the Baltic governments and parliaments themselves. The stuggle for independence in Latvia and Estonia left the Russian-speaking populations extremely vulnerable. Their self-identity remained based upon an often contradictory mixture of Soviet, Baltic, Russian-speaking and ethnic elements,[57] and in opposition to the rise of Baltic nationalism, the Russian-speakers had little from which to construct a new identity and remain politically and socially effective, other than Soviet values and institutions. Russian-speakers who participated in the independence movements were committed to the general ideals of democracy and independence but as the Popular Fronts became increasingly nationalist, their distinctive identity as non-indigenous loyalists and democrats was undermined. By autumn 1991, the communities were disoriented by the collapse of the USSR and almost completely lacking in internal organization. Following independence there have been contrasting experiences of independence for the non-autochthonous populations in Estonia and Latvia.

The Latvian approach to the settler issue had two main consequences. First, the bureaucracy has grown increasingly powerful as the main arbiter of decisions. Since a requirement to work in the bureaucracy is fluency in Latvian, it has been steadily purged of non-Latvians. The Russian settlers are now at the mercy of civil servants who are unaware of their problems or even opposed to their presence in the country.[58] Second, faced with an unsympathetic bureaucracy and lacking moderate non-Latvian organizations, the Russian population has been forced to rely on more confrontational organizations such as Equal Rights for their protection.

While Estonia certainly manifested many of the same trends of ethno-nationalism as Latvia, and the bureaucracy was also guilty of insensitivity and occasionally deliberate acts against the non-Estonian population,[59] inter-ethnic policy in the country has achieved two notable successes. First, vitally important bridges have been built between the Estonians and Russian-speakers, both in terms of institutions and in the creation of a Russian-speaking elite with Estonian citizenship. Russian-speakers can now campaign for their interests within the system and areas of tension can be handled more effectively. Second, the Russian-speakers have begun to develop their own political, cultural and economic organizations.

The historical-cultural base for Russian identity in Latvia is far more solid than in Estonia, yet the Estonian Russian-speakers are emerging with a far stronger community and identity.[60] The distinctive non-Estonian community in Estonia grew as a result of pressure placed upon the non-Estonians by a series of harsh legislative initiatives, which mobilized Russian-speakers in protest, coupled with assistance from

Estonian politicians and the Estonian state to create new institutions within the minority community. The success of this approach is manifest in growing loyalty for Estonia among Russian-speakers.[61] In response to this combination of developments a Russian identity in Estonia appears to be developing, primarily in territorial-political terms.[62] Russian-speakers' appeals for recognition as a community have been based primarily on human rights rather than on group consciousness. Their calls for participation stress their attachment to Estonia as people who simply live and work there. It is an identity with amorphous boundaries, and is generally tolerant and inclusive in its attitudes.

However, even in Estonia the degree of integration should not be overstressed. The majority of Russian-speakers remain unsure of their future. The integration of Russian-speakers into Estonian and Latvian society is at an early stage, which makes the efforts of political groups in Russia to obstruct the process particularly dangerous. To date Russia's approach has not seriously aimed to solve the basic problems of the settler communities and has been based primarily on diplomatic pressure, political initiatives and open threats. Small amounts of money have trickled through via business and philanthropic organizations but the sums are tiny.[63] It was the ineffectiveness of the Russian and Baltic governments to develop a coherent and constructive policy towards the minorities that opened the way for Soviet and Russian nationalists to exploit their problems for their own purposes.

The willingness of the Baltic governments and parliaments to moderate some of the harsher elements of legislation was significantly influenced by the international community. As both states sought integration into international, especially European, institutions considerable leverage could be exerted on them.[64] Despite the problems in the region, international organizations have generally approved both countries' formal legal systems of rights. Numerous international missions to the region have found no evidence of systematic persecution of minorities.[65] Rather, many of the problems have stemmed from political and social tension rather than from narrowly legal discrimination. For this reason, the development of an Estonian or Latvian national identity among the settler communities is likely to be closely tied to the efforts of governments to introduce more inclusive policies designed to help develop these communities.

Chapter 4

War, irredentism and national identity in Moldova

Introduction

In early summer 1992, one of the fiercest conflicts of the post-Soviet period broke out along the Dniester river in eastern Moldova. As fighting between Moldovan militia units and guards from the breakaway Transdniestrian region intensified, Moldova seemed to have become the site for the first ethnic conflict in the former Soviet Union between Russians and an indigenous population. In fact, the fighting was only loosely related to ethnic rivalries.[1] The conflict between the authorities in Chisinau and Tiraspol was more a struggle for political power and above all a fight for control of the industrial wealth of the country.

Immediately following independence, Moldova was faced with a particularly complicated set of challenges. Central among these was the need to establish a viable notion of nationhood. The complex history of the region, in particular its location at the confluence of a number of different empires, had over the centuries fostered the emergence of diametrically opposed sets of interests and perceptions of belonging within Moldovan society. During the Soviet period, these basic differences were reinforced by the imposition of a system of social, economic and political stratification that was informed by ethnicity and that also served to shape ethnic identities.

As a result of this past, in the late 1980s Moldovan politics came to be dominated by two diametrically opposed political movements: one that looked to unification with Romania and one that sought a retention of the Soviet Union and close ties with Moscow. Although both these movements were ethnically based – the former relied on ethnic Moldovans and the latter on a loose alliance of Slavic (Russian and Ukrainian) and

Distribution of Russian settlers in Moldova

Turkic peoples (the Gagauz) – ethnicity was not necessarily the sole or indeed defining character of either.

This struggle had two main elements: first, competition for control of the central state apparatus and leading positions in Moldovan society, particularly education, the main battleground being language policy; and, second, a struggle between the centre and two peripheral regions – Transdniester, located mainly on the left bank of the river Dniester, and the southern areas populated mostly by the Gagauz. While issues of ethnicity formed a common thread running through these conflicts, there were also a variety of cross-cutting economic and political interests that prevented ethnic polarization within Moldovan society.

57

The intricate political, economic and ethnic relationships were exacerbated by the important position of Moldova within the post-communist system of states. Along with irredentists within Moldova, the central authorities were faced with the involvement in Moldova's internal affairs of three powerful states with potential territorial and diaspora claims on the country: Romania, Ukraine and, most important, the Russian Federation.[2]

Within the Russian Federation, the fighting of 1992 in Moldova fed directly into the domestic debate about Russia's relationship to the settler populations and responsibility for Russians abroad. Under intense domestic pressure, the Russian government was forced to become politically involved in the conflict and eventually to dispatch a peacekeeping force there. Following the fighting, Russian policy towards the Russified settler populations of the former Soviet Union underwent important changes. From summer 1992, Russia began to adopt a far more assertive set of policies towards neighbouring states, particularly over the Russified settlers.

The fighting also had a profound effect on domestic politics, proving a catalyst for the emergence of a Moldovan nationalism that has paradoxically formed the basis of an inclusive national identity. The replacement, after the fighting, of political organizations promoting unification with Romania with ones supporting an independent Moldova (based on the belief that Moldovans constitute a community distinct from Romanians) with close economic ties to the CIS provided a foundation for the reintegration of the non-Moldovan sections of the population marginalized by developments in the late *perestroika*/early independence period.

Bessarabia, Moldova and the creation of a new state

As with the other former Soviet republics, many of the contemporary problems of Moldova are rooted in the experience of imperial conquest and Soviet domination. Moldova's geopolitical position ensured that over the centuries its lands were controlled by a variety of conquering forces including the Ottomans, the Russian Empire, Romania and the Soviet Union. Except for a few months in 1918 – and even then only within right-bank Bessarabia – Moldova had never existed as an independent political entity prior to 1991.[3] The legacy of external control for Moldova was a society arranged around a complex series of loosely interconnected socio-economic, political and ethnic subsystems often organized on the basis of divergent sets of interests. In consequence, it has faced one of the most complicated processes of nation- and state-building in the former Soviet Union.

Central to its contemporary difficulties is the separate imperial history experienced by the people living on the Moldovan territories east of the Dniester river (the left bank) and those to the west (see map). In 1793, the eastern lands were absorbed into the Russian Empire. Following a brief period of autonomy after the Bolshevik revolution, in 1922 the left-bank territories were joined to the USSR. The area therefore enjoyed close links to Moscow, with only a minor interruption, until 1991. In 1812, the lands to the west of the river, known as Bessarabia, were annexed by Russia. Although the region remained part of the Russian Empire for over a hundred years, after 1918 Bessarabia was reunited with Romania and remained under Bucharest's rule for the next twenty years.

The eastern territories of Moldova occupied a particularly important position within the USSR. On 12 October 1924, the All-Ukrainian Executive Committee of the Communist Party established the Moldovan Autonomous Soviet Socialist Republic (MASSR) on the left bank of the river Dniester, which then formed the border between the USSR and Romania. The city of Tiraspol subsequently became the capital of this new political entity. By uniting the majority of ethnic Moldovans in the USSR within the MASSR, the Soviet authorities sought to indicate that all nationalities enjoyed rights of autonomy. Later, the existence of the MASSR provided an ethno-political justification for extending Soviet influence into Romanian-controlled Bessarabia.[4] As there were very few indigenous communists in this area, loyal personnel (largely Slavs) were sent to the region to bolster the new regime.[5]

In the interwar period, the MASSR was renowned for the conservatism of its leadership and the region emerged as a centre for orthodoxy at the height of Stalinism. The experience of the left-bank population therefore contrasted significantly with that of the right bank. While Bucharest exerted a harsh form of rule over Bessarabia, the organization and culture of the two communities diverged in important ways. Their eventual fusion under Soviet control in the postwar period proved to be a difficult process. In particular, the extension of Soviet power over Bessarabia gave significant advantages to the left-bank territories and the leadership of Tiraspol.

In summer 1940, the USSR annexed Bessarabia as part of the Molotov–Ribbentrop pact. Subsequently overrun by Axis forces, the area was reconquered in 1944 by the advancing Red Army. The bulk of Bessarabia was united with the territories of the MASSR (although the Bukovyna region in the north and Budjak in the south were given to Ukraine) to form the Moldovan SSR. After 1944, Soviet policy aimed to integrate the region into the all-Union economy as quickly as possible – entire industrial plants and their predominantly Slavic workforces were moved there – and into the Soviet polity.

As Bessarabia had been under Romanian control in the interwar years, there were few communists there, especially in the rural areas. The extension of Soviet political power relied on a personnel policy with two distinct characteristics: the transfer of loyal personnel to the west from the eastern regions, the former MASSR; and from the cities to the villages. Soviet loyalists from outside the republic were also drawn into the area by the new economic and political opportunities. This personnel policy led to the institutionalization of Soviet power in the urban areas and the east of the republic.

Prior to the Second World War, the territories of modern Moldova were divided into rural areas populated by Moldovans and urban areas populated by Russians, Germans and Jews. The right bank was largely rural and Romanian, while the left bank was more urbanized and under the influence of Sovietized Slavs and Soviet-Slavic culture. By the end of the war, the structure of the urban population in the area had altered dramatically. The indigenous Jews had been destroyed by the Nazis, as had the small urban Moldovan intelligentsia, as a result of the war and Stalinist purges, while the German population had departed with the retreating Axis forces. Almost all the urban centres in Moldova were therefore left dominated by Slavs and small numbers of Russified Moldovans.

In the postwar period, there was a steady rise in the Sovietized Slavic population of the region and a system of economic and political domination from Moscow emerged, fostering ethnic divisions within the republic. Ethnic Russians made up 27% of the republic's urban population and only 4% of the rural dwellers.[6] The Sovietized and urbanized Slavic sections of Moldovan society became the foundations for the extension of Soviet control in the region and came to dominate the political economy of the republic. The settler elite, combined with the much weaker rural-based indigenous Communist Party, formed the heart of the Soviet system of control in the republic from the mid-1940s until the mid-1980s.

Soviet political and economic control of Bessarabia in the post-Second World War period was accompanied by the propagation of a particular version of the development of the peoples of the region. Soviet theoreticians constructed in the Moldovan SSR a special conception of history, chiefly a history of Russian-Moldovan interdependence through the centuries, which relied on the notion that the Moldovan population was in fact different in important ways from Romanians in terms of ethnicity, history and even language. Soviet rule thus represented a liberation from domination by Bucharest for the Moldovan people.

The creation of the Moldovan SSR as a separate political unit therefore involved welding together a variety of disparate communities with diverse interests and separate histories. Faced with this challenge, the Soviet authorities relied upon the Russian-speaking community and the passive acquiescence of the rural Ukrainians to ensure control over the region. As a result, important geographic and ethno-political differences were institutionalized as the organizing principles of the new republic.

Perestroika and the drive for unification with Romania

The peculiar political geography of Moldova, especially the relatively recent annexation of Bessarabia from Romania, and the particular form of Soviet domination exercised in the republic during the Soviet period, combined to produce a unique political dynamic in the republic during the *perestroika* period. In many of the Soviet republics in the Brezhnev era, indigenous elites came to dominate key political institutions and to infiltrate the Russified urban areas. In Moldova, as a result of the extremely powerful position of the Russian-speaking settlers, these twin processes were far less advanced. Political and economic institutions continued to be dominated by the settlers until the late 1980s.

In some other areas of the USSR, control of the republic-level communist parties by indigenous elites provided a check on the ambitions of the radical nationalists, promoting more moderate national aspirations. In Moldova, the weak position of the indigenous Communist Party meant that no ex-Soviet institution was sufficiently powerful to promote the cause of Moldovan independence. Instead, a small group of intellectuals who pressed for unification with Romania were able to dominate the immediate post-independence political agenda.

As in a number of the other western republics, the reforms of the late 1980s spawned new political groupings to support *perestroika*, which were later transformed into pro-independence organizations. The Popular Front of Moldova (PFM) promoted an agenda similar to the Fronts in the Baltic republics and Ukraine. The PFM campaigned for independence and the promotion of Romanian culture.[7] On 31 August 1989, a new language law was introduced which downgraded the status of Russian to be 'the language of inter-ethnic communication'. Plans were also announced to replace the Cyrillic script with a Latin one. These changes were particularly unpopular on the left bank of the Dniester where

61

Cyrillic characters had been used almost continuously since the fourteenth century.

As the drive for independence gathered pace, the aims of the PFM began to change. In 1989–90, a radical pan-Romanianist minority whose aim was the 'restitution of the Unitary Romanian State' seized control of the movement for an independent Moldova. Unification with Romania rapidly became the PFM's leitmotif.[8] Following the August 1991 coup in Moscow, the Moldovan Communist Party was banned, leaving politics in the republic dominated by the PFM. After independence, with little effective opposition in the country and with the Popular Front beginning to lose support, efforts to Romanianize society and the campaign to unify Moldova with Romania were accelerated.[9] These twin trends were only halted with the onset of war in mid-1992.

Although a zero option for citizenship was adopted on 5 June 1991, the drive to unite Moldova and Romania was greeted with alarm in key sections of the non-Moldovan population. In particular, declarations by the PFM leadership that the left bank and Gagauz regions would also be joined to Romania caused alarm among the elites of Tiraspol and Komrat, the Gagauz capital. As the PFM gathered strength in the late 1980s, both these regions grew uneasy about the future.

In January 1990, the Tiraspol leadership organized a referendum in the city and surrounding region on the creation of a free economic zone. Later, a similar referendum was conducted in the city of Bendery and a number of other towns in the area. Although it was on the right bank of the Dniester, Bendery has been populated by Slavic settlers, particularly the families of Soviet 14th Army personnel. On average 90% of the votes were cast in favour of creating an economic zone separate from the rest of Moldova.

In September 1990, the Transdniester leadership declared autonomy and began to set up workers' detachments drawn from enterprises on the left bank. In the south of the country, the Republic of Gagauzia was declared in five districts in August 1990. Although the all-Union referendum on the future of the USSR on 17 March 1991 was boycotted by Chisinau, it was held on the left bank. More than 93% of those who voted supported retention of the Union.[10]

As moves towards unification with Romania gathered pace following the Moldovan declaration of independence on 27 August 1991, alarm about the future further intensified in the two regions. On 2 September 1991, six days after Moldova declared its independence, the Second Extraordinary Session of People's Deputies of the *Dniester* area declared the five districts of the left bank an independent republic – the Moldovan Transdnistrian Republic (the PMR). On 1 December 1991, Tiraspol declared full independence, following a referendum in which 97.7% voted for the creation of the PMR.[11] Following the declaration of independence and in an atmosphere of growing tension with Chisinau, Tiraspol quickly became the focus for a range of pro-Soviet and radical Russian nationalist politicians and groups.[12]

While the drive for secession was in part motivated by the Russified settlers' fear of forced assimilation by Romania, ethnic differentiation was heavily underpinned by a range of political and economic interests that separated Tiraspol from Chisinau. The PMR formed the economic core of the Moldovan political economy producing 33% of the country's industrial goods, 56% of its consumer goods and 90% of its energy. The left bank also occupies a vital strategic position as almost all of the communications to the east are routed through it. At the same time, much of the economic strength of the left bank was dependent on links to the Russian Federation. Industry there was closely tied to the Soviet military-industrial complex and relied on large amounts of subsidized energy from Russia. Together, these factors combined to produce a conservative pro-Soviet elite in the PMR region.

The conflict with Chisinau was therefore as much a struggle to protect Tiraspol's economic power as to retain Slav ethnic dominance. The factory bosses of the left bank depended for their position on ties to Moscow. The proposed absorption into Romania constituted a central challenge to this position. The political changes of the early 1990s therefore threatened a fundamental shift in the balance of political power in the republic. In the postwar period, Transdniester had controlled Moldova. Until 1989, no first secretary of the Moldovan Communist Party had ever come from Bessarabia.[13]

The central political institution that emerged to protect the interests of the left bank was not the Communist Party but the United Council of Workers Collectives (OSTK), an organization based on the workforce of the region's large factories and led by the management of these enterprises.[14] Intent on preserving the economic basis of the old Soviet system and the political order that supported it, the Tiraspol leadership opposed the rise of the Democrats in the Russian Federation and supported the August 1991 coup. With independence for Moldova, the leader of the OSTK, the industrial manager Igor Smirnov, was elected President of the PMR.

Escalating tension in the east of the country after independence was matched by increasing friction between Komrat and Chisinau. The Gagauz elected their first President, Stepan Topal, in December 1991 and planned independent political institutions for the region. Unlike the PMR, the Gagauz irredentist movement was based on fear of loss of ethnic identity. Subsequently, both areas formed a loose alliance to resist Romanianization.[15]

Political conflict and war

Growing tension between Chisinau and Tiraspol/Komrat led to a rise in armed skirmishes from the end of 1991. Following the declaration of independence in 1991, the PMR authorities moved swiftly to consolidate the region's rudimentary state structures.[16] The election of a president, increased activity by parliament (Supreme Soviet), the establishment of military formations (the Dniester guards), the entrenchment of the network of district and city councils, and the introduction of a currency (the suvorov), all helped to extend the power of the regime. Eventually, tension erupted into intense fighting along the Dniester river in summer 1992.

That the conflict between Tiraspol and Chisinau was only partly about ethnic rivalry is confirmed by the important differences between the more Russified Moldovans on the left bank and those on the right bank. Of the PMR's 800,000 residents only 25.5% are Russians, while 28.3% are Ukrainians and 40.1% Moldovans.[17] A significant number of Russified Moldovans have found important positions within the leadership of the PMR, including the Speaker of the Supreme Soviet Grigorii Marakutsa and Defence Minister Stefan Kitsak. Once fighting broke out, there was no simple division into opposing ethnic groups. Moldovans, Ukrainians and Russians participated on both sides.[18] However, it is also important to note that much of the rural Moldovan population of the left bank has been resistant to the establishment of the PMR.

A key element to the emergence of PMR was the dovetailing of the interests of the remnants of the Soviet 14th Army in the region and the leadership in Tiraspol. During the fighting of 1992, the separatists allegedly received assistance from the local military (which became the Russian 14th Army in April 1992 and developed close ties to the PMR security services).[19] This was not surprising given the links between the army and the local population. Up to 40% of officers and 90% of NCOs in the 14th Army were from the area and many subsequently transferred with their weapons to the Dniester defence force.[20] The large number of military families in Bendery may also have contributed to informal intervention by the Russian Army.[21] At the peak of the crisis in 1992, Russian Foreign Minister Andrei Kozyrev claimed that the Russian

Army was unofficially shipping equipment to insurgents.[22]

The intervention of the 14th Army during the fighting was, however, central to the ceasefire agreed on 7 July 1992, although the continued presence of the Russian military then served to freeze the conflict and allow the Tiraspol regime to consolidate its power. Following this intervention, military matters became central to the internal and international politics of Moldova.[23] A multilateral peacekeeping force – Russian, Moldovan and Transdniestrian – was established in the region in July 1992 under the supervision a Trilateral Control Commission.

The appointment of the controversial General Lebed to head the 14th Army in June 1992 was widely supported by the population of the PMR, although his subsequent attacks on corruption within the Tiraspol leadership led Marakutsa to accuse the army of trying to destabilize Tiraspol.[24] An accord on a staged withdrawal of the army from Moldova was agreed in October 1994, but the Tiraspol leadership opposed it.[25]

The emergence of a Moldovan national identity

While developments affecting the settler and minority communities most clearly demonstrated the turmoil within Moldova following independence, the core political issue was Moldovan national identity. The drive for unification with Romania established in Moldova a nationalist dynamic unique in the former Soviet republics. The move from a political agenda built on freedom from Moscow to one embracing control by another 'external' power – Romania – was greeted with suspicion not only in the Russified settler communities but also among much of the indigenous population.

Thus, while Moldova has experienced the same broad features of post-Soviet development as other ex-Soviet republics on the western rim of the USSR – a wave of anti-Moscow nationalism subsequently moderated by the imperatives of economic reconstruction and integration with the Russian economy – this experience has been considerably muddied by a fierce political struggle within the ethnic Moldovan community. The changes brought about in political, socio-economic and ethnic identities in the country from the late 1980s caused a rift between key groups in Chisinau and other sections of the country. In particular, Moldovan political and economic elites whose position would have been considerably weakened in the context of a united Romania proved hostile to unification. Following the fighting of 1992, these elites emerged as a significant force in Moldovan politics.

The development of an indigenous intelligentsia and urban political and economic elite – those sections of Soviet society that were most supportive of nationalism – was less well advanced in Moldova than in other ex-Soviet republics. The Moldovan elites had their base in the rural areas, cut off from the events of the early 1990s. Together with the complicated history of the region, these factors meant that a powerful and well-organized Moldovan nationalist movement initially failed to materialize.

With the ban on the Moldovan Communist Party following the August 1991 coup, the only countrywide political organization of any significance was excluded from the political process. In this political vacuum politics came to be dominated by the only other organizations capable of mobilizing sizeable numbers: the radical organizations of the Popular Front, the Russian settler organization Interfront, and the Tiraspol and Komrat regimes. With the political system highly fragmented, the narrow group of intellectuals that led the Popular Front was able to promote a rapid, if somewhat cosmetic, Romanianization of Moldova and the Front seemed to be preparing for rapid integration with Romania.[26] These policies were stopped only by the violence of summer 1992.

The extreme disquiet among the Russified settler population, which was prepared to accept life in an independent Moldova but not to become a marginal group in Romania, was matched by growing disillusionment within the Moldovan population itself. The bloody Dniester conflict which finally halted Romanianization also served as an important catalyst for the emergence of Moldovan nationalism as a significant political force. Whether as a result of Soviet propaganda, genuine differences or developments from the late 1980s, it became clear that rather than seeing themselves as Romanians, large sections of the population of Bessarabia had come to think in terms of being Moldovan and were against unification.

A number of Moldovan historians have suggested that even prior to the annexation of Bessarabia, Romanian national identity in the region was rather weak, especially in rural areas.[27] Indeed, regional and local identities were far more important and subsequently it is these that have fused together to provide the basis for a distinct Moldovan identity. The version of history propagated by the Soviet authorities served to reinforce these local identities and to channel them into an identity separate from the Romanian. Memories of the harsh treatment of Bessarabians while under the control of Bucharest in the interwar period, exacerbated by the superiority exhibited by some Romanians towards their Moldovan 'co-ethnics' following independence, have also fostered this separate identity.

While the Dniester war was instrumental in the emergence of Moldovan nationalism, it was the former Moldovan *nomenklatura* that was crucial in transforming it into a coherent political force in the form of the Agrarian Democratic Party (ADP) after summer 1992. Built around the core of the former rural party/state organizations, the ADP became the main supporter of a Moldova separate and distinct from Romania and the ex-USSR and the leading advocate for rebuilding economic ties with the former Soviet republics, especially Russia. Although the ADP has supported economic integration with the CIS, political integration has been strongly resisted. This suggests that the Moldovan authorities are sincere in their commitment to Moldovan sovereignty not least because the new opportunities available to the Moldovan elite since independence will not easily be sacrificed.

The first sign of a Moldovan identity alternative to the vision articulated by the Popular Front was the development of a political movement against unification. Following the Dniester conflict, Moldovan and settler organizations formed an alliance to undermine the dominance enjoyed by the pro-Romanian forces. The new national consensus built up by this struggle led to the formation by winter 1992 of a new government composed largely of ex-communists, and quite different to the pro-Romanian governments of Mircea Druc (1990–1) and Valeriu Muravschi (1991–2).[28] During 1993, the struggle to unseat the remnants of the Popular Front spread to parliament and culminated in the calling of a national election and 'opinion survey' on Moldovan independence in early 1994. These resulted in the final defeat of the Popular Front. This opened the way to serious discussion of the Gagauz and Transdniester problems.

The parliamentary elections of February 1994 were crucial in the political evolution of post-Soviet Moldova. The triumph of the ADP with 53.2% of the popular vote and an absolute majority of 55 seats, followed by the largely settler-based political alliance, the Socialist-Unity bloc (22% or 27 seats), indicated that the drive to unify with Romania had lost almost all significant support. A 'non-binding' plebiscite conducted shortly after the election confirmed this trend. Following the election, the Romanian anthem was replaced with a new Moldovan one. Low support for the organizations that had emerged from the Popular Front – the Bloc of Peasants and Intellectuals 9.2% (eleven seats) and the Christian Democratic and Popular Front 7.5% (nine seats) – showed that its PFM's main legacy, the language and educational policies, was also under threat.[29] Language testing for state employment, due to begin in April 1994, was cancelled three days after the election.

Following the election, the ADP became the country's main centre of political power. With the close cooperation of the parliamentary speaker, Petru Lucinschi, the party set out a programme stressing national integrity, the rights of minorities, economic integration with the CIS and market reform.[30] In 1994, President Mircea Snegur joined the ADP in a move designed to help his re-election in the forthcoming presidential contest. With the ADP firmly in control of the domestic political situation, a new constitution was introduced in July 1994 which contained no reference to an ethno-national identity for the country, choosing instead to speak of the 'people of the Republic of Moldova'.

The elections of early 1994 were significant because they suggested the emergence of an independent Moldovan identity. However, the sizeable vote for the Socialist-Unity bloc (an electoral alliance between elements of the former Communist Party – socialists – and the renamed Interfront-Unity – see below) also indicated that those with an interest in retaining a special place for the Russian language, particularly the settler population, had also managed to organize themselves effectively for the first time.[31]

Russified settlers and minorities in the new Moldova

The issue of the non-Moldovan populations has two interrelated dimensions. First, there are a number of questions about what identity the settlers and minorities will adopt. Will they identify as ethnic Russians or Ukrainians living within Moldova? Or as Russian-speakers? Will either of these identities be compatible with loyal Moldovan citizenship? What form will the relationship between these communities and potential kin states of Russia and Ukraine take? Second, what form of autonomy will the PMR and Gagauz regions enjoy in the territorial organization of the Moldovan state? While these issues are inextricably linked, different answers are likely to emerge in different ethnic and geographical settings.

A variety of non-Moldovan populations have long histories of settlement in the region. Ukrainians have been there for hundreds of years, particularly on the left bank. Although Ukrainians in the urban areas have been largely assimilated to the Russified settler culture, Ukrainian villagers continue to speak Ukrainian as their first language. The territory of contemporary Moldova was also the site for migrations by Russian Old Believers fleeing religious persecution before Russian imperial conquest. After Russia annexed Bessarabia in 1812, Russian settlers moved to the urban centres, a process that continued until the collapse of the Russian Empire. In the late nineteenth century, much of the region's urban working class came from Russia.[32]

Sustained Soviet rule from 1944 marked an important change in the structure of the population of Moldova. The Russian percentage of the population grew from 6% in 1940 to 10.2% in 1959 and 13% in 1989. According to the 1989 census, 48% of the Russians and 33% of the Ukrainians then resident in Moldova were born outside the republic. However, from the middle of the 1970s the inflow of Slavic migrants began to dry up.

Migrants enjoyed a particularly powerful position. Not only did the left-bank Slavs exert a significant economic and political influence over the republic; domination of the urban areas, especially the capital, meant that the Sovietized Slavs occupied the most prestigious socio-economic positions in Moldovan society. In addition to political and economic offices, much of the educational and cultural apparatus of the country was under the control of the settlers.

The emergence of a pro-Romanian movement that aimed to Romanianize Moldovan society, particularly through language policy, constituted a direct challenge to the powerful position of the Sovietized settlers. Unlike the Baltic Popular Fronts, which actually encouraged the involvement of 'Democratic' settler groups, in Moldova the radical pro-Romanian line of the Popular Front squeezed out the more moderate non-Moldovans. As a result, the principal vehicles for mobilizing the settler community were Soviet or pro-Soviet. On the left bank, the all-Union factories provided the basis for resistance to control by Chisinau; while in the capital, the settler-dominated professions offered the main opposition to the Popular Front. In particular, the Interfront became the main political force representing the settlers on the right bank.

The Interfront was formed in 1988 by a group of history lecturers in the Moldovan Academy of Sciences led by Professor Anatoli Lysetsky, and including Petr Shornikov, Vilei Nosov, Valeri Solonar and Vasili Yakovlev. This group, who had been responsible for teaching the Soviet/Russian version of Moldovan history in Russian, and were therefore threatened by the Romanianization of society, provided the organizational core of the settler resistance. The main impetus behind the organization came from the proposed changes to the position of Russian language in the republic. The language law of 1989 made Romanian, using the Latin script, the state language of Moldova. This new law provoked strikes by settlers working in the transport and industrial sectors of the economy.[33] The Interfront rapidly spread to other sections of the Russian-speaking professions, especially those linked to teaching and culture.[34]

The leaders of the Moldovan Interfront enjoyed close contacts with their Baltic counterparts. The Moldovan Interfront was more pro-Soviet than pro-Russian, but not as reactionary as those in the Baltic republics. Although bankrolled by Tiraspol, there is little evidence that the organization was initiated by the KGB but it was certainly subsequently infiltrated by the security forces.[35] Although the Interfront represented only a small percentage of the settler community during the *perestroika* years, it laid the foundations for the organization of post-independence settler politics.[36]

Despite strong opposition to the Russian Democrats during the August 1991 putsch, the Interfront made no official declaration in favour of the Moscow plotters. It was therefore not banned after the collapse of the coup. Following independence, the settlers on the right bank faced a complicated new situation. Efforts to retain the Union had clearly failed and the pro-Soviet policies of the Interfront were no longer appropriate. As a result, settler politics began to undergo a reconfiguration. From the second half of 1991, the Interfront and other pro-Soviet organizations began to lose support and suffered defections to the reformed communists who had regrouped as the Socialist Party.

When leading members of the Interfront, including Vasili Yakovlev, the chief ideologue, fled to the PMR after the Moscow putsch, Shornikov and Solonar emerged as the main leaders of the movement, now renamed Unity (*Edinstvo*). As the 1994 elections approached, the move away from a pro-Soviet agenda to one that addressed the new political and economic concerns of the Russian-speakers in Moldova gathered pace and led to an alliance between the Socialists and Unity.

Although the two organizations had important policy differences – Unity was more pro-market reform than the Socialists – they shared a broadly similar agenda built around a return to the rouble zone, protection for the Russian language, closer ties with Russia (especially economic integration) and a continued role for the Russian army in Moldova. The alliance of the Socialists and Unity marked the consolidation of economic and ethnic questions within the Russian-speaking community of the right bank. However, although the Socialist-Unity alliance emerged as their main political organization, its position was challenged, mainly by a variety of cultural organizations within the settler community.

In 1990, one of the leaders of the Interfront, Alexander Belapotapov, left because of its 'excessive internationalism'. He wished instead to promote the Russian national idea and established the Russian Centre in Chisinau with the aim of promoting the self-identity of Russian peoples.[37] It was intended as a purely cultural organization that sought to 'provide a sense of stability for people who felt uncomfortable in the context of a rapid Moldovan national rebirth'.

The centre has sought to protect the position of Russian schools and education in Moldova, to promote Russian festivals and also to arrange resettlement for those who wish to move to the Russian Federation.[38] It has generally supported the Moldovan government and is primarily interested in promoting a revival of a Russian identity within an independent Moldova. In summer 1993, with help from the Russian Foreign Ministry, the activity of the Russian Centre was expanded and a Russian Society created to foster the emergence of a broadly based Russian community in Moldova.[39]

Initially, relations between the Russian Centre and the pro-Soviet Interfront were hostile. For much of the post-independence period, Unity and the Russian Centre competed for the loyalty of the settler population. In 1993, in response to an initiative from Dmitri Rogozin of the Russian Federation-based Congress of Russian Communities, Unity set up their own Russian Society to rival the Russian Centre. But before the 1994 elections, there was some reconciliation between the different organizations, their leaders having recognized their mutual interdependence.[40]

The settler community is further divided by groups which aim to promote ethnic identities other than Russian. Anatoli Lysetsky, one of the founders of Interfront, established a Ukrainian society in 1991 aiming to promote a Ukrainian identity among the large number of Ukrainians in the country. Its leadership has had little contact with the Russian groups and indeed is hostile to them. The majority of Ukrainians in Moldova supported Moldovan independence but were against unification with Romania. With no indigenous political organization of their own, the Ukrainians have, however, tended to vote for the Interfront and then the Socialist–Unity alliance.[41]

The other main ethnic group with an important impact on the settler community and its politics is the Gagauz. The Gagauz felt particularly vulnerable to the process of linguistic Romanianization because between 1979 and 1989 the percentage of Gagauz speaking their own language dropped from 96% to 91%.[42] In 1961, the Gagauz schools had been closed; this was followed in 1963 by the closure of Ukrainian schools. The language law of 1989 was therefore viewed in Komrat as a direct challenge to the future of the Gagauz *ethnos*. An organization – the Gagauz-Halki – was established to resist the policies of linguistic and cultural Romanianization.

Intense efforts were made by the Chisinau authorities to involve the

Gagauz areas in the 1994 elections. On the eve of the elections, Prime Minister Sangheli and President Snegur visited the region to encourage Gagauz participation. Following promises of special rights for the region, the Gagauz leadership agreed to hold the elections. The population of the Gagauz areas voted for the Socialist-Unity bloc. Negotiations following the elections led, in early 1995, to a referendum conducted in the southern areas on the formation of a Gagauz autonomous area.

The settler community has also been politically weakened by the division between the eastern and western regions of Moldova. The historical separation of Bessarabia and the left bank and the split between the two areas since the fighting of 1992 meant that the settler community was divided into two, with that in the PMR in a very different position from that in the rest of Moldova. Although the left bank and Bendery both have large numbers of Russians and Ukrainians, there has been almost no official support for the creation of pure Russian or Ukrainian organizations and the Tiraspol regime has continued to support the Soviet settler culture of the pre-independence period. In contrast, settlers on the right bank have moved to develop less Sovietized – whether as Russian, Ukrainian or Russian-speaker – identities.

Strong political and economic ties to Russia continue to exert a powerful pull on the PMR. Sheltered by the presence of the 14th Army, a strong psychological barrier remains among much of the urban population, especially the elite, against reunion with Moldova. However, although leaders of the anti-Yeltsin Russian opposition have visited the area, since the destruction of the Supreme Soviet in Russia in October 1993 the importance of the PMR for Russian domestic politics has steadily diminished.[43] Diplomatically isolated and threatened by the proposed withdrawal of the Russian Army,[44] the Tiraspol regime has been keen to promote Russian citizenship within the PMR.

Internal politics have also begun to call into question the future of the PMR. The Tiraspol leadership was built on a series of power structures created in response to the perceived threat of Romanianization and loss of control of the local economy to Chisinau. The core socio-economic base of this system of power was the technical intelligentsia composed of Sovietized Slavs who were most threatened by the proposed language tests. As the language threat has receded, the bonds that held this coalition together have begun to weaken. The core of the Tiraspol regime, the OSTK, has splintered and the PMR is increasingly run on the criminalized clan structure built up after 1940.[45]

The nature of the Russified minorities in Moldova therefore remains uncertain. The unification drive and the war of 1992 have channelled the identity of the non-Moldovans in a variety of different directions. In Moldova, unlike in some of the other former Soviet republics, it is difficult to speak of a settler community as a whole. On the right bank, the emergence of Moldovan nationalism has provided the basis for the development of an inclusive Moldovan national identity that embraces the Gagauz and the Russian-speaking settlers. In the PMR, new political identities continue to be defined against a perceived Romanian identity in Moldova. However, as well as internal factors, interstate relations have played a central part in the politics of the area.

The international context

The conflict in Moldova has been one of the most international of all those in the former USSR. Not only have a significant number of external actors been involved – Romania, Ukraine and Russia have all played important roles – but, at one point, potential external claims on its territory and people seemed to call into question the viability of Moldova as a sovereign state. Although its relationship to these external actors has moderated, the interaction of internal and external factors was central to the country's shift to the east in 1992 and the new identity established after the war of 1992.

Initially, relations with Romania dominated Moldova's external policy. As close contacts were built up between the Popular Front and Bucharest and as Moscow gradually lost its control over Chisinau, Moldovan unification with Romania seemed inevitable. However, as conflict over Romanianization gathered pace, other external actors entered the internal affairs of Moldova, the Russian Federation being much the most important.

The rise in tension in Moldova coincided with and accelerated the political struggle in Moscow between the Democrats in the government and conservative elements in the Supreme Soviet to determine Russian foreign policy. From late 1991, the PMR became a centre for anti-Democrat forces from the Russian Federation. The eventual outbreak of hostilities between the forces of the PMR and Moldova occurred precisely as President Yeltsin and his government were under intense domestic pressure from parliament over the issue of Russian-speaking settler communities outside the Russian Federation.[46]

The fighting in early summer 1992 therefore played directly into the hands of those opposing the policies of the Russian Foreign Ministry.

Members of the Red/Brown alliance were able to use events in Moldova to support their criticism of the government.[47] The visit of Vice-President Aleksandr Rutskoi to the conflict zone was particularly important and marked the beginning of a clear split between him and President Yeltsin. Rutskoi advocated that Moscow recognize the PMR as an independent state. On 30 June, in the midst of the crisis over Crimea and the PMR, Kozyrev published an article warning of the dangers of a coup against the Russian state which stemmed directly from events in the PMR.[48] The Moldovan leadership considered that Rutskoi had encouraged the actions of the Russian army in the conflict of 1992.[49]

Although there is little evidence of direct involvement by the Red/ Browns and other Russian-based groups in the Moldovan conflict, there is little doubt that the Tiraspol leadership received at least verbal support from radicals in Russia.[50] However, not only the rightist forces in Russia were active in the conflict, which also caused a deeper shift in Russian politics with especially important effects on the Democrats. In particular, fighting in Transdniester contributed to the development of a new assertiveness in Russia's external policy.[51] The agreement regulating the conflict, signed between Presidents Yeltsin and Snegur in July 1992, marked the beginning of Russia's direct involvement with Moldova and of a process of re-engagement between Moscow and Chisinau.[52]

The activity of the 14th Army and the subsequent introduction of Russian peacekeepers was one of the first occasions for the use of Russian troops in an external role. Henceforth, close Russian involvement with other newly independent states, and on occasion the use of Russian military forces outside Russia, became part of Russia's new identity as the dominant regional power.[53]

While it was unclear how far General Lebed was under Moscow's control, the simple involvement of the 14th Army in the region helped Russia maximize its influence in Moldova. On the basis of the protection of the Russian Army, the *de facto* independence of the Tiraspol regime was secured.[54] The political and military pressure exerted on Moldova was reinforced by economic problems after the war, when the country was bankrupt – there was a \$25 million trade deficit[55] – and was forced to seek closer economic ties with Russia and the CIS.[56]

The conflict also had an important impact upon Ukraine's external role and relationship to Ukrainians outside Ukraine. Although Ukraine has made important initiatives to establish links with the sizeable Ukrainian population in Moldova and to promote a stronger Ukrainian identity, the ethnic pull to become involved has been considerably moderated by other considerations.[57] Ukraine was deterred from supporting the seces-sionist aspirations of the PMR (despite the anxiety about Romianization felt by large numbers of Ukrainians in the area) for fear of establishing a precedent for Russian secessionism in Crimea. Nor did it wish to open the questions of Bukovyna and southern Bessarabia, territories awarded to Ukraine after Bessarabia was annexed. It therefore followed a policy of cooperating with Chisinau to prevent the creation of a Russian outpost to its west.[58] The decline of the Romanianization campaign was also broadly welcomed in Kiev.[59] The Ukrainian authorities have also been resistant to calls from Ukrainians in the PMR to make provisions for dual citizen-ship because of the precedent this would establish for the large number of ethnic Russians in Ukraine.

The complicated relationship of Moldova to Romania has effectively blocked any moves to establish dual citizenship provisions within Moldova. While Russia exerted considerable diplomatic pressure on Moldova to accept dual citizenship proposals, to establish such a right for Russians could also mean granting Moldovan citizenship to at least a million people living in Romania with some connection to Bessarabia.[60] Given the efforts of the authorities to separate Moldova from Romania, such a policy would be most unwelcome in Chisinau.

Despite the broadly favourable outcome for Russia of the conflict of 1992, Russian policy towards Moldova and its non-Moldovan population has remained cautious. Behind this caution lies uncertainty about Russia's relationship to the Russian-speaking settler communities in Moldova and ambiguity among the settlers about their own identity. After the war along the Dniester river, the Russian government sought to develop links to the settler community following the general approach outlined by Sergei Stankevich in his policy document and using the Russian embassy as the centre to coordinate policy.

In July 1993, with the assistance of the Russian embassy in Moldova, an organizing conference of the Russian (*Russkaia*) Community of Compatri-ots in the Republic of Moldova was undertaken.[61] This organization was to be built around the Russian Centre led by Belapotapov. However, while the Russian government has sought contacts with the moderate settler groups, these remain weak in Moldova. The main focus of political power among the settler community has developed through organizations founded in opposition to the Russian Democrats and their anti-Soviet policies. Never-theless, despite the history of opposition between the Russian Democrats and the ex-Interfront leadership, there has been gradual reconciliation between the two sides, blurring the political fault lines of the *perestroika* period. The Russian embassy in Chisinau has in particular developed good relations with the Socialist-Unity bloc. The Russian government has also worked to isolate the PMR and to work with Chisinau to negotiate a settlement of the territorial dispute. The fact that volunteers from the PMR helped defend the Moscow White House from the assault by Yeltsin's troops in autumn 1993 reinforced Moscow's anti-PMR policies.

The Congress of Russian Communities has worked with Unity to broaden the party's base beyond a narrow political one. Dmitri Rogozin, leader of the Congress, has also been involved in developments in the PMR, although he has distanced himself from the Tiraspol leadership, seeking instead to develop close contact with General Lebed. In 1994, the Congress of Russian Communities appeared to be in competition with the Russian government to develop different identities within the settler community in Moldova. Rogozin worked with the more radical groups to foster political identitification with Russia among the settlers – a *Rossiiskii* identity – while the Russian government sought to promote a broadly based pro-Russian community anchored within Moldova.

Conclusions

As in the Baltic states of Estonia and Latvia, the Russian-speaking settler community became central to the development of Moldova from the late 1980s. However, unlike in the Baltic states the political dynamics within Moldova and the complex ethno-political situation soon called into question the territorial integrity of the country. Although the future shape of the Moldovan state remains uncertain – whether it will become a federation or even confederation or whether the PMR and Gagauz region will simply enjoy extensive autonomy – its future as a single unit now seems beyond question.

The stability that emerged in Moldova depended on the creation of a political order capable of integrating the diverse sets of interests and communities within the country. This was contingent upon the development of Moldovan nationalism among key sections of the indigenous elite. The fighting in summer 1992 served as a catalyst for the emergence of Moldovan nationalism as a significant force and also served to channel national identity into inclusive non-ethnically defined forms. The need to defeat those who advocated unification with Romania and to avoid further conflict have ensured that since late 1992 the indigenous political and economic elites on the right bank have sought accommodation with the Russified settlers and the Gagauz. The Moldovan case therefore suggests, somewhat surprisingly, that in certain circumstances war and nationalism can actually favour the integration of minority communities.

The continued existence of the Interfront after the summer 1991 coup gave the settler community an organization capable of challenging Romanianization, while its generally left-wing orientation prevented it from becoming a purely Russian-speaking organization. With a developed internal political organisation and ensured of support from the Moldovan nationalists, the Russian-speaking settlers of the right bank have become increasingly committed to Moldova.

The issue of the PMR continues to cause difficulty. Nevertheless, the conditions that combined to produce the Tiraspol regime have begun to change in fundamental ways. The eventual departure of the 14th Army will weaken the separatists. Moreover, the forces that created the PMR (fear of Romanianization and the desire to retain control of the economy of the left bank) and the organizations established to promote secession (which were built on the political and economic relationships of the Soviet period) are being undermined by new developments. Marketization, privatization and the engagement of Chisinau with the international political economy (the IMF, World Bank and European Union) mean that the right bank is becoming more vital economically than the unreformed and criminalized PMR. Economic groups on the left bank have begun to look to Chisinau as well as to Moscow. At the same time, Chisinau has proposed a special autonomous status for the PMR that would give the region broad executive and legislative powers and special language rights. This suggests that even some of the formerly radically pro-Russian sections of the PMR elite could eventually come to identify with Moldova.

The fact that the conflict of 1992 was contained and eventually had a positive influence on developments in Moldova owes much to the Russian government. The powerful support commanded by the PMR leadership within sections of the Russian political establishment and the intense pressure on the Russian government to protect 'Russians' during the fighting of 1992 could well have led to more extensive Russian involvement. Instead, the Russian government helped to isolate the Tiraspol regime and to promote pro-Moldovan settler organizations on the right bank. The events in Moldova also had a fundamental effect on Russian external policy, forcing greater engagement between Moscow and the ex-Soviet republics and fostering a sense of Russian national identity which included as one of its main elements protection of the diaspora. This developing sense of national identity was also encouraged by events in Ukraine.

Chapter 5

Russians, regionalism and ethnicity in Ukraine

Introduction

Russia's relationship with Ukraine has emerged as one of the central questions facing the two countries in the post-Soviet period because from a historical, geographical, and ethnic point of view, they are extremely difficult to separate.[1] Since independence Ukrainian domestic politics and interstate relations with Moscow have therefore often hinged upon a debate about the political significance of the historically intertwined genealogical, linguistic and regional identities in the area.

The imperial knots that bound the territories of modern Ukraine to the Russian Empire also served to structure and reinforce the close cultural and ethnic ties between their people. While Soviet rule created the Ukrainian SSR – the first time that the bulk of the lands that constitute contemporary Ukraine had been united on broadly ethnic lines and formally separated from Russia – in practical terms, Ukrainian and Russian territories continued to function as a single political, economic and cultural unit. Indeed, from the 1930s the highly centralized nature of the Soviet state ensured that Ukraine and its people were even more closely integrated with Russia than in Tsarist times and almost nothing was done at an official level to develop separate identities.

The intermeshing of Ukrainian and Russian, Slavic and Soviet, identities within Ukraine and in the settler communities elsewhere in the USSR meant that when independence came at the end of 1991, there was little clear sense of what an independent Ukraine would stand for or look like. The country's disparate communities contained varying regional, ethnic and linguistic mixes with very little understanding of themselves as political or national communities distinct from their neighbours. The

78

Distribution of Russian settlers in Ukraine

weakness of the new Ukrainian state, the absence of significant non-Soviet institutions to connect different sections of society,[2] and the lack of a sense of common purpose provided little to integrate the population into a single national community.[3]

The internal political situation in Ukraine has been considerably complicated by the debate in Russia about its own national identity and its role in the territories of the former USSR. Ethnic intermixing in the regions along the Russian and Ukrainian border, coupled with large-scale Russian settlement of eastern and southern regions of Ukraine, has led sections of the Russian political establishment, as well as significant numbers of Russians, to conclude that a distinct Ukrainian nationality is a fiction; that there is little justification for a sovereign Ukraine independent from Russia. This has been reinforced by the chronic economic situation in the Ukraine and strong irredentist movement in Crimea.

However, within Ukraine, despite periodic crises in Crimea and inflammatory statements by Ukrainian and Russian nationalists, compared with many other former Soviet republics ethno-nationalism has played a secondary role. Faced by manifold problems after independence, the use of ethno-nationalism to mobilize popular support to defeat political opponents might have seemed a highly attractive option to Ukraine's leadership. Indeed, Leonid Kravchuk tried just such a tactic in the presidential campaign of 1994, and lost. Why, then, has ethnic-based nationalism not been a viable political tool in Ukraine? Unlike some other ex-Soviet republics, Ukraine has no clear fault line between different ethnic groups. Certainly there are poles of ethnic differentiation – Crimea and Western Ukraine – but, in between, the mixing of languages and cultures, as well as intermarriage, has created a series of interwoven communities. Russians and Ukrainians mix extremely closely and polls suggest that both groups have generally positive attitudes towards each other, although Russians tend to be a more sceptical about an independent Ukraine.[4] In this environment, ethnicity operates in the form of a gradual gradient from more Russified in the East and South to more Ukrainianized in the West.

That is, ethnicity is the central strand that runs through almost all the issues in contemporary Ukraine, but the particular configuration of linguistic, hereditary, cultural and economic elements that constitute ethnicity in different forms across the country serves to reinforce diverse geographical identities more than genealogically defined ethnic ones. Regional competition rather than ethnic polarization forms the substructure of Ukrainian politics. Indeed, ethnicity is given a different definition in each region.[5] With no obvious ethnic schism – except in Crimea and in the West – the Russian question affects Ukraine in two main ways.

First, since Ukraine has never existed as a unitary state and regions form the political and economic foundation of the country, determining the internal political organization of Ukraine becomes critical. A federal or confederal structure may be most appropriate for a state with such diverse ethno-regional identities. Second, because Russia's role in the former Soviet Union has yet to be decided conclusively, ethnic Russians and Russian-speakers are likely to continue to be used as a 'special interest' that legitimates a close Russian engagement with the internal affairs of Ukraine.

The intermixing of history and identity

The contemporary problems of political identity in Ukraine are derived from the long-standing borderland status of the area – indeed *Ukraina* means borderland – and its history as a region contested by other powers. Since the thirteenth century, Ukrainian lands have been at the intersection of shifting empires – the Grand Duchy of Lithuania, the Ottoman Empire, the Polish-Lithuanian Commonwealth, the Crimean Tatar Khanate,

Austro-Hungary and Russia. The resulting legacy of different religions, cultures and languages has provided little in the way of common institutions (political, economic or social) to mediate them. Ukraine is the land not just of the Zaporizhzhian Cossacks but also of New Russia – the northern shore of the Black Sea incorporated into the Russian Empire under Catherine the Great – as well as the industrial East, the rural West and the linguistically and ethnically mixed centre. Ukraine is and always has been a melting pot for different peoples and cultures.

The various histories that have divided modern Ukraine's territories have also created different, and often mutually exclusive, beliefs among the people about their place in the world, fostering multiple loyalties and demands for differing degrees of autonomy or even independence. Support for Ukrainian independence is weakest in those lands that were part of the Russian Empire. West Ukrainians, the most active supporters of Ukrainian independence, were never part of the Russian Empire.[6] Thus current tension in the country is, to a large extent, a legacy of imperial political geography.

The prevailing Ukrainian historiography, the version supported particularly by Ukrainians in the West and members of the intelligentsia, identifies the emergence of a Ukrainian people clearly separate from the Russians.[7] It claims that this separate identity manifested itself on three occasions when something resembling an independent Ukraine was established. First, from the eighth to the thirteenth centuries, Kiev ruled a large territory called Rus. Although eventually destroyed by internal division and dismembered by Mongol invasion – Kiev was sacked in 1240 – Kievan Rus provides a powerful founding myth for the modern Ukrainian state. Second, from the sixteenth to the eighteenth century, Zaporizhzhian Cossacks established a number of largely autonomous territories within what is today Central and East Ukraine. Caught between far more powerful neighbours, these territories were always under threat. Finally, in 1654 the Ukrainian Cossack *Hetman*, Bohdan Khmelnytskyi, signed the Treaty of Pereiaslav which stipulated that in return for protection against Poland, the Cossacks would recognize the suzerainty of the Muscovite Tsar. Under the Treaty of Andrusovo in 1667 Russia and Poland divided up the remaining Cossack territories along the Dnipro river.

Although the left-bank Cossacks initially enjoyed some autonomy under Russian overlordship, following the battle of Poltava in 1709 Russia gradually asserted direct control. By the end of the eighteenth century, any form of independent Ukraine had ceased to exist. Not until the early part of the twentieth century did Ukrainian territories again acquire some autonomy. With the collapse of the Russian and Austro-Hungarian Empires in 1917–18, followed by the Russian civil war, various powers vied for territory in Ukraine. Amidst this chaos, a number of 'Ukraines' came briefly into existence before being crushed by external forces. By the early 1920s, the territories that constitute modern Ukraine were divided between Romania, Poland, the Soviet Union and Czechoslovakia.

Many in Russia, however, do not take the Ukrainian desire for independence seriously because Ukraine, both territory and people, is seen to have been historically an organic part of Russia.[8] From this perspective, the Ukrainian association with Poland and the Austro-Hungarian Empire is viewed as a historical aberration. Generations of Russian intellectuals and politicians have believed that any sense of Ukrainian identity was invented by politicians in the Austro-Hungarian Empire or Poland as a way to destroy the Russian Empire from within.

Most Russian historians take Kievan Rus to be the forerunner of the modern Russian state. For this reason, Kiev occupies a central place in Russia's political mythology and reclaiming 'Russian' territory lost with the Mongol invasion has been an important justification for Russian expansion to the west. The territorial vision is reinforced by an ethno-cultural theory that links Ukrainians, Russians and Belarussians as 'three brotherly peoples', who together constitute the general Russian people (*obshcherusskii narod*) of Kievan Rus which was artificially divided after the twelth century. Indeed, the whole of Russia's relationship to Ukraine is interpreted through this framework. The annexation of Ukrainian lands by Russia and the settlement of Russians in the region has therefore been seen in terms of reunification rather than conquest or the extinction of Ukrainian independence.

Thus, in Imperial Russia the common founding myth of Kievian Rus and the close linguistic, religious and cultural links between Ukrainians and Russians underpinned Russian dominance over Ukrainian lands. This territory, which was known as *Malorossiia* (Little Russia) or New Russia, together with Russia itself and Belarus, constituted the natural territory of the Russian state.[9] By the nineteenth century, much of contemporary Ukraine was divided between three Russian provinces: Central Black Earth; Ukraine; and New Russia.[10] At the same time, Moscow-inspired policies of modernization were gradually integrating the Ukrainian borderlands into the political and economic core of the Russian Empire.

The Russian interpretation of history justified the often enforced introduction of Russian language, culture and institutions to Ukraine.

Ukrainian was viewed not as a separate language but as a dialect of Russian, and in Tsarist Russia its use as a means of public communication was heavily restricted. The local intelligentsia was also drawn steadily into the Russian cultural orbit. The Ukrainian Autocephalous Orthodox Church was absorbed into the Russian Orthodox Church in the late seventeenth century and although it was briefly revived in the 1920s, it was not to re-emerge fully until 1990. Thus by the nineteenth century there was little prospect of an independent Ukraine.

The Soviet period

While Ukrainian lands remained subordinated to Moscow following the 1917 revolution, Bolshevik rule brought an important change in the relationship between Russia and Ukraine. For the first time, the view that Ukrainians, Belarussians and Russians constituted a single people was officially repudiated in Moscow and three separate Slavic republics were established.[11] This decision, coupled with Stalin's later territorial annexations, the unification of Ukrainian lands during the Second World War and Khrushchev's transfer of Crimea to the jurisdiction of the Ukrainian SSR, provided the basis for modern Ukraine.

Initially, Soviet rule changed Ukraine's relationship to Moscow. In addition to the establishment of Ukrainian territorial integrity, from the early 1920s until 1933 a policy of Ukrainianization was pursued by the Ukrainian Communist Party. However, as power was increasingly centralized in the Soviet state, the pro-Ukrainian policies were reversed. Under Stalin, Soviet nationality policy and historiography, which in the 1920s had condemned Russification and the 'civilizing mission' of Russia, reverted to Tsarist views of Russia's role in the area.[12] In most practical matters, Ukrainians and Russians continued to be viewed as a single people – although Ukraine was singled out for particularly brutal repression in the 1930s – and Ukrainian settlers were sent to other republics to support policies of Sovietization/Russification. Russian language was taught in secondary schools throughout the republic and it became increasingly difficult to publish material in Ukrainian.

After the establishment of Ukraine as a separate unit, perhaps the most significant development under Soviet rule was the three-stage territorial annexation along its western border.[13] In 1939, the Red Army occupied the predominantly Ukrainian territories of Poland, bringing 7 million Ukrainians (5 million according to Polish statistics) into Ukraine. In 1940, Soviet Ukraine was extended to include the one million Ukrainians of northern Bukovyna and Bessarabia (from Romania). Finally, in 1945 union with Transcarpathia was effected, bringing 500,000 more Ukrainians into Soviet Ukraine. While Southern Bessarabia had been Russian imperial territory (1795–1917), Transcarpathia, Galacia and Bukovyna had never been part of the Russian Empire.

Thus, by the end of the Second World War, Ukraine was a formally separate political unit with a largely ethnically Ukrainian population. For the first time almost all the lands that nationalists considered historically Ukrainian had been gathered together. At the same time, despite the formal separation of the three Slavic peoples, the assumptions underlying the Russian imperial belief in a common and united Slavic identity – usually presented as an all-Russian identity – continued to inform Soviet policy. Under the Soviet system, the intermixing of Ukrainians and Russians accelerated. Many Ukrainians left Ukraine and settled in the Russian-speaking immigrant communities in other republics, while significant numbers of Russians travelled to Ukraine and settled in the heavily Russified East, South and Central regions.

The re-emergence of Ukrainian nationalism

While Ukrainian resistance to external rule was manifest in the period 1917–20, during the collectivization of the early 1930s and again in the Second World War,[14] contemporary Ukrainian nationalism as a broad-based and relatively powerful movement dates primarily from the postwar years. In this period, demographic and social changes created a wider constituency for nationalist ideas,[15] while the newly annexed West Ukraine served as an important base for nationalist sentiments.

The growth of nationalism was also facilitated by the policies of Petro Shelest, First Secretary of the Ukrainian Communist Party from 1963 to 1972, which led to the Ukrainianization of parts of the cultural and educational establishment. In addition, the pretence that Ukraine operated as an autonomous political unit – a Ukrainian Foreign Ministry was established in 1944 and in 1945 Ukraine became a member of the United Nations – helped to foster a sense of a separate identity.[16] In 1972 Shelest was dismissed and replaced by V. V. Shcherbitsky, who launched a drive to re-Russify education and the media and initiated a purge of the cultural *apparat*.[17] Shcherbitsky, who remained in position until 1989, played an important role in keeping nationalist and anti-Soviet forces in check.

Perestroika

With *perestroika* it was largely Ukrainians who became involved in the new social and political movements, and the main centres of political activity within Ukraine tended to be in largely Ukrainian areas. Russians were active in a variety of organizations but in smaller numbers. In 1989 *Rukh*, the leading independence movement, was formed. Although not overtly ethnically based, occasional anti-Soviet and anti-Russian sentiments in its propaganda and a new law on the Ukrainian language passed in 1989 provoked considerable anxiety in the Russified East.

Despite concern about Ukrainian ethno-nationalism, large numbers of Russians and Russian-speakers voted for independence in the Ukrainian referendum on 1 December 1991: 90% of the electorate supported independence. But the fact that so many Russian-speakers voted for independence did not necessarily imply a strong sense of Ukrainian (in the civic sense) national identity. Rather, the vote stemmed from a combination of other factors including a wish to escape an impotent central Soviet apparatus, to take control from a system that was collapsing, to vote against totalitarian rule and for the economic improvement promised with independence.

Post-independence

Despite the importance of nationalism from the late 1980s, the Ukrainian state that came into existence at the end of 1991 was not ethnically defined.[18] An independent Ukraine was justified by the right of self-determination for a territorially and legally constituted nation. An important factor that promoted this definition of Ukraine was the re-emergence of national-communism which had been important in the 1920s and 1960s. The territorial notion of Ukraine was introduced by the Ukrainian Communist Party and utilized the 'zero' citizenship principle – whereby everyone resident in Ukraine prior to independence would be granted citizenship – formulated by *Rukh* in 1990.[19]

The fact that ethnicity has played a significant part in Ukraine since independence but has not become the primary means of mass political mobilization implies other more important forms of identity. In particular, class, language, economics, sense of history and notions of genealogy have fused to make regionalism the primary fault line in Ukrainian society. Each of the main regions of the country – Crimea, East, South, Centre and West – has an individual identity woven from these diverse elements and each has developed a different relationship to the new Ukrainian state. Ethnicity thus plays different roles in different areas and means different things across the country.

While in the West and, to a lesser extent, in Crimea ethnicity is defined in largely genetic terms, in the East, South and Centre regions it is intermixed with language; thus Russified Ukrainians are more similar to local Russians than the non-Russified Ukrainians of the West. In the Donbas, local identity has a significant class element reflecting the industrial basis of the region, as indicated in strong support for left-wing and economic-based parties rather than nationalist ones.[20] There are clear differences between heavily Russian-populated regions such as the Donbas, the developing financial centre of Kharkiv, the emergent service- and trading-based areas of the south, and the recent migrants who populate Crimea. Ukrainian politics is about the relationship not simply between Slavs, Ukrainians or Russians but also between Donbassites, Odessites, Kharkovians, and so on.

Russians in Ukraine

The multi-dimensional nature of ethnicity in Ukrainian territories makes identifying the arrival of the first settlers from Russia problematic. Proto-Ukrainians and Russians had clearly been mixing in the area for hundreds of years before distinct ethnic identities emerged. The first significant numbers of recognizably modern Russians came to what is today Ukraine in the first half of the seventeenth century, settling in the Kharkiv region. While a mixed group of Russians, mostly peasants fleeing serfdom, had settled in southern areas in the sixteenth century, they were quickly absorbed into the Cossack communities that dominated this area.

With the rapid industrialization of the late nineteenth and early twentieth centuries, significant numbers of Russians moved to urban centres in Ukraine. Between 1890 and 1930, two million Russians moved to Ukraine, particularly the Donbas.[21] In the 1930s, a further one million Russians were sent to the region as factory workers, administrators and managers, and to ensure Ukrainian acquiescence in Soviet rule. This Soviet-Russian community gradually absorbed other national minorities, notably Serbs, Greeks and Jews.

While most Russian migration to Ukraine took place before the Second World War, significant numbers of Russians also moved there in connection with postwar reconstruction, especially in the Eastern industrial regions.

Between 1959 and 1989, the percentage of Russians in the Ukrainian population rose from 16.9% to 22.1% (7.1m to 11.36m). By comparison, the percentage of ethnic Ukrainians fell from 76.8% in 1959 to 72.7% in 1989. In this period, most Russians went to Crimea, particularly the south.

As a result of these migrations, Russians reinforced their traditional dominance of industry, administration and education in the urban areas of the East and South as well as in Kiev. By 1989, although Russians were in the majority only in Crimea, they formed sizeable minorities in many of the other regions – Donetsk (43.6%), Luhansk (44.8%), Kharkiv (33.2%), Dnipropetrovsk (24.2%), Zaporizhzhia (32%) and Odessa (27.4%). This numerical strength has been reinforced by the importance of the Russian language in the republic.

The 1989 Soviet census suggested that 66.3% of Ukraine's population considered Ukrainian their native language, 31.3% Russian, and 2.4% other languages. Thus, almost 11% of ethnic Ukrainians considered Russian to be their first language. In addition, many of those who identified themselves as Ukrainian-speakers also knew Russian very well. Bilingualism was and continues to be extensive.[22] Russian was particularly used in areas heavily populated by Russians, especially Crimea, where Ukrainian schools and publications were scarce during the Soviet period.

The mixed history of Russian settlement in Ukraine has created a complex set of overlapping and competitive identities among the Russian communities. The majority of Russians in Ukraine were born there and have therefore been subject to at least six potentially political identities: a generic Slavic identity; an ethno-linguistic Russian one; a genealogical or 'pure' ethnic Russian one; a civic-territorial Ukrainian one; a local-regional one; and a Soviet one. In addition, the various economic interests of different social groups and geographic areas have created a variety of competing identities within the Russian community.

While the nationalist politics of pre- and post-independence Ukraine and Russia fostered a growth of ethno-linguistic identities in the Russified communities – notably in Crimea and Western Ukraine – the internal politics of Ukraine and the more recent policies of the Russian government have helped to counter this trend. While ethno-politics has certainly been important, the political mobilization of the Russified communities has taken many different forms, all heavily informed by ethnic identity, but to varying degrees. Only when confronted by extremist elements of the Ukrainian nationalist movement or by initiatives from Kiev aimed at removing local powers do Russians and Russian-speakers across the country find common cause. For this reason, except in Crimea and the West, specifically Russian or even Slavic organizations have played an insignificant or at best secondary role in the mobilization of the Russian-speaking population.

Ukraine's main regions

The East
With its traditionally close relationship to Moscow, geographical position adjacent to the Russian Federation, large number of ethnic Russians and dominant Russian language, the East has often been seen as an area ripe for irredentism. In response to the rise of the Ukrainian nationalist movement and the introduction of a law to make Ukrainian the state language, the East became one of the main centres for resistance to Ukrainianization. Eastern sections of the Ukrainian Communist Party sought to undermine the policies aiming to alter the status and position of Russians and Russian-speakers in Ukraine. In reaction to the Ukrainian language law of 1989 an Interfront was established in December 1990.

The anxiety of many in the East regarding Ukrainianization did not initially translate into a strong desire to unite with Russia or remain under the control of Moscow. In the referendum on independence on 1 December 1991, 83.9% of the population of the heavily Russified Donetsk region of the East supported independence. Since independence, the population of Eastern Ukraine has not so much supported an ethnicization of Ukrainian politics by supporting ethnically Russian politicians, as voted for candidates who would protect local interests on issues such as the economy and the Russian language. This has usually meant voting for an ethnic Russian or Russified Ukrainian.

Traditionally, politicians from the East have played a leading role in Ukrainian domestic politics. However, following the ban on the Communist Party after the August 1991 Moscow putsch, the Eastern political elites were disoriented and effectively disempowered. As a result, the nationalists of the West were able to exert considerable influence on Kiev. The expansion of nationalist power from the end of 1991 prompted a fear of Ukrainianization, especially of education (which has subsequently proved largely groundless). In part driven by these anxieties, from autumn 1992 the East began to regain some of its political strength and internal organization.[23]

From late 1992, a variety of largely left-wing parties based primarily in the East began to appear. The Civic Congress was launched in Kharkiv in summer-autumn 1992 and quickly spread to Luhansk and Donetsk. In

1993, the Communist Party of Ukraine began to revive in the East and South, and was officially registered in October.[24] The miners of Donbas continued to be an important political force. Their strike against price rises in summer 1993 showed their power and close ties to the local administration.[25] All these organizations support a similar political agenda: equal status for the Russian and Ukrainian languages, notably in education; stronger links with Russia, especially economic ties; dual citizenship; and a federal Ukraine.

Besides a common ethno-linguistic identity, important sections of the East's population were initially also bound together by economic concerns. Both workers and managers supported retention of subsidies for Eastern industries. This mixture of interests encouraged the East to vote for Leonid Kravchuk in the presidential elections in 1991 when he was seen as the main opponent to the radical nationalists. In the 1994 presidential election, the bloc Union (*Soiuz*) was established – uniting the Communist Party, Socialist Party, Labour Party, Civic Congress, United Unions, Rus Society, and the Party of Slavic Unity – to campaign for Leonid Kuchma and his non-nationalist, economic-based agenda.[26]

The fusion of socio-economic and ethno-linguistic issues in the East has prevented the emergence of nationalist parties.[27] Although small organizations such as the Party of Slavic Unity and the Rus Society have been set up, they are extremely weak and have almost no influence. The prospects for ethnic mobilization in the region are also being undermined by emerging splits – geographical, economic and political – within the Eastern political camp. Strong centrifugal trends are coming to characterize the politics of the East, especially among the elite. In particular, important differences of interest are emerging between the intelligentsia and new businessmen of Kharkiv,[28] the miners and workers of Donbas,[29] and the former Red Directors, the managerial elite of Dnipropetrovsk. The left-wing parties are also far from united. The Communist Party and the Socialist Party are competing between themselves and have tended to stress socio-economic issues,[30] while the Civic Congress's main goal is building links with Russia and the CIS.[31]

Political interests in the East are being remoulded by the changing economic situation. A number of parties based primarily on the economic interests of industrialists and the new business class have been established,[32] and have supported a programme based on privatization, reforging links to business and industry in Russia, and protecting the Russian language. Support for federalization has also been expressed, although this is largely seen as a way to retain tax resources in the region and ensure that local elites control privatization, rather than as a means to secede from Ukraine. These organizations support closer economic ties with Russia, but not political union.

The re-emergence of powerful left-wing parties based particularly in the East and the rising significance of economic factors are also helping to foster political divisions. In 1994, the Communist Party gained important support among the working class of Donbas, who are vulnerable to marketization, and in the countryside, where it draws on the conservatism of the peasantry. The Socialists, based largely on the technical intelligentsia, are also concerned about the implications of marketization. There is also growing unease among left-wingers about Russia's pro-market, anti-socialist leadership,[33] while the comparative strength of the Russian economy has led some local politicians and business leaders to fear for their region's ability to compete with Russian industry.[34]

The apparently strong separatist tendencies that are often manifest in the region may therefore not be as threatening as made out by Ukrainian nationalists. Although the East is heavily Russified, it is not an area of Russian nationalism. Economic and linguistic concerns provide the main contours of its identity.[35] It is the threat posed to this regional identity, by political and economic control from Kiev coupled with Ukrainianization, that has fuelled calls for a federal structure for Ukraine.[36]

Crimea

Like the East, Crimea has been seen as a centre for secessionist movements because of its large Russian population. According to the 1989 Soviet census, Russians make up 68.4% and Ukrainians 25.6% of the region's population. In addition, 47.4% of Ukrainians on the peninsula considered Russian their native tongue. In 1991, only 54% of the population of Crimea voted for Ukrainian independence, compared with the national figure of 90%. Of this 54%, most are likely to have voted for independence for socio-economic rather than political reasons.[37] In contrast to the Eastern areas, political mobilization in Crimea has primarily taken place through organizations based on ethnicity defined in genealogical terms. Russians, Tatars (returning to what they consider to be their homeland) and Ukrainians, who are largely settled in the north of the peninsula, have all sought to establish their own exclusive organizations.

While current tension between the different communities stems from disputed histories – Russians root their claims to the peninsula in the period following their conquest of the region in the eighteenth century, while Tatars and Ukrainians concentrate on the years before Russian imperial expansion – it is also a reflection of the Crimea's difficult socio-economic position. The region, one of the poorest in Ukraine, is overpopulated. The increased pressure on resources brought about by the return of the Tatars from Central Asia has emphasized genealogically defined ethnic identity among other groups and channelled social and economic competition into a dangerous ethno-political confrontation. The final destabilizing element has been the support of leading Russian politicians for the more extreme Russian nationalists on the peninsula.[38] However, although the period 1990–94 was marked by serious confrontations, since early 1994 important splits have appeared within the Russian nationalist movement in Crimea and between it and other regions of Ukraine.

In the early phase of confrontation with Kiev, the peninsula was divided between two main political camps: the national-communists and the Russian/Crimean nationalists.[39] The first moves to decouple Crimea from Ukraine began in early 1991, the Communist Party providing much of the impetus. On 20 January 1991, Nikolai Bagrov, First Secretary of the Crimean Communist Party, organized a referendum on whether to revive Crimea's status as an autonomous region (*oblast*) within the Ukrainian SSR. Of those taking part, 93.26% voted for a change of status. On 4 September 1991, the Crimean Supreme Soviet voted to declare sovereignty over Crimea. The main Russian nationalist organization, the Republican Movement of Crimea (RDK), also campaigned for the referendum. Founded in 1991 and led by Yuri Meshkov, the RDK provided the driving force by which Russian became the official language of Crimea in July 1991.

In February 1992, the movement for Crimean independence gathered pace. With the Communist Party removed from politics after the August 1991 coup, nationalist parties on the peninsula were in a position to set the political agenda. The RDK reached the height of its influence in mid-1992. On 5 May 1992, the Crimean parliament declared independence (although this was subsequently suspended). However, the organizational weakness of the nationalist movement was already becoming apparent. Fragmented from its inception, by early December 1993, the RDK had split into four factions: Meshkov's Republican Party of Crimea; the Russian Party of Crimea; the Russian Society of Crimea; and the Russian Language Movement of Crimea.[40]

Although unity was temporarily restored with the establishment of the Russia Bloc in December 1993 to promote Meshkov's presidential campaign, the alliance among nationalists remained weak.[41] Their position was also challenged by the re-emergence of the local Communist Party, led by Leonid Grach, which joined the Communist Party of Ukraine at its founding congress in Donetsk in June 1993. Although resistant to any Ukrainianization of the region, the Communist Party is oriented more to socio-economic issues and supports the reconstitution of the Soviet Union rather than unification with Russia.

The election of Meshkov as president of Crimea in January 1994, with 70% of the vote, increased the tension between Kiev and Simferopol as Crimea seemed to be moving towards independence.[42] On 7 March a majority voted in support of the 'consultative' questions that Meshkov had placed on the ballot. Three-quarters of voters supported a plan for dual citizenship on the peninsula and for relations with Ukraine to be conducted on the basis of bilateral agreements. The bloc *Rossiia* also won a large majority (54 of 94 seats) in the Crimean parliament. While these results appeared to set the stage for a major confrontation, they were in fact the prelude to a dramatic disintegration of the Russian nationalist movement, brought about by increasing disputes over economic reform, in particular control of privatization on the peninsula.

In June 1994, the growing role of economic questions was indicated by the election of V. Semenov as the new mayor of Sevastopol, ahead of Aleksandr Kruglov, leader of the fiercely pro-Russian National Salvation Front.[43] Significantly, Semenov declared himself neutral on the Russia-Ukraine question and identified his primary concern as economic well-being.[44]

In 1994, primarily economic-based parties began to emerge on the peninsula. The Party for the Economic Renaissance of Crimea (PEVK), which was close to the Eastern Ukrainian New Ukraine group and generally pro-market reform, began to play a far more important role. PEVK was formed around a group of industrialists promoting closer economic ties with Russia, federalization of Ukraine, membership of the CIS, especially its economic institutions, but opposing the separation of Crimea from Ukraine. From early 1994 Crimea's leading economic actors began to distance themselves from the more radical pro-Moscow line of Russian nationalist groups.

In autumn 1994, the dispute about economic policy came to a head in a bitter confrontation between parliament and the president. Following his election victory, Meshkov had appointed a group of Moscow economists led by Evgenii Saburov to launch economic reform on the basis on a programme of economic integration with the Russian Federation and rapid privatization. Saburov's economic agenda caused significant resentment within the nationalist coalition and among local economic interests which feared exclusion from privatization; leading members of the Communist Party and some nationalists were also ideologically opposed to radical economic reform. Saburov was forced to resign and was replaced by a local political figure, Anatolii Franchuk. As Crimea's nationalist movement disintegrated towards the end of 1994, tension was further reduced by growing cooperation on the Crimean issue between Moscow and Kiev.

Agreement between these two capitals on the status of Crimea and the Black Sea Fleet had given way to a tense dispute following independence.[45] This was exploited by a range of Russian politicians to enhance their credentials as patriots. Close contacts developed between Crimean nationalists, the Russian parliament and Russian nationalist organizations.[46]

In April 1992, Vice-President Rutskoi visited Crimea and called for its secession from Ukraine. On 21 May the Russian parliament voted for a resolution that termed the 1954 transfer of the pensinsula to Ukrainian jurisdiction illegal. Tension in Crimea began to rise at the beginning of 1993. Its main source was economic decline, notably the price rises on staple goods of January 1993, which were manipulated by nationalists; but another central factor was the decision of 7 December 1992 by the Seventh Congress of People's Deputies to re-examine the status of Sevastopol. In July 1993, it agreed to prepare a bill granting federal status to Sevastopol within the constitution of the Russian Federation. In June 1993, Russia and Ukraine agreed to divide the Black Sea fleet, causing further tension in the region.

With the destruction of the White House in October 1993, the Russian government gained sole responsibility in Russia for managing the Crimean confrontation. It has generally supported the Ukrainian position, fearing that Crimean secession would establish a dangerous precedent for areas in the Russian Federation such as Chechenia and Tatarstan. Following Meshkov's election, it was made clear to him that Moscow would not agree to secession but would support measures aimed at closer economic integration with Russia.[47] The appointment of Saburov as Prime Minister was designed to foster this process and promote radical economic reform to undermine the nationalists. Although this policy failed, it had the indirect result of splitting the nationalist forces in Crimea and thereby diminishing the challenge to Ukrainian–Russian relations.

The West

Like Crimea, Western Ukraine has witnessed mass mobilization along narrowly ethnic lines, but for different reasons. As in Crimea, the majority of Russian settlement dates from after 1945. The small number of

Russians in the West, coupled with fierce Ukrainian ethno-nationalism, prompted the creation of ethnic Russian organizations in L'viv earlier than in the rest of Ukraine. The leading Russian group, the Pushkin Society, was set up in the late 1980s, and produced its own paper, *Sovest*. In August 1991, the council of the Pushkin Society produced a draft document on national-cultural autonomy, education and culture,[48] and it was the first organization in Ukraine to advocate dual citizenship for Russians.[49] Leaders of the Pushkin Society were quick to look for contacts in Russia and attended the Congress of Compatriots in St Petersburg in September 1992 organized by the Council of Nationalities.[50]

Perhaps because Russians in the West have felt vulnerable and been subject to hostility from radical Ukrainian nationalists, organizations such as the Pushkin Society have not advocated separatism. In addition, there is a strong sense among the Russians in this area that they are Central Europeans rather than Russians of the Russian Federation.[51] Their main interest has been to protect themselves from radical Ukrainian nationalism and to promote strong Russian social and cultural institutions.

Although the West and East of Ukraine are clearly important, because of the complicated ethno-regional nature of Ukrainian politics the role of ethnic politics in Ukraine will largely be decided in the key areas of the South and Centre. These regions hold the balance of power between East and West and are likely to mediate between them.

The South

Southern Ukraine has a particularly complex history,[52] having been tied to European powers, enjoyed prolonged periods of independence and become the New Russia region – a virgin lands project for Slavic settlement – under the Russian Empire. The important Jewish influence, particularly in Odessa, has added a further dimension to its character, discouraging ethnic polarization between Russians and Ukrainians. Clearly less pro-Russian than Crimea and more moderate than the East as regards reintegration with Russia, the South has nevertheless opposed Ukrainianization, favoured Russian as a second state language, supported rebuilding economic links to Russia within the context of the CIS, and has also looked westwards for ties with Central and Western Europe. In the 1994 elections, the local electorate voted for Kuchma and a significant number of independent parliamentary and local government candidates.

The South has been less interested in nationalist politics, of whatever hue, than the East and West, and local politics has been driven far more by economic issues. Odessa, in particular, has emerged as a centre for trade and new private economic activity. In 1994, city-wide elections brought in a local government committed to pursuing privatization and radical economic reform. The main interest of this region has been to gain national support for economic liberalization or, failing that, political independence to achieve that aim itself.

The Centre

The Centre is perhaps the most contested area in Ukraine. Ukrainians are in a majority in the cities but they are often heavily Russified. Left-wing parties with different political/economic agendas from those of the Russian and Ukrainian nationalists control the largely Ukrainian villages. Like the East, this is an important region for the Socialist Party led by the parliamentary Speaker, Oleksandr Moroz. Ties through left-wing parties, forged in a generally Russian ethno-linguistic context, provide a vital connection between the East and the heartland of Ukraine. If Ukrainianization accelerates in the Centre, it is likely to alarm and isolate the East.

Ukrainian domestic politics

While the developments within each region and the ties between the Russian communities across Ukraine will be of significance to the whole question of the territorial integrity of the country, developing a broad set of all Ukrainian political, economic and social institutions that can manage these complex relations will also be of paramount importance. Since independence Ukraine has faced a variety of simultaneous and interconnected crises – economic, political-state, nationalities and social. Together these problems effectively blocked serious economic and political reform. The presidential and parliamentary elections of 1994 were crucial because they marked the return to power of the traditional political elites of the republic. This helped to unlock the complicated ethnic/regional confrontation that had built up after independence and had prevented essential economic and political reform.

Following independence, one of the central political problems facing Ukrainian leaders was the distribution of power in the country. This struggle was fought out at two main levels: first, between the parliament and the president, and to a lesser extent the judiciary, to determine authority at the centre of the system; and second, to establish the relationship between the centre and the regions. These contests were, however, linked.

Although this battle for political power arose from the personalities involved, at a deeper level it was the product of a struggle between different elites within Ukraine. Following the collapse of the USSR, a new correlation of political forces came to dominate Ukrainian politics. With Moscow's direct control removed, power passed to an alliance between the Kiev bureaucrats and nationalist forces from the West. Unfortunately, this coalition could provide little practical direction. The Ukrainian nationalists were essentially weak with their power base largely confined to western areas while the state bureaucrats were subject to corruption and nepotism and had little interest in reform.

Kravchuk's attempts to impose a presidential system during his term in office reflected in part a desire to bring the regions under the control of this new political arrangement of Ukrainian elites.[53] However, within the context of economic deterioration and the ethno-regional basis of power in the Ukraine, the Centre was unable to establish effective control over the regions. Although prominent Eastern politicians were brought into this ruling bloc – Vitold Fokin (1990–92), Leonid Kuchma (1992–3) and Efim Zvyahilskiy (1993–4) – they faced considerable opposition from within the government and the centralized bureaucracy. By the end of 1993 an economic and political stalemate, with the Centre unable or unwilling to push through the needed reforms,[54] was provoking increased ethnic tensions, which in turn held up the reform process and encouraged further regionalization of Ukraine.

The 1994 parliamentary (March–April) and presidential elections (June–July) were important because they marked the reintegration of the diverse ethno-political and economic interests in Ukraine within a system with the potential to manage them. This was not simply about changing personalities at the pinnacle of the system; the elections marked a more fundamental change in the distribution of political power.

The results of the elections and the regional distribution of voting that produced them – the Russophone South and industrial East voted for candidates who wanted to restore ties to Russia – showed that the nationalists in the West were increasingly isolated. However, the voting did not suggest an ethnic split so much as a division between the Russophone industrial zones and the agricultural West.[55] The elections produced an important political shift to the East. That is, the former system of power forged from ethnic, regional, economic and political interests reasserted itself. The Centre was subsequently able to introduce a reformist agenda because the new political elite could rely on the compliance of the East and South.

Although there was broad support for Kuchma, his political coalition was centred on the country's industrial and managerial elites, many of whom have strong interests in economic reform, primarily privatization. At the end of 1993, Kuchma became head of the powerful Union of Industrialists and Entrepreneurs which had been created earlier by major industrialists – notably the former Red Directors of Dnipropetrovsk who moved to join the reform camp, representatives of the state sector, key sections of middle management, and other sources of private capital tied to trade and with important financial links to Russia.[56]

Kuchma couched his economic programme in national, but not ethno-national, terms. At the same time, there is little evidence of rapid or enforced Ukrainianization.[57] The President has thus been able to reassure the key political constituencies that their future is safe in his hands, freeing him to push his new deal of accelerated economic reform.[58] Despite the regional nature of voting in the elections, with the appointment of the Socialist leader Oleksandr Moroz as the new parliamentary Speaker after the elections, parliament did not break into regional factions. Instead, the Communist, Agrarian and Socialist fractions formed a close grouping. The re-emergence of these left-wing parties has been important because they tend to view Ukraine in territorial rather than ethnic terms – as a state constituted by the *people of Ukraine*, not the *Ukrainian people*.

Russian–Ukrainian interstate relations

Although the relationship between the Russophone regions and the Ukrainian state has largely turned on factors internal to Ukraine, the relationship between Moscow and Kiev has also been been of crucial importance. Determining its relationship with Ukraine is fundamental to Russia's search for its post-imperial role. Without Ukraine and Belarus, Russia's claim to be a European power becomes very weak.[59]

Interstate relations between Russia and Ukraine began on a positive note. In November 1990, a bilateral treaty was signed that recognized the inviolability of the two country's borders, and at discussions on 23 June 1992 there was broad agreement on a range of issues including the protection of minorities and division of the Black Sea Fleet.[60] However, as the struggle for power intensified within Russia, relations with Ukraine worsened. Groups opposed to the government seized on the issue of the Russians in Ukraine and especially the question of Crimea's status as a means to challenge President Yeltsin and his supporters.

While, at least prior to autumn 1993, the Russian parliament's decisions increased tension between the two countries, on the whole the Russian government has acted to calm the situation, especially as regards Crimea. In response to the July 1993 decision of the Russian Supreme Soviet which claimed Sevastopol for Russia, President Yeltsin made clear his support for the territorial integrity of Ukraine.[61] The dominance of the centrist vision of Russia's interests within the government – preservation of existing borders and maximum influence over neighbouring countries – ensured strong opposition to radicals who have sought the revision of borders. The election of President Kuchma has also facilitated Ukrainian–Russian relations. Thus, the assertion of direct rule over Crimea by Kiev in March 1995 was treated as an internal Ukrainian affair by the Russian government, although Konstantin Zatulin, head of the Duma Committee for CIS Affairs, was active in organizing opposition to Ukrainian actions in the Russian parliament.

The question of integration

The election of Leonid Kuchma placed the issue of integration between Ukraine, Russia and the CIS firmly on the political agenda. For most of the voters in the East and South and in Crimea, integration was one of the key issues in the election. For many in the East, the election of Kuchma was seen as the first stage in a process that would lead to a Ukraine tied politically to the Russian Federation through the structures of the CIS and a network of bilateral treaties. At the same time, it would also eventually lead to a federalization of the country, with East Ukraine and Crimea steadily integrated into the economy of the Russian Federation.[62]

Initially, there were signs that this indeed was the direction Ukraine was taking. In September 1994 Ukraine, along with the majority of former Soviet republics, joined a new CIS committee on economic policy. It was suggested that this was the first CIS institution with powers superior to those of the individual governments.[63] Although this committee proved moribund, Ukraine's continuing economic dependence on Russia – Russia has provided more than $5bn in import financing for Ukraine, mostly in the form of unpaid energy bills – suggests that it will have little option but to accept closer bilateral ties. However, disagreements between the two countries on dual citizenship have highlighted the fact that sovereignty will not be easily forsaken by the new Ukrainian political elite, even with a leader who looks favourably on closer ties with Moscow.[64]

Conclusion

At the end of 1993 the question of whether Ukraine could survive as an independent state was being asked more and more frequently. Faced with the huge task of reforming a centrally planned, inefficient, militarized economy, with high levels of inflation and dependent on external energy supplies that could not be paid for, the government seemed trapped within a web of regional and ethnic issues that effectively blocked necessary economic and political reform. Simmering tensions on Crimea, strong anti-Kiev sentiments in the East and South, nationalist demands from the West and an often tense relationship with Moscow suggested that the territorial integrity of Ukraine was under serious threat.[65] However, by mid-1995, despite continuing chronic problems, especially economic, Ukraine seemed unlikely to disintegrate and the prospect of ethnic conflict had receded.

This more optimistic prognosis stems from two interlinked developments. The national elections of 1994 brought to power a political leadership more able to push through reform without fostering a division of society along ethno-regional lines. At the same time, Ukraine's internal political order is becoming increasingly complicated. Changes, principally economic, within the regions have undercut potential ethnic, ethno-linguistic and ethno-regional bonds and helped to create new alliances. Crimea remains something of an exception because of its highly ethnically polarized nature. However, even here the pressures of economic change and the rise of crime have pushed the ethnic issue down the agenda of immediate political problems. Moreover, the disintegration of the Crimean political establishment has allowed Kiev to reassert control.

Although feelings of ethnic and national identity in Ukraine remain weak, the legacy of close historical and cultural intermixing, and the patchwork of local, linguistic, genealogical and economic ties among the various peoples of the area, suggests that there is a basis for a Ukrainian national identity built on diversity, a multi-ethnic history and strong regional interests. At the same time, new economic and political elites from the regions, which have much to gain from controlling an independent Ukraine in terms of privatization and political careers, could provide a cement to hold the country together.

Chapter 6

The formation of a Russian diaspora identity in Kazakhstan

Introduction

The large size and geographical location of the Russified settler population in Kazakhstan[1] – the majority of the non-Kazakhs live in the north and east of the country in areas coterminous with the Russian Federation – has made the future of these communities a central question in Kazakhstani society. The initial peaceful transition from Union republic to independent sovereign state fostered the misleading impression that inter-ethnic relations in Kazakhstan were largely harmonious. But this calm disguised a series of basic difficulties. Since early 1993, these unresolved problems have had an increasingly deleterious effect on ethnic relations in the country.

Russian and Soviet colonization of the Kazakh Steppe not only brought large numbers of non-Kazakh settlers to the region, loss of independence and a steady process of Russification, it also created the foundations for Kazakh nationalism and ultimately the emergence of the modern Kazakh nation. Since independence, without Moscow's interference to restrain the spread of nationalism, the development of a state and society giving priority to Kazakh interests has gathered pace. The main instrument for effecting basic changes in the distribution of power between different ethnic groups has been the policy of nativization (*korennizatsiia*). Colonization of state structures by Kazakhs is being used to shape political and economic change in areas of the country that have been controlled by non-Kazakhs for over 150 years. With Kazakhs taking charge of the country's central social, political and economic organizations, the majority of the settler population has been steadily excluded from the main Kazakhstani institutions.

At the same time, Russia's claim to have a special right to protect the large number of non-Kazakhs, coupled with the need to retain close economic links with Russia and the landlocked position of Kazakhstan, have made good relations with Moscow a central priority in Almaty since independence. Preventing the settler problem from becoming a major issue has therefore been of paramount importance for the Kazakhstani authorities.

National identity has been developing in Kazakhstan against this complex backdrop. Publicly at least, President Nazarbaev has been keen to foster an inclusive national identity based on citizenship rather than ethnicity. However, in fact little has been done to address the accelerating polarization of society along ethnic lines. Indeed, the majority of government policies have actually furthered this development by giving support for Kazakhization. As a result, there is little sign of the emergence of an inclusive Kazakhstani identity; instead it is exclusive ethnic Kazakh, and politically (*Rossiiskii*) but not necessarily ethnic (*Russkii*) Russian, identities that are coming to dominate. The new identity of the Russified settlers is being built around a series of myths about the colonial period and colonial superiority. These myths serve to define the settlers as separate from the Kazakhs and to tie them firmly to Russia.

Russians, Kazakhs and colonialism

It is the colonial legacy that provides the basis for the competing and largely irreconcilable claims to territory being made by the country's different communities. For much of its history, Kazakhstan was treated by Russians as a simple extension of Russia and many today continue to view large parts of the country as essentially Russian. Colonial expansion into the region put down deep roots, both in terms of the introduction of the settler population and also in the form of an ideology of colonization built on a series of beliefs about the superiority of the educated European (Christian) colonist and the illiterate Asian (Muslim) nomad.

Russian colonization

The genesis of the Kazakh people is complex and contested largely because there has been extensive intermixing of peoples in the area for hundreds of years.[2] Around the beginning of the sixteenth century the Kazakhs seem to have emerged as a distinct people separate from the Uzbeks and to have divided into three khanates or *Horda* organized on patrilateral lineages: the Great Horde (*Ulu zhuz*) in the Semirechie area in the south; the Middle Horde (*Orta zhuz*) in the Central Steppe region; and

Distribution of Russian settlers in Kazakhstan

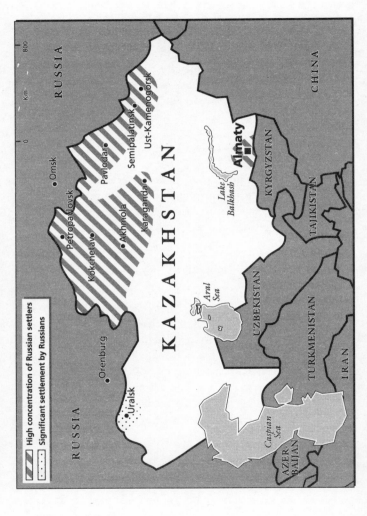

the Little Horde (*Leishi zhuz*) east of the river Ural. From the beginning of the eighteenth century, Kazakh lands came under intense external pressure. The region was gradually encircled by the territorial expansion of two great powers, Russia and China, from the west, north and east, and by Central Asians in the south.

The conquest of the Kazakh Steppe was the first phase of the two-stage Russian colonization of Central Asia. It saw the establishment of permanent Russian settlement along the periphery of Kazakh lands and scattered, small-scale settlement across the north. These enabled Russia gradually to extend control across most of the Kazakh-populated region by the middle of the nineteenth century. The second phase took place during the nineteenth century and relied upon the network of settlements established in southern Russia and Kazakhstan as bases for further expansion. The eventual conquest of the whole of Central Asia brought a flood of Russian settlers to Kazakh territories and began the intense process of Russification of the Steppe region which continued until the 1960s. This quickly shifted the demographic balance in favour of the Russified population, forcing the indigenous community to assimilate, move to the margins of society or migrate to the south.

Faced with increasing pressure from all sides and intense raiding from the east by the Jungari from China and in the west by Kalmyks from the Volga, the Kazakh Khans turned to Russia for protection. By the end of the eighteenth century, a large Russian protectorate had been established across the west of Kazakhstan while in the east a small Manchu protectorate had been created on part of the Great Horde territory. Although these protectorates were not strictly controlled, especially in the Russian case, their establishment effectively marked the end of Kazakh independence. Most importantly, the manner in which Russian power was extended into the Kazakh Steppe has allowed Soviet and Russian histories to stress that Russian colonization of the region was by voluntary agreement of the Kazakh leadership.[3] In 1847, the Greate Horde finally lost its remaining independence and was forced to pledge allegiance to the Tsar. From this time, the character of Russian colonization in the area began to change significantly.

Following the abolition of serfdom in Russia in 1861, peasants started to move eastward to work and settle on the Kazakh Steppe. Indeed they were actively encouraged to do so by Tsarist policies. Overall close to two million Slavs came to the area around the turn of the century, particularly in response to the Stolypin reforms (1906–12), by which 19 million hectares of land in Kazakhstan were set aside for farming, prompting a new wave of mass settlement by Slav peasants.[4]

Kolarz argues that it was during the period 1893–1912 that Russian colonization of Kazakhstan was achieved.[5] Between 1896 and 1916, the Russian population grew by 214% (1,257,672), considerably more in northern and eastern areas, while the native population increased by only 14% (351,051). The Slavic immigrants spread over Kazakhstan introducing agriculture, ploughing up the most fertile land – which was seen as unoccupied – and dispossessing the Kazakh nomads of their grazing lands. Many Kazakhs were forced from the Steppe to the south or into China.

Soviet colonization
Although nationalism had been rising among Kazakhs since the late nineteenth century, the First World War and the exile to the Kazakh Steppe of nationalists from other parts of the Russian Empire greatly accelerated its development. During the February revolution of 1917, the Kazakhs formed a semi-independent state called *Alash Orda*, the autonomy of which ended in 1920 when the Bolsheviks took complete control of the Kazakh Steppe.

In 1924 the Autonomous Socialist Soviet Republic of Kazakhstan was established as part of the RSFSR, thereby officially incorporating the Kazakh region into the Soviet state. As part of a later administrative reorganization of Turkistan, Kazakhstan became a full republic in December 1936 and the Kazakhs were recognized as a nation of the USSR. However, to prevent Kazakh nationalists from taking control of the new republic, the borders were drawn to include large areas of non-Kazakh settlement in the north and east, creating a firm Slavic bloc to keep the republic anchored to the Russian Federation.

The rural collectivization of the early 1930s, combined with efforts to destroy the last vestiges of the nationalist movement which opposed settlement and collectivization, proved a disaster for the Kazakhs. Between 1926 and 1939, the number of Kazakhs in the Soviet Union dropped by 869,000. While some fled into the Xinjiang region of China, collectivization rapidly led to famine and more than one million people are estimated to have starved to death. This huge demographic blow was further aggravated by the influx of deported peoples (Volga Germans, Poles, Koreans from the Far East and Crimean Tatars), political prisoners and kulaks. Final control of the Kazakh Steppe region was achieved in the 1950s with the Virgin Lands Scheme, under which the remaining high-quality grazing land was ploughed up and non-Kazakh settlers were encouraged to move onto the Steppe. This caused protest among the Kazakhs, resulting in the removal of the First Secretary, Z. Shaiakhmetov, and his replacement by a Russian, Leonid Brezhnev.

Extension of Soviet control into the countryside was accompanied by the industrial development of the north and east. The city of Karaganda became the third largest coal-producing centre of the USSR, and oil and mineral production was rapidly developed in various localities. Large numbers of Russian and Ukrainian skilled workers, engineers and technicians were imported to work in the new enterprises. The urban population of Kazakhstan rose from 9% in 1926 to 17% in 1936 and 27.7% in 1939. The expansion and Sovietization of the urban centres served to consolidate control over the countryside. In addition, the settlement of migrants in towns and cities impeded the spread of industrial employment and urbanization among the indigenous population, confining them to the low-pay, low-status and backward sectors of the economy.

By the end of the 1950s, the Kazakhs had been marginalized in the unproductive rural areas of the north and east or forced into the infertile lands of the south. In many places, they faced demographic obliteration. Between 1926 and 1970, the number of Slavs in Kazakhstan increased from 2 million to 6.5 million, among whom the number of Russians rose from one million to 5.5 million.

Cultural and political change under Russian and Soviet rule
Russian and Soviet colonization of the region did not simply rely upon the introduction of large numbers of non-Kazakhs into the area and strict external control. The apparently primitive way of life and imperfect practice of Islam among the Kazakhs seemed to suggest that this region was especially suitable for Russian cultural penetration.[6]

Russian colonization rested on an ideology of liberation – bringing civilization, Christianity and progress to backward peoples – which legitimated expansionism in the region. Later, many of the myths underpinning Russia's colonial mission in Kazakhstan merged with Communist ideology to justify Soviet rule. These ideas gave support for the enduring Russian belief that they were bringing civilization to backward lands and the idea that economic development could be accompanied only by reliance on Russian specialists, the 'Elder Brothers'.[7] This version of Kazakhstan's history also gained important adherents among Russified Kazakh intellectuals.

The re-emergence of Kazakh nationalism
Following the tightening of Soviet rule at the end of the 1920s, there was little opportunity for political resistance until the 1960s, when a powerful Kazakh leader emerged in the person of Dinmukhammad Kunaev and fundamental changes took place in Kazakh society. From the 1950s,

demographic change and modernization began to have important political, economic and social consequences for Kazakhstan.[8] Rapid population growth among the Kazakhs together with a general decline in fertility in European Russia and among Russian-European settlers meant that the trend which had been established between the 1890s and 1959 was reversed. In 1926, Kazakhs numbered 3, 968,289; by 1939 their number had fallen to 3,098,800 and by 1959 the Kazakh share of the population fell to 30%. Since then, their numbers have begun to increase relative to the settler population.[9] With the age structure of the country skewed heavily in favour of the Kazakhs – a large number of whom are under 18 years old – as well as Kazakhs returning from the diaspora and sizeable out-migration of non-Kazakhs, the demographic balance of the republic is continuing to swing in favour of the native population. This factor and the development of a sizeable Kazakh intelligentsia fostered the revival of Kazakh national identity.[10]

By the middle of the Brezhnev period, these factors contributed to a change in emphasis in the national movement. National self-preservation was no longer seen as a serious problem. Instead, the furtherance of national rights in such areas as cultural self-expression, the preservation and fostering of national heritage and national traditions and the enhancement of the Kazakh role in republic and national affairs became leading goals in the Kazakh national resurgence. As part of the general pattern of advancement for native elites in the USSR during the Brezhnev years, Kunaev emerged as a powerful local actor. He became First Secretary in Kazakhstan in 1960 and was the first native Kazakh to rise to membership of the Politburo. Under Kunaev, the standard of living rose steadily in the republic, while reforms of higher education brought the indigenous population into universities in unprecedented numbers. In addition, Kazakh political networks were extended in the republic and high-level support was provided for the development of Kazakh culture. By the early 1980s, Kazakhs were already over-represented in many spheres in the republic. In this sense, the process of Kazakhization originated in the 1960s and it was the attempt by Moscow to reverse aspects of this policy that induced the first ethnic violence of the *perestroika* period.

Perestroika

The emergence of unrest came as a shock: Kazakhstan had seemed an extremely successful melting pot for different nationalities and a likely location for the emergence of the new human genus long predicted by the communist authorities, 'the Soviet people'. But in fact, as noted above, a distinct Kazakh national identity had been steadily developing from the late 1950s. The *perestroika* years did much to accelerate this development and to transform the nationalist movement into a political force. The first indication of the strength of Kazakh national feeling came with the riots of 16 December 1986 in Almaty, sparked by the promotion of Gennadi Kolbin, a Russian from Ulyanovsk, to replace Kunaev as First Secretary.[11] Calm was only restored on 10 January 1987 when Nursultan Nazarbaev, a Kazakh who had been part of Kunaev's patronage network, was appointed as Second Secretary.[12]

Kolbin's rule was marked by twin policies which threatened many of the previous advances made by Kazakhs; the anti-corruption drive struck at the heart of the tribe and clan power structure that had infiltrated the Communist Party under Kunaev's rule, while the stress on a return to 'internationalism' was a thinly disguised attempt to re-Russify key sections of the Communist Party. To many Kazakhs, the direct and high-handed intervention of Moscow in the republic's affairs was tantamount to a reassertion of Russian power and served to politicize Kazakhstani society along ethnic lines.[13] The growing confrontation in the republic was reflected in a political struggle around two central issues: language and sovereignty.

As in many other Soviet republics, the issue of language became the basis for the first major battle between indigenous and settler populations. In September 1989, the Supreme Soviet of Kazakhstan adopted a law which stipulated that Kazakh was to become the official state language. Immediately, leaders of the Russian-speaking and largely ethnic Russian settler population began to lobby for changes to the bill.[14] Opposition to the new legislation focused on the requirement of fluency in Kazakh for completion of secondary education and employment in the public sector. However, before changes to the law could be made, the issue of language became intertwined with the question of sovereignty.

As republic-level independence movements gathered force across the Union, a debate began in Kazakhstan in September/October 1989 about the relationship with the USSR.[15] With radical Kazakh nationalist groups such as *Alash*,[16] *Azat* and *Zheltoksan* stressing the exclusive historic right of Kazakhs to live in Kazakhstan, Russians such as Viktor Kozlov of the Moscow Institute of Ethnography revived Russia's claim to northern and eastern Kazakhstan.[17] In the middle of the sovereignty debate, Alexander Solzhenitsyn published his essay on the future of Russia which argued that northeast Kazakhstan was part of a historic Greater Russia.[18]

Kazakhstan

After an intense debate, on 25 October 1990 a new version of the sovereignty bill was passed which, rather than stressing Kazakhstan as the Kazakh homeland, described the Kazakhs as the *first* among the republic's nationalities. While this represented an important compromise, the legislation on sovereignty meant acknowledging that Kazakh language, history and culture should have a special place in Kazakhstan and that Russian culture and language would have to play a diminished role.

Kazakhstan following independence

Nation-state building and Kazakhstani identity
The sudden collapse of the Union at the end of 1992 raised basic questions about the nature of the ethnic compromise implied in the sovereignty law. With independence, many of the issues which had seemed rather abstract during the debate on sovereignty suddenly became of great pertinence. Once again, the central question was the relationship between ethnic Kazakhs and Kazakhstani state and society. Was the new nation to be defined primarily in ethnic terms – the Kazakh nation – or as the civil expression of the variety of different groups living within the former republic?[19]

The battleground was provided by the debate about the new constitution, the most controversial part of which concerned the state language. After protracted negotiation, it was agreed that while Kazakh was to be the state language, Russian was to be 'the language of communication between nationalities'. However, Article 1 of the Constitution also proved controversial, providing the key justification for the construction of an ethnocratic state. It states:

The Republic of Kazakhstan (Kazakhstan) is a democratic, secular and unitary state. The Republic of Kazakhstan as a state system is self-determined by the Kazakh nation and guarantees equal rights to all its citizens.

That is, the basic foundation of the Kazakhstani state is the right of the Kazakh nation to self-determination and Kazakhstan is a unitary state.[20] President Nazarbaev has spelt out the contradiction at the heart of this arrangement in greater detail:

Kazakhstan's sovereignty is of a complex ethnological and legal nature. It is a unique synthesis of the national sovereignty of the Kazakhs (restoring to them their national origins and traditions) and the sovereignty of all the people of Kazakhstan as a single ethno-political community.[21]

Despite the careful linguistic hedging, the right of the Kazakh people to self-determination means that Kazakhs enjoy priority and greater rights within Kazakhstan; indeed in key areas the state is to promote the interests of the Kazakh nation above those of other nationalities. In addition, neither the constitution nor the President will accept forms of regional autonomy that might allow the preservation of a dominant Russian cultural-linguistic space in settler areas.

These principles have been used to legitimize the government's most controversial policy: nativization. It consists of four elements. Since independence, a steady process of marking territory has been under way. Justified in terms of fostering the 'cultural-spiritual' rebirth of the Kazakh people, the underlying agenda of this policy, especially in the settler-dominated north and east and in the Russified capital, has been to assert a change in control of the land. Formerly Russian and Soviet street, town and district names have been replaced by Kazakh ones. At the same time, the construction of a network of mosques has received high priority – with the assistance of external funding, particularly from the Middle East – especially in areas of minority Kazakh settlement.[22]

The second major aspect of the policy of nativization has been the considerable efforts made to encourage the immigration of the one million ethnic Kazakhs living in countries beyond the former USSR, the majority in China – 907, 582 according to the 1982 Chinese census – but significant communities are also found in Mongolia, Afghanistan, Turkey, Western Europe and the USA.[23] Substantial numbers have returned to Kazakhstan.[24] Many are being resettled in the European-Slav areas in order to redress the demographic imbalance.[25]

There has also been a gradual extension of the Kazakh language through television and radio and a rapid decline in Russian-language broadcasts. Schools and institutes of higher education have begun to stress the 'Kazakh' version of history and Kazakh culture. However, the primary source of resentment among settler groups is what is termed the 'secret' or gradualist nationalism, in particular the increasing domination in the state of ethnic Kazakhs. Their political and economic control is perceived as a direct effort to drive the settlers to the margins of society.

Clear priority is given to the promotion of ethnic Kazakhs within all spheres of public administration. Kazakhs now dominate the leading central ministries, the judiciary and the financial sector.[26] The rise of

Kazakh personnel has been particularly pronounced in the law enforcement agencies, notably the police. The national picture is mirrored at the local level with control of many of the regional *(oblast)* administrations in the hands of Kazakhs. Increasing the number of Kazakhs in the state apparatus does not simply ensure control over the settler population. The administration has a fundamental role in shaping the future of Kazakhstani society, particularly in terms of who will benefit economically from privatization. With representatives of the settler population being steadily forced out, political and economic power is being rapidly concentrated in the hands of a single ethnic group.

While nativization is perceived by non-Kazakhs as a policy designed to advance the interests of the Kazakh nation, the policy provides a framework for, and is fostered by, a fierce struggle for power within Kazakh society. The forces that underlie the rise of Kazakh nationalism – demographic growth, urbanization and increased education – have created an apparently insatiable demand in Kazakh society for positions of power. While independence created new opportunities for Kazakhs, fierce competition has built up to obtain new posts. The competition for these positions has developed along the traditional social fault lines of Kazakh society – family, clan and tribe – which have been reanimated since independence.

Among Kazakhs in the west, north and east – the Small and Middle Hordes – nativization is often seen as a cover for the advancement of the interests of the Great Horde or southerners. Many of the Kazakhs appointed to high and middle-level positions are from the south. On the other hand, within the southern group, especially in the capital, there is intense competition for posts between members of the various clans, leading to constant pressure to extend patronage networks into every corner of Kazakhstan. As a result, non-Kazakhs have been squeezed out of leading positions to make way for representatives of one Kazakh group or another. However, while external pressures have had an important effect on the non-Kazakh population, the extremely weak sense of identity and chronically poor internal organization among the settler community have also played a significant role in its growing marginalization.

The internal political and social structure of the settler community
The history of Russian and particularly Soviet settlement has played an especially important role in discouraging autonomous political organizations among the non-Kazakhs. Although nominally part of a separate republic, during Soviet rule the north and east were viewed largely as an extension of the Russian Federation, so the interests of the local popula-

tion tended to be articulated through Moscow-based institutions rather than those in Almaty. Of these, the Communist Party was the most important. Following independence, it might have served as the basis for the political organization of the settler community. However, its particular nature in the republic militated against this.

During the Soviet period, there were essentially two communist parties operating in Kazakhstan. The republican party drew its power from the *oblast* party organizations, particularly in the south and the rural areas of the north and east, and was largely controlled by ethnic Kazakhs. As a result, during the Kunaev years it became steadily fused with clan-based and regional Kazakh political networks. The party that operated in the large industrial enterprises of the north and east rested upon the power of factory leaders who were closely tied to the all-Union party organization in Moscow and drawn exclusively from the settler population. Control of these enterprises and the industrial economy of the north and east by the settler population was ensured by the Moscow ministries and the Central Committee bureaucracy of the CPSU. With the economic and political focus of the north and east firmly on Moscow, there was little in the way of formal institutions to link the settlers to the rest of the republic.

Following the collapse of the Union in 1991, the Communist Party was discredited as a means of totalitarian control, seen by many Kazakhs as an instrument of Moscow's rule and crucially weakened by its dual organizational structure. On 7 September 1991 it was dissolved. Although the Socialist Party was quickly established as its successor, leading Kazakh politicians and party members were reluctant to join, leaving it to assimilated Kazakhs and settlers.[27] The collapse of the Communist Party represented the failure of the single organization that might have served to bring important segments of the Kazakh and non-Kazakh populations together. It also left the settler population without an organization to speak on its behalf. The subsequent co-option of the settler economic elite – the former *nomenklatura* – into the President's patronage network through the establishment of the People's Union of Kazakhstan (SNEK) served further to isolate the settler population.

Deprived of the Soviet organizations and leadership, there was little in the settler community to provide the basis for any alternatives. The fact that the non-Kazakhs of the north and east are a settler population meant that the institutions of civil society were practically non-existent on the eve of independence. The large-scale immigration of previous decades had ensured that the social structure of the settler community was in a state of continual flux and periodically suffered severe shocks, such as the inflow of settlers as a result of the purges in the 1930s and the Virgin Lands Programme in the 1950s. This constant stream of new settlers meant that consolidating the social organization of the community and establishing broad social networks was extremely difficult. The majority of the settler population comprised industrial workers, technical specialists or farm labourers brought in to work on the state farms (*sovkhozy*). Very few of them were drawn from either the humanitarian or cultural intelligentsia, the people most likely to create social organizations outside the workplace.

Many of these characteristics are not unusual to Russified settler populations of the former USSR. The weak development of political organization among the settler community in Kazakhstan is explained by two particular developments. Under President Nazarbaev, Kazakh pro-independence sentiment was channelled through the Communist Party, while radical movements such as *Alash* and *Azat* were carefully controlled. This less confrontational approach did not threaten the settlers and little was done to organize Interfronts or develop a political infrastructure – Democratic or reactionary – among them. The collapse of the Communist Party at the end of 1991 therefore revealed the political vacuum at the heart of the settler population. Second, attempts to create new organizations were thwarted by strict state control of political activity by non-Kazakhs. In Almaty, despite numerous attempts, the largely settler organization Unity (*Edinstvo*) repeatedly had its registration blocked, while the most important settler political organization – *Lad* – had to conduct clandestine meetings for the first year of its existence.

Political development among the Russian community since independence

Faced with growing pressure from the Kazakhstani state and Kazakh society, leaders in the settler community sought to develop political and cultural organizations to combat their growing marginalization.[28] From 1993, a variety of such political organizations have emerged. However, these are not political parties with clear programmes and well defined constituencies. Rather, they are broad umbrella organizations that serve as vehicles to coordinate and channel the political activity of the non-Kazakh population.

The most radical settler organization is the Russian Community, officially registered in September 1992. While its expressed function was the defence of human rights and the collection of information on rights abuse, in fact the Russian Community has followed a narrowly ethnic Russian agenda underpinned by a fierce Russian nationalism.[29] Its centres of support were the Russian-oriented cities of the north and east, especially Petropavlosk and Ust-Kamenogorsk. Reflecting the strongly pro-Russian orientation of the organization – the leader of the Northern Kazakhstan section of the Russian Community, Boris Supruniuk, has taken Russian citizenship – its leadership has maintained very close links with radical Russian nationalist politicians and organizations.[30]

On 12 April 1994, Supruniuk was arrested in Petropavlosk on charges of promoting ethnic hatred through articles in his paper *Glas* and, most controversially, for fierce criticism of contemporary developments in Kazakhstan made at a meeting of the Cossack Circle in Omsk in late 1993. At the end of 1993 registration was withdrawn so the Russian Community could take no official part in the February elections, although the Almaty section was granted registration on 18 April 1994. After considerable pressure from Russian organizations, Supruniuk was released in May 1994 and has become something of a hero for Russian nationalists.

Although the Russian Community has a charismatic leader in Supruniuk, it is plagued by a chronically weak internal organization. Essentially a loose arrangement of radical Russian nationalist organizations which operate on the fringe of the non-Kazakh population, like other extremist groups, the Russian Community has a tendency to splinter into ever smaller but more ideologically pure factions. These characteristics coupled with intense pressure from the Kazakhstani authorities suggest that the Russian Community is unlikely to emerge as an effective political force, but its leaders have exerted an important influence on the political situation by stirring up the nationalities issue.

The most successful organization to emerge among the the non-Kazakh population has been the Slavic movement *Lad*, initially established to coordinate the various Slavic cultural centres that had developed among the settler communities in the later years of *perestroika* and the immediate post-independence period. Unlike the Russian Community, *Lad* sought to cultivate a constituency based on an all-inclusive Slavic and Russian-speaking identity rather than a narrow ethnic Russian one. Indeed, the leadership of *Lad* has claimed strong support among Russian-speaking Kazakhs, although the electoral evidence of this is weak.[31] While nominally a republican organization, *Lad*'s attention has been focused almost exclusively on the non-Kazakh populations of the north and east.

Following registration and spurred on by the 1994 parliamentary elections, *Lad* adopted an openly political agenda. Hampered by the poor coordination among the non-Kazakh communities, its main task was to consolidate its organizational base in the north and east. Slavic and Russian cultural centres, the initial units for organization, were inadequate for the broader political agenda being pursued by the *Lad* leadership, so political organizations were planned to work with the cultural centres. The campaign launched in early 1994 to collect signatures in support of the creation of dual citizenship rights for all Kazakhstan's population[32] helped mobilize and organize activists across the north and east. *Lad* activists claim to have collected nearly 500,000 signatures.[33]

However, the most important factor encouraging the consolidation of a political infrastructure among the settler population was the national and local elections that took place in the first half of 1994. Despite considerable barriers, legal and illegal, erected against the participation of independent, especially non-Kazakh, political organizations in the elections, the group of candidates loosely affiliated with *Lad* achieved important success at all levels, especially in the cities of the north and east.[34] Problems registering candidates with a clear party affiliation meant that officially four *Lad* candidates were elected to the national parliament, although up to eight deputies are closely linked to *Lad*.[35]

While all these were of Slavic origin and most were from the north and east, *Lad* did support a number of other candidates including Tatars and Kazakhs.[36] However, the ethnic polarization of Kazakhstani society meant that voting was generally conducted on the basis of a candidate's last name rather than party affiliation.[37] Despite the intentions of the *Lad* leadership, the movement has thus become a vehicle for further ethnic polarization. Nevertheless, the victory of independent candidates from the settler population marked an important change, lifting the isolation of the north.

Although the settler population generally has an uncertain identity and poorly developed social organization, one group constitutes an important exception. The re-emergence of the Cossack movement in Kazakhstan has created well-organized communities with a clear identity that can challenge Kazakh social organization. Perhaps for this reason, the Kazakhstani authorities have employed particularly harsh sanctions against Cossack organizations. Three Cossack hosts were settled on the territory of what is today Kazakhstan – the Uralsk, Siberian and Semirechie. Although all part of the Cossack movement, there are important differences between the three.[38]

The Russia–Kazakhstan border divides the Siberian Cossacks in two. The bulk of the host is located in the Russian Federation and headquartered in Omsk, while the remainder is settled in the northeastern part of Kazakhstan. The Siberian Cossacks have emerged as the most openly radical of all Cossack organizations, although they also have the weakest support in Kazakhstan. At a meeting in Omsk in early 1994, the differences between the various hosts were apparent, with speakers from the Siberian organizations adopting a far more confrontational approach than those from Ural'sk. The other two Cossack hosts have a stronger social base than the Siberian group. Thirty-two of the 36 *stanitsii* that constituted the original Ural'sk host were located on land currently inside Kazakhstan and a considerable number of these survived the Soviet period as Cossack villages. Leaders of the Ural'sk host claim that today there are 15,000 Cossack families in West Kazakhstan.[39]

Established in 1862, the Semirechie host is scattered across the area south of Almaty and along the northern border of Kyrgyzstan. The earlier settlers were responsible for the construction of Vernyi, now Almaty. Cossacks from Semirechie claim that today there are 38,000 Cossacks in the Semirechie host.[40] Although settled in the area as an integral part of Russian conquest, the Semirechie host have never been involved in military action against the Kazakhs. Under strong pressure from Kazakh nationalists, who see the revival of the Cossacks as a thinly disguised return to Russian imperialism, President Nazarbaev has taken a strong line against them.[41] The Society for the Support of Cossacks of the Semirechie was registered in June 1994 and then suspended in November. The Semirechie Cossacks themselves remain unregistered.

Beside these three main settler organizations, there are others which draw heavily on support from the settler population. The most important are the Socialist Party, the revived Communist Party,[42] the independent trades union movement *Birlesu* and Legal Development of Kazakhstan.[43] Although nominally working for the same ends, conflict and competition between these organizations makes forging a single bloc to campaign on behalf of the settlers extremely difficult. These organizations have poor direct links to the majority of the population, partly reflecting simple lack of coordinating political infrastructure, but also the result of more fundamental sociological, ethnic and geographical fault lines within the non-Kazakh population.

Different social groups among the settler population have responded in different ways to similar problems. Undoubtedly their key political weakness has been the passivity of the non-Kazakh economic elite. Unlike in the Transdniester region, where the corps of directors provided vital support for the political leadership of the left bank, in Kazakhstan the equivalent group has been largely coopted by the government. The creation of the President's party SNEK, with its roots firmly in the former *nomenklatura*, coupled with Almaty's tight financial control over the enterprises of the north and east, served to neutralize the old economic elite. The effectiveness of this strategy was highlighted by the success of the presidential list during the 1994 parliamentary elections. Drawn largely from the old *nomenklatura*, candidates on the list included a significant number of non-Kazakhs, whose subsequent election served to drive a political wedge into the settler population and provided a powerful counterweight to the emergence of independent settler politicians.[44]

This division was reinforced by the conduct and outcome of the local elections. Relying on the larger number of Kazakhs in the rural areas, the control that the *nomenklatura* is still able to exercise over rural communities and parts of the urban population, and backed by tight control over the electoral process, local authorities were able to ensure that Kazakh and non-Kazakh deputies closely tied into the ruling power structures dominated the *oblast*-level councils of the north and east. With the *nomenklatura* less able to control the urban areas, independent deputies have often taken control of town and city local councils, some of which are almost 100% non-Kazakh.

Beside the sociological stratification within the settler population, there are also important ethnic divisions. The settler community is composed of a mishmash of different ethnic groups with varying degrees of ethnic identity, diverse loyalties and different interests. The core of the non-Kazakh population is made up of Slavs – Russians, Ukrainians, Belarussians. However, Slavic solidarity in the republic is not altogether seamless. Ethnic revival among the Russian population and the creation of Russian cultural centres across Kazakhstan has been matched by a similar, but weaker, development of a Ukrainian ethnic identity,[45] though this generally merges into the overall setter identity. However, the creation of Ukrainian centres has sometimes highlighted the tensions underlying the apparent solidarity of the Slavs.[46] The settler communities also contain other important ethnic groups – Koreans, Tatars, Bashkiris, Germans and Poles.[47]

The regional character of the settler population

The vast majority of the settlers are concentrated in the urban areas of the north and east. However, the distribution, size and political orientation of these populations is far from uniform. Broadly, they may be divided into three regions: the pro-Russian and irredentist towns of the north and east; the marginal settler towns; and Almaty, its surrounding area and Taldy Kurgan.[48]

The 'Russian' cities of the northwest, north and northeast

Uralsk, Petropavlosk, Pavlodar and Ust-Kamenogorsk have emerged as the main centres for pro-Russian sentiment. The cities of the north were built by Slavic settlers from the eighteenth century onwards and are closely linked to Russian notions of homeland, feelings reinforced by the continuing numerical dominance of non-Kazakhs in the region. Kazakhization of areas traditionally controlled by non-Kazakhs has caused particular anxiety and an ethnically divided local political system. In the Pavlodar city council *(Maslikhat)*, for example, there are 30 deputies of whom one is a Kazakh, one an Azeri and 28 are Slavs. Significantly, most of the Slav deputies are independent. In the *oblast* council, only 19 of the 50 deputies are Kazakhs, largely from rural areas, but 36 are factory directors and almost all of them are connected to SNEK. The different composition of the councils reflects the tension between the settler-populated towns and the Kazakh countryside and the old and new settler elites.

During the Soviet period, the northeastern economy was tied closely to the all-Union economy and the collapse of that system has negatively affected it. Urban and rural areas have faced severe economic difficulties since links with Russia were severed and the Kazakhstani currency, the Tenge, was introduced in place of the rouble. Local entrepreneurs have faced a series of bureaucratic barriers apparently designed to prevent the emergence of a non-Kazakh bourgeoisie. With the region's economy on the edge of collapse, the settlers look to Russia for economic salvation.

These trends are favouring the development of a Russian (*Rossiiskii*) national identity in the region. Significantly, the historical sense that this area is Russian land is being linked by the settlers to this sense that they are Russian to create a Russian (though not in the exclusively ethnic sense) territorial identity and to foster a belief that the north and its people are an inalienable part of Russia.

The watershed of European-Slavic settlement

The line of non-Kazakh settlement that extends down from Petropavlosk through Kokchetav, Akhmola and Karaganda marks a break with the more radical politics of the northeast and northwest. Despite the large settler population in the central northern region, the non-Kazakh population regards this area as the fault line of European-Slavic settlement.

Akmola marks the edge of what the settlers consider Russian territory. During the Virgin Lands campaign of the 1950s, Akmola was renamed Tselinograd and became the centre for what many Kazakhs saw as a crude Russification drive. The proposed transfer of the capital there symbolizes Kazakh reclaiming of the territory.[49]

Karaganda is situated within the borders of large-scale Russian settlement but unlike in the towns further to the north and east there is little sense that the land here is Russian. The ethnic profile of the area is diverse, with large numbers of Ukrainians, Germans and Poles as well as the usual Russians. The settler community is also divided by important socio-economic splits. The industrial and social heart of the area is mining, with 35,000 miners directly employed in its 24 pits. The miners identify not as Russians or Kazakhs but as workers locked in a struggle with management over economic issues. The political weakness of the settler community is also accentuated by the general desire among the non-Kazakhs to leave, either for the cities of the north or, better still, the Russian Federation.

Southern settler communities
Originally a Cossack fortress, Almaty quickly became a centre for settlers moving to the south of the country. The settlers' dominance in the city was gradually lost as Kazakh political, cultural and educational elites took control from the late 1960s. Following independence, further Kazakhization of the state bureaucracy encouraged settler out-migration from the city. However, although many have left or plan to leave, the fact that Kazakhization of the city began earlier and has been more gradual has prevented the sense of panic that exists in the northeast. The Cossack population living around the city (Semirechie host) also has a strong commitment to the area.

Confrontation and integration

Since independence, migrations have accentuated ethnic compactness.[50] Large numbers of non-Kazakhs have emigrated – 200,000 Russians are reported to have left Kazakhstan in 1994[51] – especially from the southern cities of Zhambul, Chimkent and Almaty, or have moved to the northern and eastern *oblasty* while the Kazakhs have consolidated in the southern *oblasty* and advanced in the cities of Almaty and Leninsk.[52] As a result, the country's already highly polarized geography of settlement has been further heightened and this has fed into the growing sense of confrontation between Kazakhs and non-Kazakhs. Although, as yet, there is no unified political movement openly advocating such options, the growing confrontation between the north and Almaty and between the cities and the *oblast* authorities is fuelling demands for the creation of parallel power structures within the settler communities to circumvent central control.

Against the background of economic, political and social disintegration within Kazakhstan along broadly ethnic lines – indeed disintegration is forging new notions of ethnic communities – certain political developments, often unintentional, have helped to contain the strong centrifugal tendencies. These may be divided into four groups: the construction of multi-ethnic political institutions, primarily parties; the holding of elections and the election of legislatures at the national and local level; a series of symbolic gestures by the leadership designed to promote an atmosphere of tolerance; and changes in the international environment.

Although dependent on ethnic Kazakhs for their core support, two political parties can claim to have some support, even if extremely patchy, from sections of the settler population. Following the collapse of the Communist Party of Kazakhstan, President Nazarbaev gave guarded support for the creation of the People's Congress of Kazakhstan (*Narodnyi Kongress Kazakhstana*) led by the poet and former leader of the Nevada Semipalatinsk anti-nuclear movement, Olzhas Sulemeinov. Support for the People's Congress is drawn from among Russified Kazakhs, especially the Russian-speakers of the north and east of the country and, in Almaty, elements of the Kazakh and Russian intelligentsia. Local leaders of the People's Congress have built close relationships with leaders of the more moderate settler organizations, based on interests shared by Russified and northern Kazakhs and the settlers, notably the continued use of the Russian language (Sulemeinov writes his poetry in Russian); protection against the expansion of the power of the southern Kazakhs (the People's Congress is based largely upon the Middle Horde); and good economic and political relations with Russia (the welfare of Kazakhs in the north is dependent on the industries in the northern cities and if conflict begins in the region the Kazakhs here will suffer most).[53]

Although Nazarbaev initially gave his support to the People's Congress, important differences soon emerged with Sulemeinov and in summer 1993 the Kazakhstan Union of People's Unity (SNEK) was established. Unlike the People's Congress, which has sought to build a new coalition of interests, SNEK was forged from two existing networks of power; in effect it represents a fusing of two of the key components of the old Communist Party: the Kazakh political elites, especially from the south, and the economic elite from the settler areas. The key identity for members is not ethnic but their former participation in the *nomenklatura*.

President Nazarbaev, as the leader of SNEK, relies on the dovetailing of the interests of the former *nomenklatura* with the state to ensure continued political control in the country. The national and local elections in 1994 were organized to ensure the continued success of this group and thereby indirectly the President. Its political dominance was guaranteed both through electoral irregularities linked to the use of state resources (the media, finances, etc.) to promote candidates and through the creation of the presidential list. The majority of candidates on the presidential list were from SNEK, whose members also dominate significant numbers of *oblast* councils.

Although the election itself was subject to interference giving candidates of the ruling elites and Kazakhs an undue advantage, it nevertheless had some important integrative benefits.[54] The electoral campaign accelerated the consolidation of non-Kazakh political movements across the north/east of the country. Although success in the national campaign was heavily curbed by irregularities, the election of a number of independent settler deputies helped to bring the non-Kazakh population into the Kazakhstani political system in Almaty. The considerable success of settler candidates in the local elections also created the basis for the first real resistance to control from the centre. The election of more independent legislatures at all levels has added a degree of complexity to Kazakhstani politics that may go some way to breaking down the growing ethnic-based confrontation. Initially, the key institution in this process appeared to be the parliament. Its abolition by presidential decree in March 1995 raises major questions about the future for ethnic integration.

The 1994 elections produced a parliament controlled by two main groups: ethnic Kazakhs and state/economic elites. Kazakhs dominated with 105 deputies, followed by Russians with 49, Ukrainians with 10, Germans with three, Jews with three, then one each for Uzbek, Pole, Tatar, Ingush, Korean and Uigur.[55] Complex ethnic, geographical and political allegiances and weak formal political organizations mean that voting in parliament was based on a number of shifting coalitions and loosely organized fractions. While the President undoubtedly dominated parliament, it was not totally in his pocket and at the end of 1994 it forced important changes in government personnel, including the prime minister.

In an increasingly polarized society and with an essentially weak state, much depends on the national leadership, particularly the president. Initially, President Nazarbaev sought to promote multi-ethnic tolerance through the use of inclusive language in his speeches. However, as the process of Kazakhization gathered pace, his initially high rating among the settler population went into steady decline.[56] With tension reaching dangerous levels, from early 1994 he launched a series of initiatives aimed at restoring confidence in a multi-ethnic future.

A number of banned political organizations, including the Communist Party and the Russian Community, were granted registration, though after the elections. A more accommodating approach to the least radical Cossack organizations was launched, and a consultative forum, the Republican Committee for Human Rights, was established by presidential decree on 9 February 1994.[57] The Russian Orthodox Cathedral in Almaty was returned to the church[58] and the President spoke of a new language law to ensure that Russian-speakers did not face discrimination.[59]

The international context of the settler issue

While the Kazakhstani authorities have been keen to develop good relations with the Central Asian neighbours to the south and China to the east, the defining element of foreign policy has been the relationship with Russia.[60] The political and economic significance of Russia for the country and the importance attached to the Russian diaspora in Moscow has meant that Kazakhstani policy towards the settler community has always been informed by Almaty's relationship with its northern neighbour.

Immediately after independence, Russia's preoccupation with domestic issues and the general Western orientation of foreign policy, coupled with President Nazarbaev's reassuring speeches about the non-Kazakh population, ensured that little attention was paid to the settlers. However, the gradual transformation of the diaspora issue into a central plank of Russian foreign policy, coupled with rising tension between Kazakhs and settlers, led to growing Russian involvement. This took a variety of forms: increasingly bellicose statements about Kazakhstan by leading Russian politicians; intensifying contacts between settlers and leading Russian political and public organizations; growing links between settlers and areas of Russia adjacent to Kazakhstan; and finally an increased assertiveness in Russian foreign policy with respect to Kazakhstan in general and the settler issue in particular.

The figure who played the key role in propelling the issue of Russia's relationship to Kazakhstan and the future of the settler communities there was Vladimir Zhirinovski. During the Russian electoral campaign of November/December 1993, he made repeated accusations about violations of the rights of Russians and of Russia's right to territory in Kazakhstan.

Since the elections, Zhironovski's position has been adopted by more mainstream politicians such as the leader of the Upper Chamber of the Russian parliament, Vladimir Shumeiko, and the chairman of the Committee for Relations with CIS States and Compatriots of the Lower House, Konstantin Zatulin.[61] At the same time, there have been increased contacts between Russian public organizations and the settler community, notably with Dmitri Rogozin of the Congress of Russian Communities. Rogozin used the case of Boris Supruniuk to highlight the issue of the Kazakhstani settler communities in the Russian media and to manoeuvre the Russian government into applying pressure on Almaty.[62]

Against this background, relations between Moscow and Almaty have often appeared tense. Russian assertiveness has been manifest in claims that it has an automatic right to participate in oil deals struck in Kazakhstan and the growing concern in the Russian government for the fate of the settler communities. The main thrust of efforts to protect the settlers has been focused on attempts to obtain a dual citizenship agreement with Kazakhstan. An initiative was launched by the Foreign Ministry before the Russian elections of winter 1993 but since then it has been given even greater emphasis.[63] From the beginning, President Nazarbaev has strongly opposed dual citizenship, arguing that it would split Kazakhstani society.[64]

He has, however, supported integration among the former Soviet republics since the collapse of the Union, and in March 1994 he proposed a Eurasian Union of the republics,[65] with a single currency, single parliament, Russian as its primary language and single citizenship.[66] However, opposition from western members of the CIS – notably Ukraine and Moldova – has significantly weakened Nazarbaev's proposal. Faced with the growing secessionist sentiments among the settlers and bleak domestic economic prospects, closer integration on terms dictated by Moscow became the only real option for the Almaty government if the integrity of the fragile Kazakhstani state was not to be threatened.[67] In January 1995, Russia and Kazakhstan signed a series of agreements that if implemented will bind the two countries closely together, although dual citizenship is not included.[68]

Conclusion

The underlying problems inherent in Kazakhstan's colonial legacy have been compounded by post-independence political and economic developments. The Russified north and east of the country have increasingly sought to be detached from Almaty, provoked by Kazakh nationalism and economic collapse. With little in the way of political institutions to bridge the void between Kazakhs and settlers, north and south, the non-Kazakhs have begun to develop an identity, which permits the settlers to define themselves as separate from the Kazakhs and most importantly as a part of Russia.[69] Notions of the Russian nation, Russian ethnicity and Russianness have merged, fusing a diversity of settler groups bound together by the Russian language, Soviet/Russian urban culture and non-Kazakh ethnicity, to create a politically Russian (*Rossiiskii*) identity.

While clearly aware of the dangers of the current situation, the Almaty authorities are restricted in the policy options they can pursue by the logic of Kazakh nationalism and the chronic problems of building a state in the post-Soviet context. Colonialism has left the legacy of a country that consists of formerly relatively advantaged settlers and poorer Kazakhs. As the central legitimacy of the Kazakhstani state ultimately resides on the right of Kazakhs for self-determination and the political power of the Kazakhstani leadership rests on this section of the population, it is the demands of Kazakhs that have been receiving priority. Of these, 70–75% live in rural areas and many of the aspirations of the poor Kazakhs, especially in the south, have taken the form of nationalist demands. The government must therefore tackle their economic problems if it is to address one of the main elements of Kazakh nationalism. However, this will mean reducing the settler population's political power and redistributing wealth from north to south.

In this context, Kazakhstani foreign policy has aimed to prevent national disintegration by offering to cede key areas of national sovereignty to some form of supranational organization – the CIS, Eurasian Union, etc. This would subdue many of the forces driving disintegration: with fully transparent borders and political institutions divorced from the polarization characteristic of Kazakhstani society, the settler community would feel less marginalized or trapped. The key question for Kazakhstan therefore becomes not so much whether it will seek closer integration with the other former Soviet republics – not to do so would be to risk the disintegration of the country – but what place Russia is to have in this new arrangement. With settlers demanding unification with Russia, Russified Kazakhs calling for a confederation with Russia and Kazakh nationalists calling for even greater independence, President Nazarbaev's task is a complex one. He must find a balance between promoting links between the north/east and Russia and retaining crucial elements of national sovereignty that will allow him to keep support in the key southern areas.

Chapter 7

Conclusions

The intense political, economic and social turmoil that followed the collapse of the Soviet system raised a series of fundamental questions about modern societies and the way in which they are organized. As a result of the sudden disintegration of the communist order, academic debate about the nature of states, nations, markets and democracy suddenly acquired an urgent practical significance for the peoples of the former Soviet Union. Among the range of pressing theoretical and practical questions facing these peoples, one of the most important to emerge was the role that nationalism, and in particular ethno-nationalism, would play in the post-Soviet order.

In the years immediately following the disintegration of the Soviet Union, the fate of the Russian and Russian-speaking settler populations located outside the Russian Federation became one of the most contentious issues in post-Soviet politics. The large number of settlers, the powerful anti-Russian sentiment that had driven many of the political movements of the late *perestroika* period and the rise of ethno-nationalist movements within many of the newly independent states, ensured that this issue quickly became a decisive factor in shaping the new social, economic and political order within the former USSR.

As tension around the settler communities in the Baltic states, Ukraine and Moldova mounted during 1992, it seemed as though the prospects for a peaceful evolution of the post-Soviet order were being increasingly threatened by the issue of the Russian communities. In fact, despite the confrontation that built up around the fate of the settlers in some areas of the former Soviet Union and during the short war in Moldova in 1992, on the whole the settler issue did not play the destructive role that some observ-

124

ers had initially predicted. The central finding of this study is that because of the poorly articulated character of Russian ethnicity, widespread conflict did not develop over the issue of the Russian settler communities.

Antony Smith has drawn a distinction between an *ethnic category* – a separate cultural and historical grouping with little self-awareness and only a dim consciousness that they form a separate collectivity – and an ethnic community or *ethnie*, which is a group defined by a variety of characteristics of which the most important are a myth of common ancestry, shared historical memories, a notion of a specific homeland and a strong sense of belonging and solidarity that can override class, factional or regional divisions.[1] At independene, Russians corresponded more to Smith's idea of an ethnic category than to that of a distinct *ethnie*.[2] The poor self-realization of Russians in an ethnic sense did not stem simply from some inadequacy but was the result of the imperial character of Russian ethnicity.

Over the past two hundred years, the dovetailing of Russians with the Russian Imperial and Soviet orders ensured that Russian ethnicity has been particularly open in form and subject to change. Within these two empires a variety of mechanisms operated to promote Russian ethnic identification. Mixed marriages (particularly of non-Russian members of the Soviet elite to Russians), forced Russification and the advantages of being identified as Russian/Russian-speaking led to a steady rise in the number of those who adopted an ethnic Russian identity. Thus, under these two political orders the borders of the Russian ethnic category were considerably expanded. This was particularly true of groups that shared similar linguistic and cultural backgrounds, such as Slavs, although other groups were by no means immune to these tendencies.

As the numbers and the boundaries of the Russian *ethnos* expanded, the significance of Russian ethnicity in terms of constituting a basis for solidarity and as a means to mobilize large numbers of people was diminished. The fusion of Russian identity with the Russian Imperial and the Soviet structures of power – the very reason Russian ethnicity was attractive to many – led to Russian ethnicity as a distinct and separate ethnic category being blurred with other identities, particularly an Imperial-Soviet one. While the ethnic identities of the titular groups in the non-Russian republics were developed, reinforced and given a political significance under Soviet rule (a process given further impetus by the independence movements of the *perestroika* period),[3] the unique position of the Russian population within the Soviet Union ensured that even in the late 1980s Russians remained ethnically unconsolidated.

The weakly developed nature of Russian ethnicity had two important consequences for the politics of the *perestroika* and post-independence periods in the former Soviet Union. First, while almost all of the republican independence movements in the USSR were heavily informed by ethno-nationalism, within the Russian Federation a weak Russian ethnic consciousness helped produce an opposition movement that was primarily civic in form. It was the influence of a territorial notion of Russian nationhood among key sections of the political establishment in Moscow after 1991 that did much to curb the use of the Russian settler issue to justify the development of an expansionist Russian foreign policy.

Second, the poorly articulated nature of Russian ethnicity had a crucial impact upon developments within the settler communities outside the Russian Federation. The formal ethnic classification of the settlers disguised the fact that their identity was not cast primarily in an ethnic form but in socio-economic and political ones. The fact that twenty-five million people were identified as Russians living outside the Russian Federation did not indicate a unity among these people or even a common understanding of what it meant to be Russian. This was true not only across the Russian populations of different republics but also within each settler community. Without a clear notion of a homeland, lacking a developed sense of Russianness and in the absence of institutions to promote non-Soviet identities, the bases for the large-scale popular mobilization characteristic of ethno-nationalist movements proved to be very weak among the settlers.

Following the collapse of the Soviet system, the forces at work shaping ethnicity in the area have undergone a dramatic reconfiguration. The shift in power to titular and other groups since 1991 has meant that Russian ethnicity has lost much of its attraction for key sections of post-Soviet society. People on the margins of Russian ethnicity have rediscovered their 'true' ethnic identities. Russian-speaking Ukrainians might now opt for a Ukrainian rather than a Russian identity, and children of mixed marriages in which one of the partners is formally Russian and the other a member of the titular population might well choose the non-Russian ethnic identity today. In this sense, the borders of Russian ethnicity have begun to contract.

However, at the same time as assimilation to Russian ethnicity from titular or other powerful groups has slowed, Russian ethnicity has begun to undergo a redefinition in other directions. Since 1991, settler communities have had ethnic identities thrust upon them by the activity of nationalist movements and the policies of the newly independent states.

Titular based ethno-nationalism was most often defined against the 'foreign' or 'colonial' settler communities and especially against the Russian language. Pressure from these movements and the state has helped to consolidate the settler populations in key ways. In particular, under external political pressure, Russian ethnicity has begun to be viewed primarily in cultural-linguistic (Russian-speaking) rather than simply genealogical terms.

Although the reconstruction of ethnic boundaries has occurred as a result of developments internal to the former Soviet republics – citizenship legislation, political movements, language laws, state support for ethnic and cultural societies – in the case of Russian ethnicity, interstate relations have also played a critical role. At least in part through the efforts of politicians and activists in Russia, Russians, Russian-speakers and others with some link to Russia or Russian civilization have been bound together conceptually and linked by Russian foreign policy to form the 'Russian diaspora'. As a result, large sections of the Russian-speaking settler communities have, for the first time, begun to think of themselves as members of the Russian nation and of the Russian Federation as their homeland.

While the ill-defined nature of Russian ethnicity has been central to the prevention of widespread conflict around the issue of the settlers, this factor alone was not sufficient. In the post-Soviet states, elite activity has had a crucial impact on the settler issue. The study of ethnicity and nationalism is in large part the study of politically induced cultural change. In this process elites and counter-elites play a central role in selecting aspects of group culture, attaching new values and meanings to them, and then using them as symbols to mobilize the group for defined political objectives.[4] In the context of post-communist societies, the action of elites has been particularly important because political and civil institutions are so poorly developed.

While key sections of the post-Soviet elites and counter-elites sought to use ethno-nationalism to enhance their political position, the opportunity to manipulate the settler issue was always constrained in the immediate independence period. The fact that many of the post-Soviet elite in Russia, Kazakhstan, Ukraine and, after the war in 1992, Moldova were drawn from the former communist system ensured that ethno-nationalism was often moderated by the influence of national-communism with its stress on interethnic accord. At the same time, fear within the newly independent states that Russia might use the settler issue to reconstitute some form of empire forced a moderation and caution even among some of the most radical nationalists in the former Soviet republics.

Conclusions

Within Russia itself, the initial political dominance of an elite that put relations with the 'far abroad' ahead of issues in the former Soviet territories also ensured that Russia, despite fierce rhetoric, did little to provoke the settler issue. Even the political defeat of the original version of interstate relations and the consolidation of the statist vision of Russia's external interests did not lead to an escalation of the issue. Despite the more nationalist agenda of the Statists, they are committed to developing Russia within its existing borders, and only economic and diplomatic sanctions are to be employed to protect 'Russians' abroad.

Since independence a crucial period has been negotiated in a relatively peaceful fashion. Nevertheless, the problem of the Russian-speaking settlers remains far from solved. Settler communities are poorly integrated within the newly independent states, and the development of national identities that can incorporate these populations remains of paramount importance for governments in the region. At the same time, since 1991 new identities and institutions have emerged among the settler populations and links to Russia have been established; that is, the infrastructure for political mobilization has been developed to a far greater extent than it was at independence. The current correlation of political, economic and social forces in the former Soviet Union suggests three possible scenarios for the future development of the issue of the settler populations:

(1) A stable evolution. Perhaps the most likely future scenario is a continuation of the present trajectory of political developments: constrained Russian engagement with the diaspora and a gradual integration of the settlers within the newly independent states. The political elite in Moscow is committed to a Russia defined by current territorial borders. Ties to the diaspora are therefore to be confined to economic, cultural and educational ties. While there are signs of increased ethno-nationalism in Russia – and future elections are likely to reinforce this tendency – there is little indication that the nationalist forces seeking territorial expansion or more aggressive policies to protect the diaspora have sufficient political support to gain control of the Russian state apparatus.

This is not to suggest that there will be no contact between Russia and the settlers. The establishment in 1994 of an official Russian policy towards the diaspora and the creation of state and public institutions committed to fostering relations with the settlers and to developing a Russian identity among them has firmly bound Russia and the settlers together. But growing contact between Russia and the diaspora does not imply that a clash between Russia and its neighbours is inevitable or indeed that Russia will use the diaspora against the interests of the other former Soviet states.

Post-Soviet governments share a broad range of interests including quelling separatist movements, preventing a large-scale migration of settlers to Russia and avoiding costly financial or military commitments to the settler issue. These common concerns have provided the basis for cooperation between Moscow and the former Soviet republics on the diaspora issue and for the development of a range of policies aimed at integrating the settlers in the newly independent states.

While the opportunities for manipulation of the settler issue have diminished, a variety of other factors have begun to influence the development of the Russian question in unpredictable ways. The use of the diaspora issue by regional elites in their relations with their metropolis and the effect of unequal economic development in the diaspora – the plummet in living standards among Russians in northern Kazakhstan in comparison to Russians on the Russian side of the border has been a major factor fostering pro-unification sentiments among settlers – are pushing post-Soviet politics in new directions.

(2) Growing nationalism in Russia. Although the actual nature of Russian national identity remains ill-defined, Russian ethnicity has come to play a steadily more important symbolic role in Russian domestic and interstate politics. Above all, it has been the transformation of the Russian-speaking settlers into a Russian diaspora and the institutionalization of this issue at the foundations of Russian external policy towards the former Soviet republics that has fostered this far greater ethnic awareness within the Russian Federation.

The use of the issue in Russian domestic politics and foreign policy is well established and has been central to the post-independence process of state-building within Russia. The elite dialogue about Russia's relationship to the settlers that reached its apogee in 1993 was one of the fundamental debates about Russia itself in the first years of independence. The vision of Russia's ties to the diaspora that emerged from this debate subsequently became part of that matrix of ideas that currently serves to define Russian statehood. Russia is a 'Great Power' in large part because of the 'need' to protect its diaspora. If Russia enters an expansionist or nationalist trajectory, the issue of the diaspora would almost certainly play a central role in justifying a hardening of foreign policy and possible territorial annexations.

The significance of the diaspora issue has, however, begun to move beyond the political elite and to enter more general public consciousness. Increasingly, elections may become the main force driving a nationalist agenda. The first signs of this change came with the strong popular vote for nationalist politicians in the 1993 parliamentary elections. Early political manoeuvring in connection with the 1995/6 elections witnessed the once-moderate Foreign Minister, Andrei Kozyrev, making particularly bellicose statements about the diaspora.[5] New political alliances, such as that forged between General Alexander Lebed, then Commander of the 14th Army in Moldova, and the Congress of Russian Communities in April 1995, are also likely to bring ethno-nationalism further into the mainstream of the Russian body politic.

(3) Conflict within a newly independent state. Although most groups and interests in Russia are currently oriented towards non-intervention in the affairs of their neighbours, an aggressive Russian nationalism could be triggered by developments within the neighbouring states or within the settler communities themselves.

Estonia and Latvia: The legalistic battle fought over citizenship thinly disguised the real basis of conflict in these two countries: a struggle for power between the Russian/Russian-speaking settlers and the titular populations. Action by the Estonian and Latvian independence movements following the abortive putsch in Moscow in August 1991 brought the two states firmly under the control of the titular elites. In subsequent years, these two former Soviet republics underwent radical political, economic and social restructuring with the Russians and Russian-speaking settlers given little opportunity to influence the form and nature of these changes.

Although Estonia and Latvia underwent the most extensive change of all the former Soviet republics, and the settler population in these two countries experienced the greatest direct pressure to adapt to the new situation, the commitment of the settlers to the newly independent states is remarkably firm. In areas such as Narva, the danger remains that socio-economic problems could be transformed into ethnic ones, but the comparative economic success of Latvia and Estonia has undergirded settler support for Baltic independence and the development of a Baltic identity among the settlers.

However, there are important differences between the settler populations in the two states. In Estonia, a nationalist drive among the Estonians that finished earlier than elsewhere, the introduction of a set of policies towards the settlers that had clear aims, and state support for the creation of a moderate pro-Estonian settler elite laid the foundations for the development of a generally loyal non-Estonian population that has been gradually integrated into the Estonian polity over the course of two elections.

Latvia, on the other hand, did little to address the problems of the non-Latvian population in the initial period of independence. From 1991 until 1994, the non-Latvians had no clear sense of their future in the country, and the state did nothing to structure settler society politically. With no support for moderate settler leaders from the Latvian side, the settlers had to rely upon pro-Soviet politicians and former Soviet institutions to represent them. Although important progress has been made following the introduction of the Law on Citizenship, the lack of moderate political organizations among the settler populations means that they may be vulnerable to extremist influence and will have little stake in Latvian political life for years to come.

Moldova: The war of 1992 effectively split the country into two, but it also played a positive role by stimulating the titular elite to promote Moldovan nationalism and by encouraging the settlers on the right bank to organize themselves more effectively. Together, these two developments have provided the foundations for a new political order in the country following the war. The complexity of the titular identity – separating Moldovans from Romanians is rather difficult – has played a decisive role in influencing the emergence of the new multi-ethnic national identity in Moldova. Anxious to provide a justification for their new positions of leadership and to undermine the arguments of those seeking unification with Romania, key sections of the titular political elite have promoted the idea that Moldovan national identity is primarily territorial rather than ethnic in form.

Although the Russian population of the right bank has been largely incorporated within the new Moldovan polity, the Transdniester question remains unresolved. Much of the current impasse between Tiraspol and Chisinau stems from the pro-Soviet orientation of the PMR leadership, but the basis for mutual mistrust between left and right bank goes deeper than personalities alone. The different histories, economic interests and experience of political power under the Soviet system lies at the heart of the opposition that developed between the two regions from the late 1980s. Nevertheless, if the Russian 14th Army is withdrawn and the economy of the PMR continues to decline there may well be popular support for a reintegration with Moldova, provided Transdniester is granted some form of special status analogous to that of the Gagauz areas.

Conclusions

Ukraine: From the late 1980s, the strong cultural and historic bonds between Ukrainians and Russians, and the large size of the Russian communities in Ukraine, made Ukraine an area of particularly complex and acute issues. Although the confrontation on Crimea has often appeared to cast the issue of national identity in Ukraine in rigidly ethnic terms, in fact developments since 1991 have highlighted the lack of unified Russian and Ukrainian ethnic communities in the former Soviet republic.

Within Ukraine, regional and ethnic interests have intermixed to produce a patchwork of loyalties and interests. Despite the efforts of both Russian and Ukrainian nationalists, the ethno-regional foundations of the Ukrainian state have made ethno-nationalist mobilization difficult. Instead, the network of regional identities across Ukraine has provided the basis for the emergence of a distinct, if still weak, multi-ethnic national identity that incorporates Russians, Russian-speaking Ukrainians and other ethnic groups as equal members of the Ukrainian nation.

The strong pro-Russian sentiments on Crimea continue to present a major challenge to Ukrainian independence, not least because of the close link between the issue of secession and that of the future of the Black Sea Fleet. However, the disintegration of the pro-Russia political elite on the peninsula in the autumn of 1994 has helped diffuse the conflict and allowed Kiev to assert increased control over Simferopol. With a political leadership in Moscow which has discouraged secessionist movements on the peninsula, there is little indication that Crimea will be able to affect adversely the gradual consolidation of a multi-ethnic Ukrainian identity.

Kazakhstan: The significant cultural divide between the settler community and key sections of the Kazakh population – particularly those in the south – and the persistence of myths of colonial superiority provided little initial basis for the development of an integrated national identity in Kazakhstan. Following independence, the Kazakhization of the state apparatus, legal and illegal measures to exclude non-Kazakhs from the political process, and the chronic state of the economy have done little to alter this situation. The dissolution of the parliament in 1995 has reinforced the development of traditional forms of politics (clan and family patronage networks) at the expense of democratic institutions and has further diminished the prospects of fostering a Kazakhstani as opposed to a Kazakh national identity.

Not only is there little indication that the settlers view themselves as part of Kazakhstani society in any meaningful way, but the Russian-speaking settlers are also increasingly developing a political identity as members of the Russian nation. Widespread support for dual-citizenship provisions with Russia and even support in some areas for a redrawing of the borders to incorporate northern and eastern regions within the Russian Federation have called into question the whole future of Kazakhstan as a unified, sovereign state. The danger inherent in this situation is one of the main forces driving the Kazakhstani leadership to seek closer ties with Russia.

Thus, in most former Soviet republics the initial wave of ethno-nationalism has passed; at the same time, the Russian and Russian-speaking populations outside Russia remain characterized by multi-loyalties and uncertain national identities. However, while there remain important issues that could cause problems in the future, in general the settler question is being effectively managed through an evolving combination of new institutions (state organizations, political parties, cultural organizations and interstate consultation) and legislation (constitutions, citizenship and minority rights laws).

The area in which the settler issue continues to pose the greatest challenge to peace and stability is Kazakhstan. The basis for confrontation is deeply embedded within a variety of political, economic and cultural relationships in the region, and for this reason forging an inclusive national identity has proved impossible. Indeed, experience since 1991 suggests that only closer ties between Kazakhstan and Russia will provide the necessary assurance to the settler population. Here, as in the other former Soviet republics, some of the initial challenges posed by the Russian diaspora have been overcome, but the settler issue continues to exert a determining influence on the country's domestic and interstate politics.

Since independence, we have witnessed the establishment of the broad parameters of post-Soviet identities both among the Russian settler communities and within the newly independent states. These new identities have also found their initial expression in the new political, economic and social institutions of the region. But such identities are, of course, not fixed, especially among minority communities who may exhibit a variety of loyalties simultaneously. Post-imperial experience elsewhere suggests that decolonization is a prolonged process. The issue of the Russian settlers is therefore likely to remain a central one well into the next century.

Statistical appendix

The main characteristics of the settler population are indicated in the tables below: mainly ethnically Russian (Table A.1); largely recent migrants (Table A.2); Russian-speaking (Table A.3) and predominantly urbanized (Table A.4). Typically the settler communities had higher rates of ethnic intermarriage than other communities in the USSR. See Robert J. Kaiser, *The Geography of Nationalism in Russia and the USSR* (Princeton, NJ: Princeton University Press, 1994), Table 6.13, pp. 302–3.

Table A.1 Ethnic Russians and Russian-speakers* in Soviet republics outside Russia in 1989

| Republic | Ethnic Russians | | Russian-speakers | |
	Estimated total	As % of population	Estimated total	As % of population
Ukraine	11,355,000	22.1	16,898,000	32.8
Belarus	1,342,000	13.2	3,243,000	31.9
Kazakhstan	6,227,000	37.8	7,797,000	47.4
Uzbekistan	1,653,000	8.3	2,151,000	10.9
Georgia	341,000	6.3	479,000	8.9
Azerbaijan	391,000	5.6	528,000	7.5
Lithuania	344,000	9.4	429,000	11.7
Latvia	905,000	34.0	1,122,000	42.1
Estonia	474,000	30.3	544,000	34.8
Moldova	562,000	14.0	1,003,000	23.1
Kyrgyzstan	916,000	21.5	1,090,000	25.6
Tajikistan	388,000	7.6	495,000	9.7
Armenia	51,000	1.6	66,000	2.0
Turkmenistan	333,000	9.5	421,000	12.0

*Persons of non-Russian ethnic origin regarding Russian as native language. Since 1989, there are likely to have been significant changes in the number of Russians in these republics as the result of out-migration.
Source: *Naselenie Rossii. Ezhegodnyi demograficheskii doklad* (Moscow: The Centre for the Demography and Ecology of Man, 1993), p. 15.

Table A.2 **Structure of the Russian population of former Union republics**

Republic	1979					1989				
			including those living					including those living		
	natives	migrants	less than 2 years	2–5 years	6–9 years	natives	migrants	less than 2 years	2–5 years	6–9 years
Ukraine	46.5	53.5	8.2	9.5	6.8	50.2	49.8	5.6	7.5	5.8
Belarus	40.9	59.1	8.6	10.2	7.7	42.3	57.7	6.0	8.1	6.4
Uzbekistan	34.7	65.3	10.9	12.5	9.5	32.5	67.5	9.8	11.5	8.1
Kazakhstan	44.4	55.6	8.0	9.8	8.3	48.3	51.7	5.0	7.3	6.0
Georgia	40.3	59.7	10.1	11.6	9.2	46.8	53.2	6.3	7.8	6.3
Azerbaijan	43.5	56.5	7.5	9.2	6.0	41.8	58.2	7.0	8.6	5.5
Lithuania	55.0	45.0	5.2	6.4	5.1	56.4	43.6	5.1	5.5	3.5
Moldova	36.5	63.5	10.7	11.4	7.7	38.4	61.6	7.6	10.8	7.9
Latvia	40.6	59.4	9.0	11.5	8.9	43.3	56.7	9.9	8.7	6.4
Kyrgyzstan	36.6	63.4	9.3	11.5	7.8	41.6	58.4	6.2	8.1	5.9
Tadzjikistan	39.3	60.7	9.8	10.8	8.9	45.3	54.7	6.5	7.7	6.2
Armenia	36.3	63.7	9.7	11.3	9.2	43.3	56.7	5.8	7.7	6.0
Turkmenistan				(no information)						
Estonia	41.2	58.8	10.2	11.2	8.1	47.1	52.9	6.4	7.8	5.4
USSR Total	33.3	66.9	9.4	10.5	8.2	65.1	34.9	2.3	4.2	4.0

Source: Naselenie SSSR, pp. 124–139, Soiuz 1990, nos. 32, 34, 39.

Table A.3 Russian and the languages of the former Union republics (in %)

Republic	Russian population in republic	Consider language of titular nationality their mother tongue	Fluent in titular national language	Are bilingual
Ukraine	22.1	1.6	32.8	77.2
Belarus	13.2	2.3	24.5	7.1
Uzbekistan	8.4	0.1	4.5	1.5
Kazakhstan	37.8	0.0	0.9	1.1
Georgia	6.3	13.0	22.5	1.6
Azerbaijan	5.6	0.2	14.3	1.1
Lithuania	9.4	4.4	33.4	2.6
Moldova	13.0	0.9	11.2	1.3
Latvia	34.0	1.2	21.1	4.0
Kyrgyzstan	21.5	0.1	1.2	0.2
Tajikistan	7.6	0.1	3.5	0.3
Armenia	1.6	1.6	32.2	0.4
Turkmenistan	9.5	0.1	2.5	0.2
Estonia	30.3	1.4	13.7	1.4

Source: 1989 data of the USSR State Committee for Statistics.

Table A.4 Urban population of the former Union republics 1959–90 (in %)

Republic	1959 the total population	1959 Among Russians	1979 Among the total population	1979 Among Russians	1989 Among the total population	1989 Among Russians
RSFSR	52	55	69	72	73	77
Ukraine	48	81	61	86	67	88
Belarus	31	73	55	86	65	87
Uzbekistan	34	84	41	93	41	95
Kazakhstan	44	59	54	74	57	77
Georgia	42	79	52	85	55	86
Azerbaijan	48	88	53	94	54	95
Lithuania	39	77	61	87	68	90
Moldova	22	67	39	83	47	86
Latvia	56	73	68	83	71	85
Kyrgyzstan	34	58	39	69	38	70
Tadzjikistan	33	87	35	94	33	94
Armenia	50	71	66	83	67	85
Turkmenistan	46	95	48	97	45	97
Estonia	56	87	70	91	71	92
USSR Total	48	58	62	74	66	78

Source: All-Union census 1959, 1979, 1989.

Notes

Chapter 1: Introduction

1 Benedict Anderson, *Imagined Communities: Reflections on the Origins and Spread of Nationalism* (London: Verso, 1983); John Breuilly, *Nationalism and the State* (Manchester: Manchester University Press, 1982); Ernest Gellner, *Nations and Nationalism* (Ithaca, NY: Cornell University Press, 1983); Eric Hobsbawm, *Nation and Nationalism Since 1780: Programme, Myth, Reality* (Cambridge: CUP, 1990); Eric Hobsbawm and Terence Ranger, eds, *The Invention of Tradition* (Cambridge: CUP, 1983); and James Mayall, *Nationalism and International Society* (Cambridge: CUP, 1990).

2 Ronald Grigor Suny, *The Revenge of the Past: Nationalism, Revolution, and the Collapse of the Soviet Union* (Stanford, CA: Stanford University Press, 1993), chapter 3.

3 In this study national identity is understood as a complex and multi-dimensional identity that is shaped by a wide range of factors. It is an identity that is simultaneously collective and personal; it refers both to those characteristics that are specific to a given national community – history, culture and way of life – and, at the same time, to individual self-awareness. National identity is structured around and reinforces a sense of homeland and of a common history derived from collective triumphs, betrayals and aspirations. In combination, these elements construct a notion of difference that separates one community from another. This notion of difference is expressed through language, symbols and sentiments that together involve the propagation of modes of group and self-perception as a nation. National identity therefore serves as one of the foundations upon which the basic socio-political and economic relationships are built.

Chapter 2: Russian identity in Empire, Union, nation-state and diaspora

1 One leading commentator even suggested that given the rise of national-ism, ethnic Russians needed a separate state to guarantee their rights. 'What is the place of Russians in Russia, CIS?', *Current Digest of the Post-Soviet Press* (henceforth *CDPP*), vol. XLV, no. 17 (1993), p. 11.

2 Finding a single term to describe the non-indigenous settler populations is difficult. The composition of the communities varies from republic to republic, but they are invariably built around a core of recent ethnic Russian, Ukrainian, Belarussian and Jewish migrants, although there may be sizeable residual communities of Slavic settlement dating back well over a century. Other groups closely tied to these communities include Greeks, Koreans, Poles and Germans. Although the Russian language dominated within the settler areas and new arrivals tended to be absorbed within a predominantly Russian culture, these were primarily de-ethnicized communities. In the settler communities rates of inter-ethnic marriage were particularly high – especially among the Slavs – suggesting that these populations came closest to the dream of creating a Soviet people. See Wesley Andrew Fisher, 'Comment – the extent of intermarriage in the Russian group', in Edward Allworth, ed., *Ethnic Russia in the USSR: The Dilemma of Dominance* (New York: Pergamon, 1979), pp. 309–11; Robert J. Kaiser, *The Geography of Nationalism in Russia and the USSR* (Princeton, NJ: Princeton University Press, 1994), pp. 301–17.

3 The relationship between Russians, the Russian Empire and the Soviet Union is examined in Walter Kolarz, *Russia and Her Colonies* (New York: Praeger, 1952). For a discussion of the relationship between national identity, nation and state and of civic and ethnic definitions of the nation, see Neil Melvin, *Forging the New Russian Nation: Russian Foreign Policy and the Russian-Speaking Communities of the Former USSR* (London: RIIA, Discussion Paper 50, 1994), note 1.

4 For an examination of the diverse and often contradictory ethnic, linguistic and cultural strands from which the notion of the Russian diaspora is woven see Melvin, *op. cit.*, pp. 17–22.

5 Kyoji Komachi, 'Concept-building in Russian diplomacy: from "Economization" to "Eurasianization"', unpublished paper, Center for International Affairs, Harvard University (3 May 1994).

6 Hannes Adomeit, 'Russia as a "great power" in world affairs: images and reality', *International Affairs*, 71, 1 (1995), pp. 35–68.

7 Despite the presence of millions of Russians in the West – primarily in the

United States and France – who consider themselves to be tied to Russia, this 'diaspora' barely figured in debates about Russia's relationship to its co-ethnics.

8　Sergei Stankevich, 'Russia in search of itself', *The National Interest* (Summer 1992), p. 47.

9　Thus, as the Empire extended beyond the traditional lands of the Russians, there was little clear distinction between 'home' and 'abroad'. The ambiguous relationship between state and ethnic territories is reflected in the overlapping use of the terms *rodina* (native land) and *otechestvo* (fatherland), both of which were used to mean homeland or state.

10　The nationalization process was most advanced in the industrial northwest, but in general was only beginning at the end of the Tsarist period. Edward C. Thaden, *Russification in the Baltic Provinces and Finland 1855–1914* (Princeton, NJ: Princeton University Press, 1981); and Dominic Lieven, *Russia and the Origins of the First World War* (London: Macmillan, 1981).

11　Jeffery Brooks, *When Russia Learned to Read: Literacy and Popular Literature 1861–1917* (Princeton, NJ: Princeton University Press, 1985), pp. 216, 241.

12　Ladis Kristoff, 'The geographical image of the fatherland: the case of Russia', *The Western Political Quarterly* (1967), pp. 941–54.

13　S. Bruk and V. Kabuzan, 'Dinamika chislennosti i rasseleniia Russkikh posle velikoi oktiabr'skoi sotsialisticheskoi revoliutsii', *Sovetskaia Etnografiia*, no. 5 (1982), pp. 3–21; and I. Gurvich, 'Sovremennye napravleniia etnicheskikh protsessov v SSSR', *Sovetskaia Etnografiia*, no. 4 (1972), pp. 16–33.

14　Frederick Barghoorn, *Soviet Russian Nationalism* (Westport, CT: Greenwood Press, 1976).

15　In the interwar period, the highest rate of assimilation was among Ukrainians and Belorussians living in the RSFSR and in the northern Caucasus region. Bruk and Kabuzan, *op. cit.* (1982), pp. 3–21, and Robert Lewis, Richard Rowland and Ralph Clem, *Nationality and Population Change in Russia and the USSR* (New York: Praeger, 1976), p. 219.

16　For a review of the size and distribution of the settler communities, see Chauncy Harris, 'The new Russian minorities: a statistical overview', *Post-Soviet Geography*, 34, no. 1 (1993), pp. 1–27.

17　According to surveys conducted by the Institute of Ethnography, during the late 1970s and early 1980s, 70% or more of Russians in Moscow, Kishinev and Tashkent considered the USSR as a whole to be their homeland (*rodina*). L. Drobizheva, 'Etnicheskoe samosoznanie Russkikh v sovremennykh usloviiakh: ideologiia i praktika', *Sovetskaia Etnografiia*, no. 1 (1991), pp. 3–13.

18 John Dunlop, *The Faces of Contemporary Nationalism* (Princeton, NJ: Princeton University Press, 1983). Dunlop has suggested that the Soviet invasion of Afghanistan and the demographic boom among the Muslims of Soviet Central Asia accelerated the decoupling of Russian and Soviet identities. John B. Dunlop, *The Rise of Russia and the Fall of the Soviet Empire* (Princeton, NJ: Princeton University Press, 1993).

19 *Russkie: Etno-sotsiologicheskie ocherki* (Moscow: Nauka, 1992).

20 As late as 1979, Edward Allworth concluded that 'Russians remain an ethnically underdeveloped people'. Allworth, *op. cit.* (1980), p. 34.

21 The peculiar position of the Russian Federation within the USSR suggests that it was never really a Russian homeland. Vadim Medish, 'Special Status of the RSFSR', in Allworth, *op. cit.*, pp. 188–96.

22 Leokardia Drobizheva, '*Perestroika* and the ethnic consciousness of Russians', in Gail Lapidus, Viktor Zaslavsky and Philip Goldman, eds, *From Union to Commonwealth: Nationalism and Separatism in the Soviet Republics* (Cambridge: CUP, 1992), pp. 98–113.

23 Dunlop, *op. cit.* (1993).

24 Many of the conflicts on the Russian periphery were encouraged, if not actually directly supported, by powerful individuals and organizations within the Russian political and military establishment. A range of shadowy Russian political organizations, including the National Salvation Front, the Liberal Democratic Party (Zhirinovski), and the National-Republican Party, established links to the settler populations. Olga Volkova, 'Russkie Legionery ukrepliaut zdorov'e', *Megapolis-Express* (24 February 1993), and Vera Tolz and Elizabeth Teague, 'Is Russia likely to turn to authoritarian rule?', *RFE/RL Research Report*, vol. 1, no. 4 (24 January 1992).

25 Suzanne Crow has demonstrated the effects of this political underdevelopment on Russia's external policy. Suzanne Crow, 'The fragmentation of Russian foreign policy decision-making', *RFE/RL Research Institute Draft Occasional Study* (2 February 1993).

26 Aleksandr Solzhenitsyn was one of the first to raise the issue of Russia's 'natural' borders, arguing that Russia included the Russian Federation, Ukraine, Belarus and northern Kazakhstan. Aleksandr Solzhenitsyn, 'Kak nam obustroit' Rossiiu. Posil'nye soobrazheniia', enclosure in *Literaturnaia Gazeta* (19 September 1990).

27 The period from the summer of 1991 to December 1993 is examined in greater detail in Melvin, *op. cit.* (1994), pp. 27–48.

28 Robert Miller, *Soviet Foreign Policy Today: Gorbachev and the New Political Thinking* (London: Harper Collins, 1991).

29 The citizenship of Russian settlers was an issue in agreements between Yeltsin and the authorities in the Baltic states in 1991 but both sides eventually agreed to support a zero option: citizenship would be awarded to all residents of each country. Riina Kionka, 'Russia recognises Estonia's independence', *RFE/RL Report on the USSR*, vol. 3, no. 5 (1 February 1991).

30 For an outline of the Democratic vision of interstate relations see the essays by Andrei Kozyrev, 'Preobrazhennaia Rossiia v novom mire', *Izvestiia* (2 January 1992), p. 3; 'Russia and human rights', *Slavic Review*, 51, no. 2 (Summer 1992), pp. 287–93; 'Partiia voiny nastupaet – i v Moldove, i v Gruzii, i v Rossii', *Izvestiia* (30 June 1992), p. 3; and 'Preobrazhenie ili kafkianskaia metamorfoza: demokraticheskaia vneshnaia politika Rossii i ee prioritety', *Nezavisimaia Gazeta* (20 August 1992), pp. 1, 4.

31 For the broad parameters of foreign policy debates see *'Natsional'nye interesy i natsional'naia bezopasnost' Rossii glazami ee politicheskoi elity (Politicheskii analiz)'* (Moscow: Tsentr analiticheskoi informatsii po politicheskoi kon'iunkture Rossii, 1993).

32 The understanding of settler issues held by members of the Red/Brown alliance and the Statists differed significantly. The Red/Browns viewed the territories of the former USSR as the natural boundaries of the Russian/ Soviet state. For them, the settler issue demonstrated the need to reunite this area under a single state. The Statists, on the other hand, believed that the Russian Federation had a dominant role to play within the former USSR because of its special interests. The diaspora was one of the most important of these interests but would not justify an annexation of neighbouring territories.

33 Powerful radicals within parliament, such as Sergei Baburin, were instrumental in organizing groups of deputies to campaign on diaspora issues. Martin McCauley, ed., *Directory of Russian MPs: People's Deputies of the Supreme Soviet of Russia–Russian Federation* (Harlow, Essex: Longman, 1992), p. xxxxix. Baburin also drafted a law on compatriots for the Supreme Soviet. *Kontseptsiia zakon o gosudarstvennoi politike v otnoshenii sootechestvennikov.*

34 The work of these writers formed the pool of ideas for the Statist vision of Russia's future. S. A. Karaganov, 'Problemy zashchity interesov rossiisko-orientirovannogo naseleniia v "blizhnem" zarubezh'e', *Diplomaticheskii Vestnik*, no. 21–22 (15–30 November 1992), pp. 43–5. Sergei Stankevich,

'U Rossii est' svoe mesto v mire', *Rossiiskie Vesti* (27 February 1993), p. 2; 'To, chto idet na pol'zu Rossii, – polezno vsemu miru', *Rossiiskie Vesti* (5 June 1993), p. 4. Andranik Migranian, 'Podlinnye i mnimye orientiry vo vneshnei politike', *Rossiiskaia Gazeta* (4 August 1992), p. 7. In all of these writings, defence of Russian communities emerges as a principal justification for Russia's need to develop 'an active post-imperial role' in the ex-USSR – what became known as a 'Russian Monroe Doctrine'.

35 Migranian, *op. cit.* (1992).

36 In February 1992, the Foreign Ministry signalled some concessions to its critics with the drafting of a document 'On the concept of Russian foreign policy' which contained a commitment to maintain ties with Russian communities in the CIS and Baltic states. Interfax, 21 February 1992. Quoted in Suzanne Crow, 'Russia debates its national interests', *RFE/RL Research Report*, vol. 1, no. 28 (10 July 1992), p. 44.

37 Boris Yeltsin, 'Nado zashchishchat' russkikh, rossiian, kotorye zhivut v stranakh SNG, no zashchishchat' politicheski', *Izvestiia* (7 July 1992), p. 3. In the middle of the Transdniester crisis, the MFA appointed Fedor Shelov-Kovediaev deputy minister of foreign affairs in charge of interstate affairs in the former Soviet Union. An important part of his brief was settler affairs. 'MID Rossii sootechestvennikov v bede ne brosit', *Izvestiia* (26 July 1992), p. 6.

38 In August 1992, 'A strategy for Russia' was issued by the Council for Foreign and Defence Policy, a semi-official think-tank with close contacts to the MFA and the Ministry of Defence. The Council included some of the leading Statists. The document placed protection of the Russian communities at the heart of Russia's foreign policy. 'Russia is unconditionally interested in the preservation and enlightenment of the Russian (*russkii*) (or Russian-speaking) diaspora in all the states of the former USSR ... in this sense the fall of the USSR, paradoxically, gave Russia a political, economic and social trumpcard of significant potential power.' 'Strategiia dlia Rossii: Nekotorye tezisy dlia doklada soveta po vneshnei i oboronnoi politike', *Nezavisimaia gazeta* (19 August 1992), p. 4.

39 The draft version of Russia's new military doctrine identified 'the violation of the rights of Russians outside the Russian Federation and of those who identify ethnically or culturally with Russia' as a *casus belli*. *Voennaia mysl'* (special edition), no. 4–5 (1992). In 1993, peacekeeping activities were also linked to the idea of protecting the Russians.

40 On 4 November Galina Starovoitova, Presidential Adviser on Nationalities Issues, was dismissed. A month earlier, Deputy Foreign Minister Shelov-

Kovediaev had been removed for his allegedly soft approach to the issue of Russian-speakers.

41 'Russia warns Balts against "Ethnic Cleansing"', *RFE/RL Research Report*, vol. 1, no. 4 (9 October 1992), p. 67.

42 In 1993, the notion of Russia's responsibility to protect its diaspora was interwoven with a range of other foreign policy ideas. In March, Yeltsin called for Russia to be granted special powers as 'guarantor of peace and stability on the territory of the former USSR', while in April 'The Basic Theses of Russian Foreign Policy', a document intended to outline the principal directions of Russia's external policy, was endorsed by Yeltsin. Defence of the rights of Russian-speakers was identified as one of the basic policy priorities. 'Natsional'nye interesy Rossii i ugrozy dlia ee bezopasnosti', *Nezavisimaia gazeta* (29 April 1993). Protection of the Russians also received important support in two public reports: the Gorbachev Foundation 'Russkie v "blizhnem zarubezh'e"', *Nezavisimaia gazeta* (7 September 1993), p. 5, and the RAU Corporation, *Natsional'naia bezopasnost' : Rossiia v 1994 gody* (Moscow: Obozrevatel', 1993), pp. 95–108.

43 Stankevich had been a leading member of the Democratic movement. In September 1992, he became political adviser to President Yeltsin. 'Sergei Stankevich the PR man', *New Times International*, no. 43 (October 1992), pp. 10–13.

44 S. B. Stankevich and D. P. Pollyeva, '"Starye" russkie v "novom" zarubezh'e', *Rossiiskii Monitor*, no. 3 (1993), pp. 35–43; Stankevich, 'Derzhava v poiskakh sebia', *Nezavisimaia Gazeta* (28 March 1992), p. 4; 'Ne dopustit' deportatsii russkikh iz Pribaltiki', *Rossiiskie Vesti* (28 April 1993), p. 1; 'Kak nam obustroit' blizhnee zarubezh'e', *Novaia Ezhednevnaia Gazeta*, no. 14 (7 July 1993); and 'U Rossii est' svoe mesto v mire', *Rossiiskie Vesti* (27 February 1993).

45 Sections of the Migration Service were to be created in each of the Russian embassies in the former Soviet republics. A state fund called *sootechestvenniki* was established to support the costs of resettling migrants. *Rossiiskie Vesti* (30 March 1993), p. 4.

46 In November 1992, President Yeltsin issued a decree instructing the MFA to develop legal agreements with governments of the former Soviet republics and an embassy/consular system to represent Russian citizens. '*O voprosakh zashchity prav i interesov rossiiskikh grazhdan za predelami Rossiiskoi Federatsii*', *Diplomaticheskii Vestnik* (November 1992).

47 Sergei Shakhrai, 'Goskomnats budet zanimat'sia problemami zashchity rossiian v strankah Balti', *Rossiiskie Vesti* (28 January 1993).

48 *Nashi* (Ours), *russko-dumaiushchee naselenie* (Russian-thinking – in the

ethnic sense – population), *Rossiisko orientovannoe naselenie* (populations oriented to Russia).

49 This term means more than simply ethnic Russians. Slavs and heavily Russified ethnic groups within the settler populations are also considered to be *etnicheskie Rossiiane*. Abdullah Mikitaev, the head of the Presidential Committee on Citizenship, has identified more than 30 million *etnicheskie Rossiiane*, 25 million of whom are ethnic Russians. *Rossiiskie Vesti* (16 August 1994).

50 On occasion, the MFA opted to describe members of the diaspora simply as *Rossiiane*. See 'Kontseptsiia vneshnei politiki Rossiiskoi Federatsii', *Diplomaticheskii Vestnik* (January 1993) (special edition).

51 Initially the Club was jointly managed by Shelov-Kovediaev and published the journal *Sootechestvennik*. Although the Club was to function on the basis of moneys raised through its own activities, on 19 March 1993 President Yeltsin issued a special order stating that the Club had the right to withdraw funds from the 'reserve state fund'. *'Rasporiazhenie presidenta RF: Voprosy nepravitel'stvennoi organizatsii "Rossiiskii Klub"' – No. 194*. On 23 December, Yeltsin issued a decree granting 100m roubles to the foundation *Sodruzhestvo*, a charity operating among the Baltic settler population under the umbrella of the Russian Club. *Ukaz Prezidenta RF: O gosudarstvennoi podderzhke fonda 'sodruzhestvo' – no. 1574*.

52 On 29–30 March 1993, Rogozin organized a meeting that brought together representatives of the settler communities and leading conservatives in the Supreme Soviet. 'Zarubezhnye diaspory ob'edinilis', *Megapolis-Express*, no. 13 (7 April 1993), p. 15.

53 *Kongress Russkikh Obshin: Kratkaia Spravka.*

54 Author's interview with Dmitri Rogozin, Moscow (7 June 1994).

55 Reference to Russia's obligation to protect Russians outside Russia could be found in most of the party electoral platforms including moderate parties. *Bloka Iablok: Predvybornaia platforma* (Moscow, November 1993), pp. 27–8, and *Partiia Rossiiskogo edinstva i soglasiia v voprosakh i otvetakh* (Moscow, November 1993), p. 41.

56 'Yeltsin gives New Year address with pledge to stand by Russian citizens abroad', *SWB B/1* (3 January 1994). In a shorter address at the beginning of 1995, Yeltsin again picked out the Russians outside Russia for particular mention. 'Yeltsin's New Year Address', *SWB SU/2191/ B/1* (3 January 1995). In a series of speeches at the beginning of 1994, the Foreign Minister made clear his conversion to the diaspora cause. 'Kozyrev details Russian foreign policy agenda', *FBIS–SOV–94–028* (10 February 1994), pp. 12–14. 'Foreign Minister Kozyrev outlines parliament's role in foreign

policy', *SWB SU/1914 B/1* (5 February 1994); 'Kozyrev warns against violations of rights of Russian minorities in former USSR', *SWB SU/1901 S2/1* (21 January 1994).

57 'Paper publishes Yeltsin's "Annual Message"', *FBIS–SOV–94–039* (28 January 1994), pp. 58–9.

58 The Commission for Questions of Citizenship was established in March 1992 and Abdullah Mikitaev was appointed its president. Throughout 1992 and 1993 the Commission had been largely invisible. Following the failure of the Stankevich initiative, a high-level decision was taken to develop a comprehensive set of policies towards the Russian communities and Yeltsin issued instructions for the Citizenship Commission to work out measures for the protection of the diaspora. 'Ne velikoe pereselenie, a dvoinoe grazhdanstvo', *Pravda* (29 April 1994), p. 2. 'Rossiia voz'met pod svoe pokrovitel'stvo milliony russkikh v novom zarubezh'e', *Izvestiia* (22 July 1994), pp. 1 and 2.

59 Abdullah Mikitaev has also called for the creation of autonomous regions in the settler areas of northeastern Estonia, Latvia and Lithuania. *RFE/RL News Briefs* (18–22 July 1994), p. 18.

60 'Russkie obshchiny namereny ob'edinit'sia', *Emigratsiia*, no. 5 (February 1994); 'Vstrecha predstavitelei obshchestvennykh organizatsii v MID RF', *Diplomaticheskii Vestnik*, no. 7–8 (April 1994), pp. 56–7; 'Zashchiti' prava vernuvshikhsia v Rossiiu', *Rossiiskie Vesti* (5 April 1994); *Diplomaticheskii Vestnik*, no. 9–10, (May 1994), p. 70; and 'Obshchestvennaia palata obsudila "baltiiskuiu problemu"', *Rossiiskie Vesti* (10 March 1994).

61 Ginsburgs has noted a change in Russian citizenship legislation from a restrictive regime designed to make settlers stay put by erecting obstacles to obtaining Russian citizenship, to one based on a dual citizenship system aimed at inducing stability by establishing Russia as a sanctuary. George Ginsburgs, 'Citizenship and state succession in Russia's treaty and domestic repertory', unpublished paper (1995). The presence of large numbers of Russian citizens outside Russia might also provide a powerful justification for future Russian involvement in the affairs of its neighbours.

62 At a conference in April 1994, Mikitaev claimed that close to 150,000 members of the diaspora had applied for citizenship. 'Sud'ba rossiian v blizhnem zarubezh'e', *Delovoi Mir* (29 April 1994).

63 The idea of dual citizenship had in fact first been mooted during Kozyrev's visit to Almaty in November 1993. S. Skorokhodov, 'Rossiia vspomnila o russkikh v Kazakhstane', *Rossiiskaia gazeta* (18 November 1993), p. 6; however, the main diplomatic offensive began in January with

Uzbekistan, 'Russian and Uzbek officials discuss issue of ethnic Russians in Moscow meeting', *SWB SU/1909/ B/2* (31 January 1994), and in February with Kyrgyzstan, 'Dispute over dual citizenship issue viewed', *FBIS–SOV–94–024* (4 February 1994), p. 57.

64 George Ginsburgs, 'The question of dual citizenship in Russia's relations with the successor states in Central Asia', *Central Asia Monitor*, no. 5 (1994), pp. 11–16. Although Russia and Kazakhstan have not been able to agree on dual citizenship provisions, an agreement on citizens' rights that allows for a swift change of citizenship has been established. 'Rossiiskaia Federatsiia prioritetnyi partner Kazakhstana', *Segodnia* (16 December 1994), p. 4.

65 *Osnovnye napravleniia programmy podderzhki sootechestvennikov za rubezhom (v gosudstvakh, obrazovavshikhsia na territorii byvshego SSSR) (Proekt)*, p. 1. See also the draft published in *Rosinformbiuro*, no. 10 (1994).

66 'Osnovnye napravleniia gosudarstvennoi politiki Rossiiskoi Federatsii v otnoshenii sootechestvennikov, prozhivaiushchikh za rubezhom', *Rossiiskaia Gazeta* (22 September 1994), p. 4. The document contains a mishmash of terms to describe the diaspora including compatriot, *vykhodtsy* (emigrants), *Rossiiane* (people linked to the Russian state), *slaviany* (Slavs), Russian-speakers and describes Russia as the historic homeland (*istoricheskaia rodina*) and native land (*rodnaia zemlia*) of these people.

67 See also the new Federal Migration Programme. *'O Federal'noi migratsionnoi programme'*, Presidential decree no. 1668 (9 August 1994).

68 The document includes the requirement that the government draft a decree to transform the public association *Rodina* into a quango for channelling Russian assistance to the diaspora. *Rodina* was intended to replace Stankevich's Russian Club, which had proved inappropriate for the complex task of building ties to the diaspora. 'Voprosy Assotsiatsii po sviaziam s sootechestvennikami za rubezhom (Assotsiatsiia "Rodina").'

69 Various ministries have begun to draw up detailed measures on the basis of this programme. E. E. Kuzmina, *Russkie v mnogonatsional'nom regione: sotsiokul'turnye problemy russkoiazychnogo naseleniia v Blizhnem Zarubezh'e (Promezhutochnyi)* (Moscow: Ministry of Culture RF/Russian Academy of Science, 1994).

70 High-level endorsement for the new programme was signalled by support from Viktor Chernomyrdin and the appointment of Sergei Shakhrai to head of the Commission for the Affairs of Compatriots Abroad. *Rosinformbiuro*, no. 10 (1994).

71 When the Latvian law on citizenship was issued, the Russian parliament was quick to pass a resolution condemning it. 'Duma appeals for Latvian citizenship law reconsideration', *FBIS–SOV–94–132* (11 July 1994).

72 'Interview with Konstantin Zatulin by Dr. Yutaka Akino', *Institute for East–West Studies* (24 March 1994).

73 Zatulin also became closely involved in settler issues in Kazakhstan. See Chapter 6.

74 'Duma Committee hearings on plight of Russians abroad', *FBIS–SOV–94–131* (8 July 1994), p. 35.

75 The head of the Congress of Russian Communities, Dmitri Rogozin, was the most vocal. Following the destruction of the parliament the CRC continued to function and remained opposed to the government line on the diaspora. Rogozin particularly argued against the Russian government's emphasis on the assimilation of the Russian communities within their host state. He believes that diaspora Russians should form part of a renaissance of Russia not on the basis of individual rights or citizenship but on the establishment of the rights of the Russian nation as a whole. 'Proekt ukaza prezidenta RF o sootechestvennikakh nesovershenen', *Nezavisimaia Gazeta* (11 August 1994), p. 7.

76 The Committee for CIS Affairs has also begun to adopt a more assertive role towards the diaspora and has put forward an alternative to the government's approach to the settlers. 'Deklaratsiia o podderzhke Rossiiskoi Federatsiei Rossiiskoi diaspory i o pokrovitel'stve Rossiiskim sootechestvennikam (proekt)', 1995.

77 Within domestic politics, debate about the diaspora moved from being an issue that fostered divisions among Russian politicians to one that encouraged greater integration. State institutions are being established and shaped around the notion of the diaspora, and the consensus on settler affairs has provided a basis for the creation of a network of regularized contacts and consultations between government, parliament, public organizations and the settlers. The membership of the Presidential Citizenship Commission indicates the broad range of political, economic, social and cultural interests being integrated within the new policy-making structures. *Diplomaticheskii Vestnik*, No. 17–18 (September 1994) pp. 39–40.

78 'Yeltsin: economic wealth key to world power status...', *RFE/RL News Briefs* (18–22 July 1994), p. 4.

79 One of the principal reasons for pursuing dual citizenship is to put Russia's relationship to the settlers – and therefore Russian policy – onto a legal basis that would be more accepted by international society.

80 Michael Cherniavsky, *Tsar and People: Studies in Russian Myths* (New Haven, CT: Yale University Press, 1961).

81 Mikitaev has noted: 'To Russia after the collapse of the USSR fell the most difficult fate because suddenly millions of ethnic Russians (*etnicheskie Rossiiane*) were outside its borders. Protection of their rights is the holy duty of our state.' 'Prava rossiian za rubezhom budut nadezhno zashchishcheny', *Rossiiskie Vesti* (16 August 1994), p. 1.

Chapter 3: Russian settlers and the struggle for citizenship in Estonia and Latvia

1 Although the settler communities are here classified as Russian, in fact they include a range of ethnic groups (see Tables 3.1 and 3.2). The majority of these communities are, however, Russian-speakers, and for many, Russian has become their mother-tongue. A Russian and Russian-speaking identity have therefore been interchangeable.

2 While researching this chapter, the author drew heavily on material published in *The Baltic Independent*, *Baltic Observer*, *SM-Segodnia*, *Panorama*, *Vechernii Kur'er*, *Latvii*, *Molodezh' Estonii*, *Estoniia* (1992–95); *Russkii Put*, *Diena* (Russian edition).

3 Stephen D. Corrsin, 'The changing composition of the city of Riga, 1987–1913', *Journal of Baltic Studies*, vol. 13, no. 1 (1983), 87.

4 Edward C. Thaden, *Russification in the Baltic Provinces and Finland 1855–1914* (Princeton, NJ: Princeton University Press, 1981).

5 Anatol Lieven, *The Baltic Revolution: Estonia, Latvia, Lithuania and the Path to Independence* (New Haven, CT: Yale University Press, 1993), pp. 38–53.

6 The grandfather of the Latvian Viktor Alksnis, the great Soviet patriot of the late 1980s, was a commander in the Soviet air force before being purged in 1937.

7 This figure is often used to tar the Russian-speaking population but of course many prisoners in the USSR were jailed for minor crimes or political or economic activities.

8 Soviet language policy was based on the decision of the Communist Party and Council of People's Commissars in 1938, 'On compulsory study of the Russian language in schools of non-Russian republics and regions'.

9 In a survey conducted in Estonia in 1988, 78% of the Russians questioned identified themselves as members of the 'Soviet nation' and only 15% as belonging to another national group. The comparative figures for Estonians were 10% and 73%. *Vikerkaar*, 5 (1988), 76.

10 Rasma Karklins, *Ethnopolitics and Transition to Democracy: The Collapse of the USSR and Latvia* (Baltimore, MD: Johns Hopkins University Press, 1994), p. 82.

11 Toomas Hendrik Ilves, 'Reaction: the Intermovement in Estonia', in Jan Arveds Trapans, ed., *Toward Independence: The Baltic Popular Movements* (Boulder, CO: Westview Press, 1991), pp. 71–83, and Karklins, *op. cit.*, 80.

12 Karklins, *op. cit.*, 79–80.

13 'Latvijas iedz votaju ekspresaptaujas rezultati', *Diena*, 22 (January 1991), 3.

14 For the results see 'Results of the March 3, 1991 referendum on Latvian independence', Nationalities Papers, vol. XIX, no. 1 (spring 1991), Appendix 2b, pp. 109–10.

15 Data from the Estonian polling organization Mainor-EMOR.

16 Aleksei Semyenov, 'Mezhnatsional'nye faktory integratsii obshchestva Estonii', unpublished paper (1993).

17 Klara Hallik and Marika Kirch, 'On interethnic relations in Estonia', *Estratto da 'Annali' della Fondazionne Giangiacomo Feltrinelli* (1992), 158.

18 'Khotyat li russkie bezhat?', *Moskovskie novosti* (27 January 1991), 12–13.

19 Hallik and Kirch, *op. cit.*

20 *The Citizenship and Alien Law Controversies in Estonia and Latvia* (Harvard University Strengthening Democratic Institutions Project: April 1994).

21 Dzintra Bungs, 'The shifting political landscape in Latvia', *RFE/RL Research Report*, vol. 2, no. 12 (19 March 1993).

22 Georgs Andrejevs, the Latvian Foreign Minister, called for the repatriation of 'colonists'. 'Biting the biter: Georgs Andrejevs and Russia', *The Baltic Independent* (12–18 March 1993), 9.

23 In 1988–9, the Popular Front created organizations to encourage the development of national cultures among non-Latvians and to foster support for the Front. In 1991, the Nationalities Department was created to develop these organizations, and act as a link to the Front and later the government. The Department was ignored by parliament and in 1992 transferred to the Ministry of Justice and downgraded.

24 Aasland highlights the diverse character of the Russian-speaking community. Aadne Aasland, 'The Russian population in Latvia: an integrated minority?', *The Journal of Communist Studies and Transition Politics*, 10, no. 2 (June 1994), 233–60.

25 Rubriks and Dimanis are ethnically Latvian while Zdanok is Jewish.

26 Equal Rights is close to the Committee on Human Rights and International

Humanitarian Cooperation. The committee has campaigned extensively in the local Russian press in support of the zero variant and in May 1993 held a press conference in the Moscow Ministry of Foreign Affairs. *Diena* (22 September 1993), 8.

27 Author's interview with Vladimir Vladov, Riga (October 1993).

28 The main groups were: the Cossack Circle which had close links to Soviet officers' organizations; the Union of Latvian Communists formed in early September 1992 from the core of the Communist Party of Latvia and the Interfront; the Union for the Defence of Veterans' Rights which was formed from the Council of USSR War, Work and Armed Forces Veterans, which had been banned in August 1991; and the Association of Russians in Latvia.

29 *Diena* (24 September 1993), 1.

30 *Diena* (6 October 1993), 1.

31 Author's interview with Janis Jurkans, Riga (October 1993).

32 'Latvia votes down Russian military factory deal', *The Baltic Independent* (4 June 1993).

33 King and Thad Barnowe found similar value orientations between Russophone and Latvian managers. Gundar King and J. Thad Barnowe, 'Complementary and conflicting personal values of Russophone managers in Latvia', *Journal of Baltic Studies* XXV, no. 3 (Fall 1994), 249–72.

34 The city's population is 65% Russian, 12% Latvian, 12% Polish, 8% Ukrainian and 3% Belarussian. Many Latvians speak Russian as their first language.

35 For details of the pre-election period see Dzintra Bungs, 'Twenty-three groups vie for seats in the Latvian Parliament', *RFE/RL Research Report*, vol. 2, no. 23 (4 June 1993), 44–9.

36 In parliament there were eight parties: Latvian Way – 36 seats, in coalition with the Farmers Union – 12 seats, making a total of 48; Equal Rights – 7 (8 if the imprisoned Rubiks is counted), Fatherland and Freedom – 6, Christian Democratic Union – 5, Democratic Party – 5, Harmony for Latvia – 13, Latvian National Independence Party – 15, making a total of 99.

37 Criticism from the Russian Federation and the suggestion that Latvian membership of the Council of Europe might be blocked if the law was not changed concentrated parliamentary minds very quickly.

38 'Latvia passes new citizenship law', *The Baltic Independent* (29 July – 4 August 1994), 1, also *Diena* (21 January 1995).

39 'Local councils shaken up in Latvia', *The Baltic Independent* (3–9 June 1994), 1 and 4.

40 The language law was passed on 18 January 1989.

41 Author's interview with Sergei Gorokhov, sociologist in Narva (October 1993).

42 An EMOR poll suggests that half the respondents in Narva were unhappy with the work of the local council – many more than in other areas of the country: 54% said the local council should work in close cooperation with the Estonian government. 'Second referendum called in north-east Estonia', *The Baltic Independent* (5–9 July 1993).

43 An official at the Russian embassy in Tallinn reported that by February 1995 there were 61,401 Russian citizens in Estonia. *OMRI Daily Report (Part II)* (7 February 1995).

44 The other places went to: Savisaar's Party – 5 mandates; Coalition Party – 14 and Tiit Vahi became chairman of Tallinn Council; and Rai-Club – 9.

45 The distribution of seats was as follows: 12 – Democratic Labour Party, 12 – Narva Trade Union, and 7 – Narva Estonian Society.

46 Andrus Park, 'Ethnicity and independence: the case of Estonia in comparative perspective', *Europe–Asia Studies* 46, no. 1 (1994), 69–87.

47 In 1994, a new Russian nationalist group emerged: the Russian Community in Estonia. The organization is built around a core of 12,000 retired Soviet officers. Led by Yurii Kotenkov, the organization has close ties with the Congress of Russian Communities in Russia. 'MP views Russian community councils statement', *FBIS–SOV–94–052* (17 March 1994), 43.

48 'Russians found political parties', *The Baltic Independent* (14–20 October 1994), 1.

49 Riina Kionka, 'Russia recognizes Estonia's independence', *RFE/RL Report on the USSR*, 3, no. 5 (1 February 1991), 14–16.

50 Stephen Foye, 'Russian politics complicates Baltic troop withdrawal', *RFE/RL Research Report*, vol. 1, no. 46, 20 November 1992, 30–35.

51 'Yeltsin officially links troops to human rights', *The Baltic Independent* (18–24 June 1993), 3.

52 'Kremlin defends its troops in Baltic', *The Baltic Independent* (19–25 March 1993), 3.

53 *Baltic News Service* (2 August 1993).

54 'Estonia grants residence rights to ex–Soviet officers', *The Baltic Independent* (26 November–2 December 1993).

55 'Party would uphold Russian rights', *The Baltic Independent* (26 November–2 December 1993).

56 'Russians to stay in Baltics, says Kozyrev', *The Financial Times* (19 January 1994), 2.

57 In 1992, Estonian sociologists suggested that ethnic Russians saw themselves simultaneously as representatives of Estonian, Russian, Soviet and world culture. See Aksel Kirch, Marika Kirch and Tarmo Tuisk, *The non-Estonian Population Today and Tomorrow: A Sociological Overview*

(Tallinn, December 1992).

58 Latvia's Department of Citizenship and Immigration was criticized by Helsinki Watch for 'serious systematic abuses' in its failure to uphold the December 1991 law on the registration of residents. 'Watchdog condemns Latvian "abuses"', *The Baltic Independent* (5–11 November 1993).

59 In 1993, the Estonian Ministry of Foreign Affairs, fearing the influence of the Russian Orthodox Church in Moscow and under pressure from Estonian ultra-nationalists, backed the Stockholm-based Estonian Orthodox Church in exile to take over Orthodox sites in the country. In an attempt to head off a split, the head of the Russian Orthodox Church in Moscow, Patriarch Aleksei II, himself an Estonian citizen, issued a special decree giving the church complete independence on 26 April 1993. 'Estonskaia pravoslavnaia Tserkov' po-prezhnemu samostoiatel'na', *Izvestiia* (6 May 1993), 5.

60 Efforts are being made by Russians in Latvia to reclaim a Russian past. I. I. Ivanov, ed., *Russkii v Latvii: Istoriia i sovremmenost'* (Riga: LAD, 1992), 1st edn.

61 Maley has found higher support among Russian-speakers in the Baltic states for their own governments than for the Russian government. William Maley, 'Does Russia speak for Baltic Russians?', *The World Today*, 51, no. 1 (January 1995), 4–6. See also 'Loyalty of local Russians has increased', *The Baltic Independent* (15–21 July 1994, 3, and 'Ethnic tensions evaluated', *The Baltic Independent* (1–7 July 1994), 2.

62 Juan Linz, 'From primordialism to nationalism', in Edward Tiryakin and Ronald Rogowski, eds, *New Nationalities of the Developed West* (Boston: Allen & Unwin, 1985).

63 The Zadornov Foundation has distributed tens of thousands of dollars to Russian papers in the Baltic, and to cultural and educational organizations and to local charities. Author's interview with Mikhail Zadornov, Moscow (October 1994).

64 Konrad Huber, 'Averting inter-ethnic conflict: an analysis of the CSCE High Commissioner on National Minorities in Estonia, January–July 1993' (Occasional Paper Series of the Conflict Resolution Program of the Carter Center of Emory University, 1994).

65 A United Nations mission to Latvia, 27–30 October 1992, found that the laws did not infringe the international norms and that there were no systematic violations of rights but that 'it would be desirable if Latvia, for humanitarian reasons, would extend its nationality to the majority of its permanent residents who express a desire to be loyal citizens of Latvia'. See also the collection of reports including that from the CSCE, *Human Rights in the Baltic States*, (Finnish Helsinki Committee), no. 6 (1993).

Chapter 4: War, irredentism and national identity in Moldova

1 According to the 1989 Soviet census, the republic's total population stood at 4,335,360 of whom 2,794,749 (64.5%) were Moldovans, 600,366 (13.8%) Ukrainians, 562,069 (13.0%) Russians, 153,458 (3.5%) Gagauz, 88,419 (2%) Bulgarians, and 65,672 (1.5%) Jews.

2 Turkey became closely involved in Moldova because of the Gagauz minority in the south who were presented by policy-makers in Ankara as a part of the Turkish diaspora.

3 I thank Charles King for making me aware of this.

4 According to the 1926 Soviet census, the ethnic structure of the new political entity stood at 48.5% Ukrainian, 8.5% Russian, 8.5% Jewish and 30.1% Moldovan. The latter figure may have been inflated to increase the legitimacy of the republic as a national homeland. Walter Kolarz, *Russia and Her Colonies* (New York: Fredrick A. Praeger, 1952), p. 149.

5 Ronald J. Hill, *Soviet Political Elites: the Case of Tiraspol* (London: Martin Robertson, 1977).

6 Chauncy Harris, 'The new Russian minorities: a statistical overview', *Post-Soviet Geography*, 34, no. 1 (1993), 1–27.

7 Vladimir Socor, 'Popular Front founded in Moldovia', *Radio Liberty Report on the USSR*, vol. 1, no. 23 (9 June 1989), 23–6.

8 Charles King, 'Moldovan Identity and the Politics of Pan Romanianism', *Slavic Review*, vol. 53, no. 2 (1994), 345–68.

9 According to opinion surveys, support for the Moldovan Popular Front fell from 21% in October 1991 to 12% by winter 1991–2. Support for Unity fell from 7% in June 1991 to 5% in November 1991 and 3% in February 1992. Vladimir Socor, 'Public opinion polling in Moldova', *RFE/RL Research Bulletin*, vol. 1, no. 13 (27 March 1992), 60–63.

10 *Russkii Vestnik* (11 September 1991).

11 Pål Kolstø and Andrei Edemsky with Natalya Kalashnikova, 'The Dniester conflict: between irredentism and separatism', *Europe–Asia Studies*, vol. 45, no. 6 (1993), 985.

12 *Ibid.*, 992.

13 Following independence in 1991, there was a rapid increase in the number of ethnic Moldovans in the state apparatus. Vladimir Solonar and Vladimir Bruter, 'Russians in Moldova', in Vladimir Shlapentokh, Munir Sendich and Emil Payin, eds, *The New Russian Diaspora: Russian Minorities in the Former Soviet Republics* (New York: M. E. Sharpe, 1994), 83.

14 For the structure and policies of the OSTK see 'Materialy III Konferentsii OSTK NMR', *Trudovoi Tiraspol'*, 2–9 March 1994.

15 From 1990, a close relationship grew up between the PMR and the Gagauz republic. In late 1993, a special economic agreement was signed between Stepan Topal and Igor Smirnov. Author's interview with Stepan Topal, President of the Gagauz Republic, Komrat (2 March 1994).

16 Barely two weeks after the August 1991 coup, the PMR leadership had begun to take control of police stations on the left bank. Vladimir Socor, 'Creeping putsch in Eastern Moldova', *RFE/RL Research Report*, vol. 1, no. 34 (17 January 1992), 8–13.

17 Kolstø et al., *op. cit.*, 973–1000.

18 Author's interview with Vadim Malakov, Presidential Adviser for Nationalities, Chisinau (4 March 1994).

19 'Carnage among the cherry trees as Moldovan conflict worsens', *Observer* (UK) (28 June 1992).

20 Vladimir Socor, 'Russia's Fourteenth Army and the insurgency in Eastern Moldova', *RFE/RL Research Report*, vol. 1, no. 36 (11 September 1992), 41–8.

21 '14-ia Armiia okhraniaet svoi sem'i i voennye gorodki', *Izvestiia* (22 June 1992), 2.

22 Andrei Kozyrev, 'Partiia voiny nastupaet – i v Moldove, i v Gruzii, i v Rossii', *Izvestiia* (30 June 1992) and 'General Lebed' stavit ul'timatum prezidentu rossii', *Izvestiia* (7 July 1992), 1.

23 'Mircha Snegur: kto mne garantiruet, chto rossiiskie tanki ne voidut v kishinev?', *Izvestiia* (9 June 1992), 6.

24 'Russian 14th Army accused of attempt to overthrow Dnestr leaders', *SWB SU/1899/ D/5*.

25 'Tiraspol' protiv soglashenii moskvy i kishineva', *Nezavisimaia gazeta* (7 February 1995), 1.

26 The flag and anthem of Romania were adopted as the state insignia of Moldova.

27 Author's interviews in the Institute of History, Chisinau (5 March 1994).

28 Vladimir Socor, 'Moldova's new government of national consensus', *RFE/RL Research Report*, vol. 1, no. 47 (27 November 1992), 5–10.

29 Neil Melvin, 'Moldova looks back to the future', *World Today,* vol. 50, no. 6 (June 1994), 102–6.

30 Author's interview with Petru Lucinschi, parliamentary speaker, Chisinau (24 February 1994).

31 While informal polls suggest that voting was divided along ethnolinguistic lines, the election itself did not have an overt ethnic colouring. The Socialist-Unity list included a number of ethnic groups. The Gagauz regions voted solidly for it. The urban areas voted for Socialist-Unity

candidates and the rural areas for the ADP. The rural areas populated by Bulgarians voted for the Agrarian Party. Up to a quarter of the Socialist-Unity vote came from Moldovans and up to a third of Russian-speakers voted for the ADP. *Department of Public Opinion, Chisinau Sociological Institute.*

32 For a history of Russian settlement in the region see Solonar and Bruter, *op. cit.*, 72–90.

33 Vladimir Socor, 'Politics of the language question heating up in Soviet Moldovia', *Radio Liberty, Report on the USSR*, vol. 1, no. 36 (8 September 1989), 33–6.

34 The Interfront leadership formed two sub-organizations: the Association for Employees in Organizations Connected with Educational/Culture and Science, and the N. I. Pirogov Association for Medical Employees.

35 Author's interview with Petr Shornikov, co-leader of Unity, Chisinau (5 March 1994).

36 In the February–March 1990 Moldovan elections, 60 of the 370 parliamentary deputies were elected on the Interfront list. Solonar and Bruter, *op. cit.*, 83.

37 A second major settler organization is the International Foundation for Slavic Literature and Culture of Moldova which was created in 1989. The organization initially faced opposition from the local Communist Party and as the Popular Front grew in strength, it came under pressure to become more political. Following independence, the society received financial assistance from the Russian Ministry of Culture although this later ceased. Author's interview with members of the Foundation, Chisinau (2 March 1994).

38 Under instructions from the Russian MFA, in 1994 the centre launched an initiative to create the Russian (*Rossiiskii*) Association for Links with Compatriots Abroad ('Rodina'). This association was designed to forge links between the diaspora communities in Azerbaijan, Kazakhstan, Moldova, Ukraine and Estonia. Subsequently Rodina became an important part of the Russian government's diaspora programme launched in late 1994 (see Chapter 1). *Slavianskaia Gazeta* No. 1, 1994, p. 1.

39 Author's meeting with the Executive Committee of the Russian Centre, Chisinau (28 February 1994).

40 On the eve of election, Belapotapov published an article in the main Russian-language paper *Kishinevskii Novosti* calling on all Russians and Russian-speakers to vote for Unity.

41 Author's interview with Alexander Tkachenko, leader of the Moldovan Ukrainian Society, Chisinau (28 February 1994).

42 Author's interview with M. B. Marunevich, Gagauz historian, Komrat (3 March 1994).

43 The Vice-President of the PMR has claimed that 'the Russian Parliament understood that it needed to put out fires on the periphery to stop them spreading to Russia'. Author's interview with Aleksandr Karaman, Tiraspol (6 March 1994).

44 On 26 March 1995, a referendum on the withdrawal of the 14th Army was conducted in the PMR. Between 91% and 93% of those who took part opposed withdrawal of the army. *CDPP*, vol. XLVII, no. 13 (1995), p. 21.

45 The Russian military claim that there are dozens of criminal gangs operating in the region and many originate from around the PMR leadership. Author's interview with Mikhail Bergman, Commandant of the Tiraspol garrison of the Russian Fourteenth Army, Tiraspol (6 March 1994).

46 'Narrow Congress victory for Yeltsin', *The Independent* (7 April 1992).

47 'Pridnestrovskii rubezh', *Sovetskaia Rossiia* (27 June 1992), 1, and 'Fakt natsional'nogo terrora', *Sovetskaia Rossiia* (23 June 1992), 2.

48 Andrei Kozyrev, 'Partiia voiny nastupaet – i v Moldove, i v Gruzii, i v Rossii', *Izvestiia* (30 June 1992), 1.

49 'Mircha Snegur obviniaet Aleksandra Rutskogo', *Izvestiia* (2 June 1992), 1.

50 Romania sent weapons to help create the Moldovan armed forces. 'Rumyniia ofitsial'no priznala postavki oruzhiia v Moldovu', *Izvestiia* (13 July 1992), 4.

51 'V Rossii skladyvaetsia nevernoe predstavlenie o sobytiiakh v Moldove', *Izvestiia* (12 June 1992), 5.

52 'Soglashenie ob uregulirovanii konflikta v Pridnestrov'e gotovo k podpisaniiu', *Izvestiia* (21 July 1992), 1.

53 'Mirotvorcheskie sily voshli v Bendery', *Izvestiia* (30 July 1992), 1.

54 'Igor Smirnov, "My schitaem sebia nezavisimymi",' *Izvestiia* (16 June 1992), 2.

55 Charles King, *Post-Soviet Moldova: A Borderland in Transition* (London: RIIA, Post-Soviet Business Forum, 1995).

56 As with Ukraine, the considerable debts to Russia for energy supplies forced the Moldovan leadership to seek closer ties with the United States following the 1994 elections. 'Prezident Snegur vstretilsia s zamestitdem directora Rossiiskogo kontserna Gazprom', *Nezavisimaia Moldova* (15 March 1994), p. 1. 'Novoe pravitel'stvo Moldovy pristupilo k rabote', *Izvestiia* (5 August 1992), 1.

57 Bohdan Nahaylo, 'Ukraine and Moldova: the view from Kiev', *RFE/RL Research Report*, vol. 1, no. 18 (1 May 1992), 39–45.

58 Bohdan Nahaylo, 'Moldova conflict creates new dilemmas for Ukraine',
    RFE/RL Research Bulletin, vol. 1, no. 20 (15 May 1992), 1–8.
59 Author's interview with Eugen Levitsky, Ukrainian Counsellor in the
    Republic of Moldova, Chisinau (12 March 1994).
60 Author's interview with Vladislav Reider, journalist at *Nezavisimaia
    Moldova*, Chisinau (1 March 1994).
61 The importance attached by Moscow to the creation of diaspora organiza-
    tions was signalled by the attendance of the head of President Yeltsin's
    Commission on Citizenship, Abdullah Mikitaev.

Chapter 5: Russians, regionalism and ethnicity in Ukraine

1 According to the last Soviet census (1989), the ethnic Russian minority in
   Ukraine was 11.4m – Europe's largest – and is very concentrated, with
   80% of the Russians living in the South and East and mostly in urban
   areas. While Ukrainians are in the majority in every district (*oblast*) except
   Crimea, if Russophones are counted as part of the Russian bloc, then they
   are in the majority in Donetsk (67.7%), Luhansk (63.9%) and Crimea
   (82.9%) and close to majority in Zaporizhzhia, Kharkiv and Odessa.
   Russians also constitute majorities in every regional capital of the South
   and East.
2 In May 1992, the Orthodox Church in Ukraine split into two – the
   Orthodox Church-Moscow Patriarchate and Orthodox Church-Kiev
   Patriarchate – thereby introducing a further social division. The majority
   of those surveyed in a poll in 1993 intended to support the Kiev
   Patriarchate. Jaroslaw Martyniuk, 'Religious preferences in five urban
   areas of Ukraine', *RFE/RL Research Report*, vol. 2, no. 15 (9 April 1993),
   52–5. To date, however, most parishes remain with the Moscow
   Patriarchate.
3 Roman Solchanyk, 'The politics of state building: centre-periphery
   relations in post-Soviet Ukraine', *Europe–Asia Studies*, vol. 46, no. 1
   (1994), 47–68.
4 Ian Bremmer, 'The politics of ethnicity: Russians in the new Ukraine',
   Europe–Asia Studies, vol. 46, no. 2 (1994), 261–83.
5 That is, there is an important difference between ethnic identification
   according to the old Soviet passport system and the everyday, popular
   understanding of ethnicity. While individuals may have identified themselves as Russian or Ukrainian in the 1989 census on the basis of genealogical criteria (parentage), in popular usage – particularly in the East,
   South and Centre of Ukraine – the terms *Russkii* and *Rossiianin* are often

employed with a far broader meaning that includes language, religion, culture, feelings of historical belonging and regional identity. Frequently, these terms encompass individuals identified formally as Ukrainian.

6 After the collapse of Kievan Rus, the West Ukrainians are thought to have formed the Galician-Volhynian state, then to have come under the rule of Lithuania, Poland and Austria, and finally under Poland again in the interwar years of the twentieth century.

7 Modern Ukrainian historiography is largely based on the work of the early twentieth-century historian and politician Mykhailo Hrushevsky. See John S. Reshetar, *The Ukrainian Revolution, 1917–1920: A Study of Nationalism* (Princeton, NJ: Princeton University Press, 1952), p. 9.

8 Jeremy Lester, 'Russian political attitudes to Ukrainian independence', *The Journal of Communist Studies and Transition Politics*, vol. 10, no. 2 (June 1994), 193–233.

9 Orest Subtelny, *Ukraine: A History* (Toronto: University of Toronto Press, 1988).

10 Hugh Seton-Watson, *The Russian Empire 1801–1917* (Oxford: Oxford University Press, 1967), p. 52.

11 Richard Pipes, *The Formation of the Soviet Union: Communism and Nationalism, 1917–1923* (Cambridge, MA: Harvard University Press, 1964).

12 Lowell Tillet, *The Great Friendship: Soviet Historians on the Non-Russian Nationalities* (Chapel Hill, NC: University of North Carolina, 1969).

13 The complex intermixing of Ukrainians and Russians along what is now the frontier made constructing ethnically defined borders extremely difficult. However, the decision to include sizeable Russian populations within the borders of the Ukrainian SSR may well have reflected a desire to establish a Russian anchor securing Ukraine to the Russian Federation. Similar considerations prevailed when the borders of Kazakhstan were drawn to include large Slavic populations in the north and east.

14 John Armstrong, *Ukrainian Nationalism, 1939–1945* (Englewood, CO: Ukrainian Academic Press, 1990).

15 The introduction of political nationalism into the Ukrainian body politic was also accompanied by a rise in the numbers of Ukrainians in cities, particularly in Kiev which eventually emerged as an ethnically Ukrainian city. Bohdan Krawchenko, *Social Change and National Consciousness in Twentieth Century Ukraine* (Basingstoke: Macmillan/St Antony's, 1985).

16 Theofil I. Kis, *Nationhood, Statehood and the International Status of the Ukrainian SSR/Ukraine* (Ottawa: University of Ottawa Press, 1989).

17 Borys Lewytzkyi, *Politics and Society in Soviet Ukraine, 1953–1980*

(Edmonton, Alberta: University of Toronto Press, 1984).

18 Roman Szporluk, 'Reflections on Ukraine after 1994: the dilemmas of nationhood', *The Harriman Review*, vol. 7, nos. 7–9 (March–May 1994), 1–11.

19 This definition of Ukraine and its people had been formulated by the Ukrainian nationalists in the 1960s and the 1970s and built on and adapted the notion of the Soviet People of Ukraine. Serhiy Tolstov, 'Dimensions of inter-ethnic relations in Ukraine', *The Ukrainian Review*, vol. XL, no. 2 (Summer 1993), 28–46.

20 Theodore Friedgut, 'Perestroika in the provinces: the politics of transition in Donetsk', in Theodore H. Friedgut and Jeffrey Hahn, eds, *Local Power and Post-Soviet Politics* (London: M. E. Sharpe, 1994), pp. 162–83.

21 T. H. Friedgut, *Iuzovka and Revolution: Vol. I, Life and Work in Russia's Donbass, 1869–1924* (Princeton, NJ: Princeton University Press, 1989) and *Vol. II, Politics and Revolution in Russia's Donbass, 1869–1924* (Princeton, NJ: Princeton University, 1994).

22 Bilingualism is a misleading term with its implication of equal knowledge of two languages. In many areas, Russian and Ukrainian have fused to create a mixed language. Moreover, in West Ukraine, Galacian and Transcarpathian dialects of Ukrainian are spoken rather than literary Ukrainian.

23 Andrew Wilson, 'The growing challenge to Kiev from the Donbas', *RFE/RL Research Report*, vol. 2, no. 33 (20 August 1993), 8–13.

24 "V Dnepropetrovske vozrozhdaiut idealy leninizma', *Segodnia* (9 August 1994), 3.

25 'Shakhtery gluboko konaiut', *Moscow News*, no. 25 (June 1993), 4.

26 There was also a referendum in Donbas in which a large majority voted for full Ukrainian membership of the CIS, federalization of Ukraine, Russian as a second state language and the preservation of Russian as the primary language in the Donbas.

27 There is little sense of the region being purely Russian. Local historians have suggested that as a result of centuries of intermixing, a specific regional identity has emerged that stretches into the Black Earth zone of Russia. There is no distinct break between the Russian and Ukrainian side of the border. When republican borders were drawn up between 1917 and 1926, large numbers of Ukrainians were allocated to the Russian Federation. Despite the intense Russification and destruction of the infrastructure of Ukrainian ethnicity in the Russian Federation from the 1930s, large numbers still consider themselves Ukrainians. Author's interviews with local historians in Kharkiv and Donetsk (September 1994) and Kursk (December 1993).

28 Liudmila Sokyrianskaia, 'Politicheskie orientatsii kharkovchan letom 1993g.', *Sovremennoe obshchestvo*, no. 2 (1993), 114–19.

29 The Donetsk local press contains numerous articles on federalization and rebuilding economic ties with Russia. See *Donetskii Kriazh* (1993–4) and *Sotsialisticheskii Donbass* (1993–4).

30 *Programma i ustav sotsialisticheskoi partii ukrainy* (Kiev 1993).

31 'Ustav grazhdanskogo kongressa ukrainy', *Grazhdanskii Kongress*, no. 2 (1994), 5.

32 In 1991, the Liberal Party of Donetsk was founded, later the Labour Party of Ukraine was created and in 1992 the Interregional Association of Industrialists was set up and is primarily focused on the seven *oblasty* of the southeast. Vladimir Grinev, who ran in the presidential elections of 1991 and has his power base in Kharkiv, became leader of the New Ukraine and Interregional Bloc of Reform. See ' . . . Ia vizhu Ukrainu federativnym gosudarstvom . . .', *Donetskii Kriazh* (6–12 May 1994) and 'Da ne sbudutsia eti slova!', *Donetskii Kriazh* (17–23 September 1993), 1.

33 Author's interviews with representatives of the Socialist Party, the Communist Party and Civic Congress, Kharkiv and Donetsk (September 1994).

34 The agreement signed between Ukraine, Russia and the United Kingdom in December 1994 included a clause that the parties would refrain from 'economic coercion'. This reflected Kiev's growing anxiety about the economic strength of Russia *vis-à-vis* Ukraine. *The Financial Times* (6 December 1994).

35 'Programma interdvizheniia Donbassa', *Nash Donbass* (January 1993), 3.

36 See the roundtable discussion between members of the Donetsk political elite. *Donetskii Kriazh*, no. 33 (24–30 September 1993), 2.

37 A survey of public opinion found little support for Ukraine as a political unit among Russians in Simferopol. Bremmer, *op. cit.* (1994), 276–7.

38 Initially, a range of leading Russian nationalist politicians made a great deal of the issues of the Crimea as a whole, the future of the Black Sea Fleet and the status of the city of Sevastopol. Sergei Baburin said he was prepared to participate in the third defence of Sevastopol. Subsequently, the issue has retreated from the forefront of nationalist political rhetoric.

39 Andrew Wilson, 'Crimea's political cauldron', *RFE/RL Research Report*, vol. 2, no. 45 (12 November 1993), 1–8. In contrast to Russian nationalist organizations, Russian democratic organizations – the Citizens Forum and the Democratic Crimea Movement – have been extremely weak and were effectively marginalized from political developments in Crimea from 1992 onwards.

40 The Russian Party of Crimea, led by Sergei Shuvainikov, grew out of the Russian Society of Crimea, headed by Anatoli Los, and was far more radical than the former, essentially cultural, organization. Los has suggested that his organization is open to all people raised in Russian culture and speaking Russian because they are all Russians (*Rossiiane*) whether of Russkii, Ukrainian or Crimean Tatar origins. Aleksandr Pilat, 'Russkaia Partiia Kryma – Partiia Russkikh?', *Nezavisimaia Gazeta* (25 February 1993), 3.

41 Andrew Wilson, 'The elections in Crimea', *RFE/RL Research Report*, vol. 3, no. 25 (24 June 1994).

42 Ustina Markus, 'Crimea restores 1992 Constitution', *RFE/RL Research Report*, vol. 3, no. 23 (10 June 1994), 9–12.

43 The National Salvation Front was very active in 1993 and established a local chapter in Sevastopol. Aleksandr Pilat, 'Front Natsionalnogo spaseniia trebuet vozvratit sevastopol pod iurisdiktsiiu Rossii', *Nezavisimaia Gazeta* (11 January 1993), 3.

44 *Nashe delo* (Sevastopol) no. 3 (1994).

45 Taras Kuzio, *Russia – Crimea – Ukraine: Triangle of Conflict*, Research Institute for the Study of Conflict and Terrorism, London, Conflict Studies 267, January 1994.

46 Roman Solchanyk, 'The Crimean imbroglio: Kiev and Moscow', *RFE/RL Research Report*, vol. 1, no. 40 (9 October 1992), 6–10.

47 Author's interview with adviser to Meshkov, Simferopol (September 1994).

48 'Polozhenie o natsionalno-kulturnoi avtonomi russkogo naseleniia Lvovskoi oblast', *Sovest* (August 1991), 2.

49 In early 1992, members of the society drafted an agreement for Russia and Ukraine on dual citizenship. *Sovest*, no. 18 (October 1992).

50 'Mezhdunarodnaia nauchno-prakticheskaia konferentsiia "Novoe russkoe zarubezhe". Problemy i perspektivy', *Sovest*, no. 20 (December 1992).

51 Author's interview with representatives of the Pushkin Society, Moscow (June 1994).

52 Patricia Herlihy, *Odessa: A History* (Cambridge, Mass.: Harvard University Press, 1986).

53 Karen Dawisha and Bruce Parrott, *Russia and the New States of Eurasia: The Politics of Upheaval* (Cambridge: CUP, 1994), pp. 135–6.

54 Vladimir Razuvaev, 'Krizis na Ukraine i Rossiia', *Nezavisimaia gazeta* (17 December 1993), 5.

55 Dominique Arel and Andrew Wilson, 'The Ukrainian parliamentary elections', *RFE/RL Research Report*, vol. 3, no. 26 (July 1994), 6–17.

56 'Kuchma i Grinev nastupaiut na Kravchuka s iugo-vostka', *Novaia ezhedelnaia gazeta* (December 1993). This group was tied to the Inter-

regional Reform Bloc, known as the Grinev-Kuchma bloc, and was very active in support of Kuchma in the 1994 election campaign. Following the election, Vladimir Grinev became Kuchma's adviser for regional policy. Grinev was instrumental in the creation of a council of regions and an association of mayors, both were attached to the President's office in late 1994 as a means to counteract the power of the Supreme Soviet at the local level. On 17 December 1994, the Interregional Bloc became a party with Grinev as its leader.

57 Roman Solchanyk, 'The politics of language in Ukraine', *RFE/RL Research Report*, vol. 2, no. 10 (5 March 1993), 1–4.

58 Andrew Wilson and Artur Bilous, 'Political parties in Ukraine', *Europe–Asia Studies*, vol. 45, no. 4 (1993), 693–703.

59 Roman Solchanyk, 'Russia, Ukraine, and the imperial legacy', *Post-Soviet Affairs*, 9, 4 (1993), 337–65; Roman Szporluk, 'Belarus, Ukraine and the Russian question: a comment', *Post-Soviet Affairs*, 9, 4 (1993), 366–74; and Zbigniew Brzezinski, 'The Premature Partnership', *Foreign Affairs* (March–April 1994), 80.

60 'Peregovory v Dagomyse', *Sovetskaia Rossiia* (25 June 1992), 1.

61 'Yeltsin calms Sevastopol row', *The Independent* (11 July 1993), 12.

62 In late 1994, dissatisfaction with the speed and form of integration being followed after the election of Kuchma triggered a campaign in the East led by the Communists, but opposed by the Socialists, to re-establish the Union. 'Kommunisty sozdali proletarskii soiuz', *Segodnia* (20 December 1994).

63 'Pervoocherednoi zadachei ukrainskikh lederov ostaetsia normalizatsiia otnoshenii s Rossiei', *Segodnia* (23 September 1994), 3.

64 On 26 January 1995, President Yeltsin announced that he would not go to Ukraine to sign the treaty of friendship and cooperation until the provisions on dual citizenship are agreed. At a meeting of CIS Foreign Ministers on 25 January 1995 Ukraine, Turkmenistan and Azerbaijan resisted signing agreements to cooperate on protecting CIS external borders. *Open Media Research Daily Digest (Part 1)*, 26 Janary 1995

65 Razuvaev, 'Krizis ...', *op. cit.*, 5.

Chapter 6: The formation of a Russian diaspora identity in Kazakhstan

1 According to the last Soviet census, in 1989 the population of the republic stood at 16,464,000, of which 6,535,000 (39.7%) were Kazakhs, 8,263,000 (50.2%) were Russians, other Slavs (Ukrainians and Belorussians) and Europeans (Germans, Poles), 332,000 (2%) were Uzbeks and 1,334,000

(8.1%) others. The Slavic movement *Lad* claims that the percentage of ethnic Russians in Kazakhstan has fallen from 44% in 1989 to 37% in 1994. *SWB /SU/2071 G/1* (11 August 1994).

2 For a contemporary Kazakh account of the origins of the Kazakhs see Nurbolat Masanov, 'My – zhiteli stepi', *Kazakhstanskaia Pravda* (29 September 1992), 2.

3 N. E. Bekmakhanova, *Formirovanie mnogonational'nogo naseleniia Kazakhstana i severnoi Kirgizii: Posledniaia chetvert XVIII – 60-e gody XIX g* (Moscow: Nauka, 1980); also E. B. Bekmakhanov, *Prisoedinenie Kazakhstana k Rossii* (Moscow: Akademiia Nauk SSSR, 1957).

4 George J. Demko, *The Russian Colonization of Kazakhstan 1896–1916* (Bloomington, IL: Indiana University Press, 1969), pp. 31–2.

5 Kolarz, *op. cit.*, 263.

6 Geoff Wheeler, *The Modern History of Soviet Central Asia* (London: Weidenfeld & Nicolson, 1964), and Elizabeth E. Bacon, *Central Asians Under Russian Rule* (New York: Cornell University Press, 1966).

7 Russian cultural domination was reinforced by the introduction of a Latin script for the Kazakh language in 1929 and a change from the Latin script to a Cyrillic one in 1940. In 1938, Russian language became compulsory in all schools in the republic.

8 Teresa Rakowska-Harmstone, 'Nationalism in Soviet Central Asia Since 1964', in George W. Simmonds, ed., *Nationalism in the USSR and Eastern Europe in the Era of Brezhnev and Kosygin* (Detroit: University of Detroit Press, 1977), pp. 272–94.

9 A. B. Galiev, 'Etno-demograficheskii Protsessy i Etno-politicheskii orientatsie v sovremenom Kazakhstane', in *Mezhetnicheskie aspektii sotsialnikh i ekonomicheskikh reform* (Almaty: Institute of Strategic Studies: 1993).

10 Allen Hetmanek, 'National renascence in Soviet Kazakhstan: the Brezhnev era', in Simmonds, *op. cit.*, 295–305.

11 Yaacov Roi, 'The Soviet and Russian context of the development of nationalism in Soviet Central Asia', *Cahiers du Monde Russe et Soviétique* XXXII (1) (January–March 1991), 130.

12 Nazarbaev became First Secretary in June 1989 when Kolbin was recalled to Moscow.

13 Hélène Carrère d'Encausse, *The End of the Soviet Empire* (New York: New Republic/Basic Books, 1993), pp. 31–46.

14 The debate on language and Kazakhstan's sovereignty served as a catalyst for the emergence of the first settler political organizations. In eastern Kazakhstan, the Organization for the Autonomy of Eastern Kazakhstan

was established. In Almaty, a similar organization called Unity (*Edinstvo*) was registered in September 1990 but its activities were severely restricted by the authorities. *Programma Mezhnatsional'nogo Dvizheniia 'Edinstvo'*.

15 Eventually, Russian legislators agreed to support the sovereignty bill in return for modifications in the language law. The new law stated that each locality could set its own language tests for schools and that fluency in Kazakh would not be required as a condition for state employment until the beginning of the year 2000.

16 Aron Atabek, *Alash i Kazahskaia Natsii* (Moscow: TOO 'KhAk', 1991).

17 V. Kozlov, 'Natsional'nyi vopros: paradigmy, teoriia i politika', *Istoriia SSSR*, no. 1 (1990), 3–21.

18 *Komsomolskaia Pravda* (19 September 1990).

19 Ingvar Svanberg, 'In search of a Kazakhstani identity', *Journal of Area Studies*, no. 4 (1994), 113–23.

20 V. Galenko, 'O nekotorykh protivorechiiakh v konstitutsii Kazakhstana', *Birlesu* 14 (1993).

21 N. A. Nazarbaev, *Strategiia stanovleniia i razvitiia Kazakhstana kak soverennogo gosudarstva* (Alma-Ata: RGZhI, 1992), 37.

22 Dilip Hiro, *Between Marx and Muhammad* (London: Harper Collins, 1994), Chapter 3.

23 Ingvar Svanberg, 'Kazakhs', in Graham Smith, ed., *The Nationalities Question in the Soviet Union* (London: Longman, 1992), p. 200.

24 Up to 2,000 Kazakh families in Iran have requested repatriation. 'Dve tysiachi semei iranskikh kazakhov vozvrashchaiutsia na istoricheskuiu rodinu', *Panorama* (Kazakhstan) (7 August 1993).

25 The head of the department for migration of Karaganda *oblast* claimed that in the previous three years 9,000 immigrants from Mongolia had been resettled in the area. 'Dym otechestva im sladok i priiaten?', *ABV* (18 February 1994).

26 Galenko has argued that the previous balance in the higher organs of management in terms of Kazakh/non-Kazakh was 52/48%, by mid-1993 this had swung to 60/40% and among the top leadership the figure was 65/35%. Galenko, *op. cit.*

27 The Socialist Party is focused almost exclusively on economic and social issues and its election platform had almost nothing to say about inter-ethnic issues. 'Zaiavlenie k predvybornoi platforme sotsialisticheskoi partii Kazakhstana', *Respublika* (20 February 1994), 1.

28 The settlers have tried to publish their own version of history to counteract the Kazakh version. A. Feoktistov, *Russkie, Kazakhi i Altai* (Moscow/Ust-Kamenogorsk, February 1992).

29 *Ustav Russkoi Obshchiny Respubliki Kazakhstan and Doklad o Narusheniiakh Prav Russkogo Naseleniia v Kazakhstane*, No. 1–4, Informatsionno-analiticheskaia Sluzhba RO: Vernyi (Alma-Ata), 1993–4.

30 Prior to its abolition, the Legislation Committee of the Russian Supreme Soviet, headed by Sergei Baburin, was developing legislation on the diaspora, in close contact with the Russian nationalists in Kazakhstan. Author's interview with Vladimir Vukolov, head of the Almaty division of the Russian Community, Almaty (June 1994).

31 Author's interview with Viktor Mikhailov, Akmola (August 1993).

32 At present, only Kazakhs living outside Kazakhstan are granted this right in the Constitution.

33 The *Lad* leadership claim that there are 10,000 activists in the movement.

34 Of the 690 candidates registered for 135 constituencies, 566 were Kazakhs. The CSCE observer mission found that the elections did not meet international standards. 'Glavi delegatsii SBSE utverzhdataet, chto vybory v Kazakhstane "ne sootvetstvovali mezhdunarodnym standartam"', *Panorama*, no. 10 (March 1994).

35 *Lad* deputies were elected from East Kazakhstan, Semipalatinsk, Pavlodar, Kokchetav, Akhmola, Karaganda, Uralsk and Chimkent. *Spravka o V konferentsii ROSP 'LAD'* (23–24 April 1994).

36 Author's interview with Alexandra Dokuchaeva, President of *Lad*, Almaty (May 1994).

37 Survey material suggests that more than 45% of the electorate voted according to nationality and only 8% identified with a party. Author's interview with Baurjan Jusvpov, Director of the Kazakh Centre for the Study of Public Opinion, Almaty (May 1994).

38 A Union of Cossacks in Kazakhstan was formed on 16 December 1993. The Ataman of the Ural'sk Cossacks, Alexander Kachalin, has stressed the multi-faith basis of the Cossacks – Muslim, Christian and Buddhist – and argued that Cossacks could be useful to Kazakhstan because of their farming skills or as southern border troops. 'My khotim ubedit vlasti v nashei zakonoposlushnosti', *Karavan* (22 January 1993), 4.

39 Author's interview with Viktor Vodalazov, Uralsk Cossacks, Almaty (May 1994).

40 Author's interview with representatives of the Semirechie Cossacks, Almaty (May 1994).

41 'Ministr iustitsii daet pravovuiu otsenku vyskazyvaniiam gossovetnika Suleimenova', *Panorama*, no. 10 (March 1994).

42 The Communist Party claims 45–50,000 members today, most of whom are in the upper age cohort, and 33% are Russians, the next largest group

being Kazakhs, then Ukrainians.

43 The former leader of Unity, Yuri Startsev, has been instrumental in the registration of a new organization called Legal Development of Kazakhstan which aims to change the 'ethnic bias' of Article 1 of the Constitution. *Ustav Dobrovol' nogo obshchestvennogo Ob" edineniia "Pravovoe Razvitie Kazakhstana"*.

44 The presidential list system operated in tandem with the more conventional 'open' electoral process. In each region the President nominated three candidates and the electorate had to choose two of them to serve as deputies. The presidential list was therefore a crude electoral device to ensure the creation of a bloc of deputies in the new parliament whose loyalty was to the President.

45 The first conference of Ukrainians in Kazakhstan took place in May 1993. 'Ukrainians of Kazakhstan have united', *Kazakhstan* (English), no. 31 (4 August 1993), 1.

46 Ukrainians in Kazakhstan settled in four waves: (a) following the abolition of serfdom, Ukrainians established compact settlements in the north; (b) during the 1920s and 1930s members of the Ukrainian intelligentsia and church were exiled there; (c) at the end of 1945, those who had assisted the Nazi occupation of Ukraine were sent there; (d) in the 1950s Ukrainians came to the north under the Virgin Lands Programme. Those who came prior to the 1930s have lost their language and are largely assimilated and many from the Stolypin era migration identify themselves in their passports as Russian. More recent settlers form the core of the Ukrainian organizations that have appeared in the last few years. There are important centres of Ukrainian settlement. The Kustanai Ukrainian Autonomous *Oblast* existed until 1934. In 1934, as part of the Stalinist policy of Russification, all Ukrainian schools were closed. West Ukrainian nationalists have established links to local Ukrainian cultural centres and are sending teachers to the region. 'Get iz 'LADa''', *Komsomolskaia Pravda (v Kazakhstane)* (21 January 1994).

47 Germans and Poles constitute a distinct section of the settler population and tend to regard Poland and Germany rather than the Russian Federation as home. Polish settlement of the area dates back to the turn of the century. Germans have been particularly successful in Kazakhstan and occupy powerful positions. However, large numbers have already migrated to Germany. The Koreans are fully integrated into the Russified settler population and have largely lost their separate cultural identity. Tatars marry both Slavs and Kazakhs. They rarely occupy the highest positions and are now squeezed between Kazakhization and Slavic resistance.

48 Philip S. Gillette, 'Ethnic balance and imbalance in Kazakhstan's regions', *Central Asia Monitor*, no. 3 (1993), 21.

49 Despite the official reasons – to be closer to the main transport routes, with an airport open all year around – there can be no doubt that the move is a political gesture designed to reinforce the territorial integrity of the country. *FBIS–SOV–94–132* (11 July 1994), 70–1.

50 'Dvizhenie – eto zhizn. Khotia my i "stareem" ...', *Kazakhstanskaia Pravda* (12 May 1994), 4.

51 *Vek* (2–8 June 1995).

52 While a primary motivation for these large population movements is undoubtedly growing ethnic tension, other important motivations are economic deterioration, the environmental crisis in parts of the country – there are large outflows from the ecologically polluted areas of Semipalatinsk and Kzyl- Orda – and the withdrawal of ex-Soviet military personnel. N. Mitrokhin, V. Ponomarev, *Demograficheskaia Situatsiia v Kazakhstane* (Moscow, 1995).

53 Akmola has emerged as a centre for links between pro-Russian Kazakh organizations and settler organizations. 'Provedeny konsultatsii', *LAD*, no. 3 (4 May 1994), 5.

54 The growing power of the former Communist elite prompted the unlikely alliance of *Azat* and the Russian nationalists in Ust-Kamenogorsk in the run-up to the elections. 'Uchastniki mnogotysiachnogo mitinga v Ust-Kamenogorske prizvali golosovat na vyborakh protiv nomenklatury', *Panorama* (15 February 1994).

55 *Vremia* (Kazakhstan), no. 5 (19 March 1994).

56 Support for President Nazarbaev fell between May 1993 and February 1994 among all ethnic groups but the drop was most pronounced among the Russians (from 88.8% to 63.6%; cf. 82.8% to 73.1 for Kazakhs). Of Russians, 31.2% said that their opinion of the President had worsened, the primary cause being a lack of trust in his promises about equal rights and freedoms for all the population irrespective of nationality. Only 35.3% of Russians trusted him to fulfil these promises, 62.% did not trust him and 1.9% did not answer. The equivalent figures among Kazakhs were: trust 63.5%; don't trust 34.1%. Among other nationalities the figures were: trust 44.6%; don't trust 54.3%; no answer 1.1%. 'Reiting prezidenta: pokazateli i tendentsii', *Karavan* (25 March 1994).

57 'Ukaz Prezidenta Respubliki Kazakhstan ob obrazovanii Respublikanskoi Komissii po pravam cheloveka', *Kazakhstanskaia Pravda* (19 February 1994), 1.

58 'Voskresenie sobora voskreseniia', *Aziia* (May 1994), 1.

59 'Kazakh leader calls for end to ethnic discrimination', *SWB SU/2021 G/1* (14 June 1994).

60 Nurbulat Masanov and Nurlan Amerekulov, 'Budushchee Kazakhstana bez Rossii nevozmozhno', *Karavan* (4 February 1994), 10.

61 Visiting Almaty as election observers, Konstantin Zatulin and Andranik Migranian spoke of the need for dual citizenship agreements with Russia and for Russian to become a state language in Kazakhstan. 'Po utverzhdeniiu rossiiskikh parlamentariev rukovodstvo Kazakhstana blagoskonno otnositsia k idee vtorovo gosudarstvennogo iazyka', *Panorama*, no. 10 (12 March 1994).

62 Rogozin spoke on Radio *Mayak* in connection with the case, organized a rally by the Union for the Revival of Russia, the Russian Congress and the Constitutional Democratic Party at the Russian Foreign Ministry and is reported to have had contacts with Sergei Stepashin, the head of the Russian intelligence services. 'Dmitrii Rogozin ob'iavil ultimatum prezidentu Kazakhstana', *Segodnia* (19 May 1994).

63 Andrei Kozyrev met the Kazakhstani Prime Minister in November 1993 to discuss this issue. 'Dvoinoe grazhdanstvo pro i contra', *ABV* (23 November 1993). Kozyrev then had further discussions on this topic during a trip to Almaty in February, *FBIS–SOV–94–030* (14 February 1994), 17, and Abdullah Mikitaev, chairman of the Commission on Issues of Citizenship attached to the Russian presidential apparatus, visited Kazakhstan in May 1994 to discuss citizenship issues.

64 'Nazarbayev rejects dual Kazakh-Russian citizenship', *FBIS–SOV–94–030* (14 February 1994).

65 Olzhas Suleimenov, 'Soiuz c Rossei – nasha sud'ba', *Karavan* (18 February 1994), 4.

66 *FBIS–SOV–94–063* (1 April 1994), 45.

67 'Rossiiskaia federatsiia – prioritetnyi partner Kazakhstana', *Segodnia* (16 December 1994), 4.

68 An extensive bilateral agreement with the Russian Federation was agreed in early 1995 including military cooperation, border agreements and provisions for increased contacts between Russian regions and the northeast of Kazakhstan. 'Rossiia i Kazakhstan khotiat vernut' "druzhbu navek"', *Segodnia* (28 January 1995), 3. The geopolitics of oil exports from Kazakhstan are also playing an important part in this process. With Kazakhstan reliant on Russian pipelines for export of the oil, Moscow is in a strong position to demand concessions from Almaty on the settler isssue. Klara Rakhmetova, 'Strategiia i politika razvitiia neftegazovogo kompleksa respubliki kazakhstana', *Kazakhstan i Mirovoe Soobshchestvo*, no. 1 (1994), 80–92.

69 Recent surveys among the settler population suggest that the majority of non-Kazakhs remain uncertain about their national identity, with the largest number of settlers identifying themselves as citizens of the USSR or the CIS, then of Russia and finally of Kazakhstan. Survey material of the Kazakh Centre for the Study of Public Opinion (Almaty), 1994.

Chapter 7: Conclusions

1 Anthony D. Smith, *National Identity* (London: Penguin, 1991), pp. 20–21.

2 John B. Dunlop, *The Rise of Russia and the Fall of the Soviet Empire* (Princeton, NJ: Princeton University Books, 1993).

3 'State-building and Nation-making: The Soviet Experience', in Ronald Grigor Suny, *The Revenge of the Past: Nationalism, Revolution and the Collapse of the Soviet Union* (Stanford, CA: Stanford University Press, 1993), pp. 84–126.

4 Paul R. Bass, 'Élite groups, Symbol Manipulation and Ethnic Identity among the Muslims of South Asia', in David Taylor and Malcolm Yapp, eds., *Political Identity in South Asia* (London: Curzon Press, 1979), pp. 35–43.

5 'Kozyrev stanovitsia "silovym" ministrom?', *Izvestiia* (20 April 1995), 1 and 3.

Select bibliography

Arutiunian, Iu. V., ed. *Russkie: Etno-sotsiologicheskie ocherki* (Moscow: Nauka, 1992).

Bacon, Elizabeth E. *Central Asians Under Russian Rule: A Study in Cultural Change* (Ithaca, NY: Cornell University Press, 1966).

Barghoorn, Frederick C. *Soviet Russian Nationalism* (Westport, CT: Greenwood Press, 1976).

Demko, George J. *The Russian Colonization of Kazakhstan 1896-1916* (Bloomington, IL: Indiana University Press, 1969).

Dunlop, John B. *The Rise of Russia and the Fall of the Soviet Union* (Princeton, NJ: Princeton University Press, 1993).

Hambly, Gavin, et al. *Central Asia* (Weidenfeld and Nicolson: London, 1969).

Harris, Chauncy. 'The new Russian minorities: a statistical overview', *Post-Soviet Geography*, 34, no. 1 (1993), pp. 1-27.

Karklins, Rasma. *Ethnopolitics and Transition to Democracy: The Collapse of the USSR and Latvia* (Baltimore, MD: Johns Hopkins University Press, 1994).

Krawchenko, Bohdan. *Social Change and National Consciousness in Twentieth Century Ukraine* (Basingstoke: Macmillan/St Antony's College Oxford, 1985).

Kolarz, Walter. *Russia and Her Colonies* (London: Praeger, 1952).

Kristoff, Ladis. 'The geographical image of the fatherland: the case of Russia', *The Western Political Quarterly* (1967), pp. 941-54.

Lewis, Robert, Richard Rowland and Ralph Clem. *Nationality and Population Change in Russia and the USSR* (New York, NY: Praeger, 1976).

Lieven, Anatol. *The Baltic Revolution: Estonia, Latvia, Lithuania and the Path to Independence* (New Haven, CT: Yale University Press, 1993).

Melvin, Neil. *Forging the New Russian Nation: Russian Foreign Policy and the Russian-Speaking Communities of the Former USSR* (London: RIIA, Discussion Paper 50, 1994).

Pipes, Richard. *The Formation of the Soviet Union: Communism and Nationalism, 1917-1923* (Cambridge, MA: Harvard University Press, 1964).

Seton-Watson, Hugh. *The Russian Empire 1801-1917* (Oxford: Oxford University Press, 1967).

Shlapentokh, Vladimir, Munir Sendich and Emil Payin, eds. *The New Russian Diaspora: Russian Minorities in the Former Soviet Republics* (Armonk, NY: M.E. Sharpe, 1994).